A Note on the Author

CLANCY SIGAL was a novelist, journalist, screenwriter and political activist. Chicago-born, he was an American GI in Occupied Germany. Working as a talent agent on the Sunset Strip in the mid-fifties, he was blacklisted, fled McCarthyism, and moved to the UK. Living in London for many years, he worked as a film critic, a playwright and a BBC correspondent. He returned to Los Angeles in the late 1980s, and later became a professor emeritus at the University of Southern California Annenberg School of Journalism. He died in 2017.

THE LONDON LOVER

My Weekend that Lasted Thirty Years

Clancy Sigal

BLOOMSBURY PUBLISHING

LONDON · OXFORD · NEW YORK · NEW DELHI · SYDNEY

BLOOMSBURY PUBLISHING
Bloomsbury Publishing Plc
50 Bedford Square, London, WC1B 3DP, UK

BLOOMSBURY, BLOOMSBURY PUBLISHING and the Diana logo
are trademarks of Bloomsbury Publishing Plc

First published in Great Britain 2018
This edition published 2019

Typeset by Integra Software Services Pvt. Ltd.
Printed and bound in Great Britain by CPI Group (UK) Ltd, Croydon CR0 4YY

To find out more about our authors and books visit www.bloomsbury.com
and sign up for our newsletters

Contents

Foreword

... and *my* weekend with Clancy Sigal lasted thirty years.

His life was filled with writing, voracious reading, illness, anxiety, colossal insomnia and depression, but also with a profound and singular vivacity and the call of the typewriter bird – his obsessive relationship with a keyboard. During those years we married, had our son Joe, went to Little League games, worked together, wrote scripts together, argued together; I edited his work, and he edited mine. He left England to live with me in California.

Yes, Clancy Sigal really did leave his beloved London. He kept a journal of dreams: zig-zagging through chaotic streets, geese flying over Primrose Hill, his flat in Princes Square, broadcasting on the BBC, pub food. He dreamt of his friends, the women he knew (keep on reading), anti-war marches, anti-nuclear marches, and even megalithic mounds. He dreamt of acid trips he took with R. D. Laing (Doris Lessing called *him* 'that poseur') and a Beatle or two, smashed on LSD straight from the Sandoz Swiss lab. Those days, it was legal, though it wouldn't have mattered either way. Clancy was frank: he said he had never slept with

Twiggy or Jean Shrimpton or Princess Margaret, but I'll let the reader decide. Nothing would surprise me.

The first time I met him – *the very first time* – I was hanging in inversion boots, a 1980s Southern California fitness fad. Upside down like a sloth, straining to do sit-ups from a metal bar in a doorway, I was clad in a silver unitard – a skintight, one-piece number – and this combination of ballet leotard and tights really didn't leave much to the imagination. We exchanged greetings: 'Hello, hello, so nice to meet you.' He came by to talk to my then-boyfriend, David Strick, a photo-journalist, for a piece Clancy was writing for the *Observer*. This was prior to his massive heart attack in 1984 after eating a Dodger [hot] Dog with everything on it, landing him in the hospital for a month. Our three-way marriage: Clancy, his dodgy cardiac health and me.

After his recovery, we ran into each other at a packed and drunken party in Venice. My silver unitard was still etched into his NHS-issued black-rimmed glasses. Woody Allen could have directed the scene: Clancy trying to hit on me couldn't be heard over the twenty noisy bodies smashed between us. Three years later, I was single, so was he. A dinner party at the Santa Monica flat of Grover and Rae Lewis. (Grover was one of the early, great *Rolling Stone* writers.) On the wall of the screened-in balcony, a few blocks from Ocean Avenue, a pink neon rainbow cast a cool light. (Gus Hasford, author of *The Short Timers*, had christened this niche, with affection, the Café Cafard.) Here, complicated – OK, neurotic – pals came to argue jazz, blues, books, and movies, and shoot the shit. Pitchers of Rae's lethal margaritas flowed. Canary Island palms with heavy dark pediments blocked out the moon. Clancy asked me to a movie. We walked out after ten minutes; I demanded our money back and … what can you say? If you have the same taste in movies, live it up: fall in love.

Clancy had many close encounters with history. It was no coincidence. He was fuelled by causes. It was in his DNA. He was always *Going Away* (the title of his second book, a runner-up for the National Book Award). He was an American Jewish soldier packing a gun, *going* AWOL to bum rush the Nuremberg Trial of Hermann Göring, meaning to kill him. *Going* to UCLA, battling his arch-enemies, future Watergate conspirators Bob Haldeman and John Ehrlichman, whom he earnestly interviewed during and after their prison terms. *Going* to Hollywood during 'the time of the toad', what Hollywood Ten blacklisted screenwriter Dalton Trumbo called the infamous period of McCarthyism. 'Communist' Clancy had the balls to get hired as a Sunset Strip talent agent who – yes he did – rejected both James Dean and the 'Hillbilly Cat' Elvis as clients. *Going* to Paris to 'fuck Simone de Beauvoir', as he boasted to his client Nelson Algren. (Nelson: 'He didn't know I'd knocked around with her, so I kept my mouth shut.')

And yes, Clancy *went* to London for the weekend …

He became *Doris Lessing's lover*; **sorry,** Doris was *Clancy's lover.* Ancient history, except for Saul Green in *The Golden Notebook.* People are still curious – who can blame them? Their three tumultuous years together forged a relationship that lasted a lifetime. They never stopped being incensed at each other, yet they corresponded warmly (mostly) up until she couldn't. In the early sixties at British *Vogue*, Clancy wore a brown wool, Friar Tuck-type monk's robe. I wondered *where* he got it – at the local Monk's Robe Shop? 'Doris made it for me.' 'What?? Doris Lessing, who went on to win the Nobel Prize in Literature, sewed you a monk's robe?' What a genius way of cursing her ex-boyfriend!

The last few years of Clancy's life were very difficult physically. Strangely, it was a most productive time. Seldom a day went by when he didn't write all day. He lost his sight in the last few months. While dictating a new book, in terrific pain, he said he was ready to die. I tried to understand: 'You want to die; you want to write?' 'Absolutely,' he said calmly. 'There is no contradiction.' Clancy died on July 16, 2017.

Why did he write *The London Lover*? *CLANCY WAS HERE* – that's why. He wrote it for our son Joe, whom he had very late in life. Doris wrote to Clancy in 2006: 'Tell me, have you wondered what sort of a labyrinth your boy will find if he ever tries to find out about you?'

Janice Tidwell, Los Angeles

PART ONE

The World in the Morning

HOMELESS AND ILLEGAL IN LONDON

Kicked out of Paris by the French police for having a cancelled US passport and no visa (and probably for speaking the language so badly). Fed up with Europe, I'm going back to Hollywood, but first a London weekend so this trip isn't a total waste. Dover's white cliffs loom over the cross-Channel ferry backing into its berth where, hiding among tourists, I purposely jostle a teenager to distract the duty Immigration Officer. Then out free on the street I grab a bus rolling up the A28. What sort of money do the English take? Constantly swivel my neck to look over my shoulder. Did it! Without permission of the US State Department. When I see my FBI file in later years, I'm proud to see I'm noted as, 'SM – SUBVERSIVE (FOREIGN INFLUENCE).'

Forty dollars remain from an original thousand. Where did it all go? Fool! Drawing to inside straights to impress my Paris girlfriend. Don't ever play poker with French intellectuals: they take forever to bet and then sucker you.

Roll into Victoria coach station. This London spring is like a Chicago winter, I'm shivering in the pale sunlight. My bones shake in the cold. Keep walking to stay warm.

ON THE RUN

An American living rough in the Smoke has a few eminent examples to follow. London Yankees like Benjamin Franklin, Henry James, Mark Twain and Hart Crane lived high; even a socialist like Jack London, posing as a sailor, sewed $100 in gold coins ($2,500 in today's money) in his jacket lining when he plunged into the slums of the East End to write *The People of the Abyss*. Smart Jacko. I'm a homeless bum, finding a snug berth under Charing Cross bridge and on Hyde Park's wet grass. I'll be gone tomorrow, Inspector, I swear.

My stuff is limited to a GI duffel with almost everything I own in it (Sgt C. Sigal 36929935), a sweat-stained almost empty money belt, and a boxed-up Corona #3 portable typewriter – Hemingway's preferred machine. Nil English contacts, and no bed for the night. And, oh, yes, those other things I brought over from America: dizziness, nausea, headaches, fainting spells, vomiting, mysterious pains and insomnia.

*

London is the anti-California. Even when the pale May sun is out I'm freezing. Should wear long johns. Bring on blue skies and palm trees. And London is filthy. Even the Thames Embankment and public buildings are blackened on every visible surface. Westminister Abbey, St Paul's, all the famous monuments … speckled in soot. Smells of stenchy fog and Dettol in every public 'convenience', and that waxy scratchy toilet paper. How can people not gag on this polluted Thames Valley air? Where is Henry James's 'friendly fog'? Cough, cough. I came to Europe for a new life, but this place looks like Akron, Ohio on a bad day.

But first, for bragging rights before I go back to Hollywood, check out: Changing of the Guard ✓, Big Ben ✓, Tower of London ✓, Kew Gardens ✓, Windsor Castle ✓, Karl Marx's plaque at 28 Dean Street ✓, Dickens's house at 48 Doughty Street where he threw out his wife after she gave him ten children – some *Christmas Carol* – ✓, train to Salisbury and tour bus to Stonehenge, no guard rails, no fences meaning I can walk up to caress the stone pillars ✓, then hop on a Green Line bus up the A11 to the Thetford, Norfolk birthplace of my main man, 'difficult, irascible' Thomas Paine, his statue holding *Rights of Man* upside down: final ✓.

What's keeping me in this godforsaken place? It can't be any liking for the cold spring drizzle that shrivels the skin. Or the food. Eel in a pie or jellied with cockles? Everywhere is seedy, shabby, grey and worn. The telephone system – Press Button B! – was invented in, what, the thirteenth century?

*

MEMO TO READER:
This story takes place a long time ago in a British galaxy far, far away, before the Internet, Pret a Manger, decimalisation, armed police and decent pub hours.

4

Insolvent, I can afford only one daily high-carb meal in a cheap (2s.6d.) caff with dirt-smeared steamy windows, don't look at the heart attack going into your stomach: fried eggs, day-old french fries, streaky bacon, burned sausage, baked beans on blackened toast, grilled tomatoes, margarine on more sliced white bread, and Camp (chicory) so-called coffee. Yuk.

Even broke, there's still one luxury I can afford.

TING-TING

> A man who, beyond the age of twenty-six, finds himself on a bus can count himself a failure.
> —allegedly, Margaret Thatcher, PM

'Are you lost, luv?'

Four years past the age of failure/success you dodge police by taking a good long snooze aboard the fuggy designated-for-smokers top deck of a number 88 bus, traveling from Camden across the river to Clapham.

'Sure yer awrigh', luv?' Jean the clippie asks again. Riding her bus has become my day job, except for when falling asleep on a fellow passenger's shoulder (''Ere now, ger orf!') while peering out of the dirty window, scanning the rain-blackened streets for the Woman of my Dream … who first appeared to me in a mononucleosis fever on the very day I quit my Sunset Boulevard job as a talent agent. Or rather it quit me. Night after sheet-drenched night, she appeared to me like Aphrodite: a sun-burnished female in a denim skirt and Pendleton blouse, one arm around a chubby little boy, inviting me, 'You there! Come on, come on! Hurry!' Oh, I do know her, she's the spitting image of actress Wendy Hiller: no classic beauty but the fierce romantic from *I Know Where I'm Going,* a defiant Eliza Doolittle in *Pygmalion*, and, my favorite, a Salvation Army soul-saver in *Major Barbara.*

I'm as sure of my Dream Woman's reality – that she's out there somewhere looking for me – as I am of my new friend Jean the clippie. 'Mind the stairs … hold tight please … ting-ting!'

In her rakish cap and trim bus conductor's uniform, a ticket machine hanging round her lovely neck, Jean looks vaguely military except for her smile, which is so ravishing, despite her bad teeth – the English defect, I'll learn.

Jean knows of a spare room.

'Tell you what, ride with me to the depot and I'll brew you a cuppa.' Thunk! Roulette ball drops into my lucky number.

Jean is amazing. In a sudden pea-souper – London still has them despite the Clean Air Act – she swings down onto the road to walk in front of the bus, guiding it through the flaky, impenetrable soot. Like her driver, I'd follow this woman anywhere.

My days are spent bucketing around inside her number 88 and nights in Jean's room in Tottenham where she inducts me into the mysteries of class, accent, sex and Ascot heaters. And, crucially, how to survive as an illegal immigrant in a 'socialist' welfare state. Such as: applying at the nearest Employment Exchange where the clerk behind the grille hands me £8 ($24) as an 'emergency payment', no questions asked; and signing on for free medical care under the National Health Service with her 'locum', a black Barbadian doctor in a walk-in surgery to whom I confess I'm a foreigner with no visa, at which he shrugs 'So what?' and issues me a little card and a lecture about how the NHS doesn't want contagious aliens running around the country infecting everyone. No fuss, no mess. Can't believe it's this easy. A single card for doctor, hospital, emergency care, this or that ... where's the money come from for all this?

I'm skittish about sex with my first Englishwoman. Is there a secret to it? Splendidly intuitive, Jean suggests a cup of tea 'before', saying: 'It calms me down and makes the day go faster, you'll see.' Faster? She sighs after taking three sugar lumps and milk with her tea, as if the ritual itself is the real pleasure, and then we're off. She's right: tea is the secret to English sex. She keeps condoms in her night table, slips one on and stares at my 'Mars and Venus', her Cockney slang for it.

'It's not very big,' I admit.

'Chaps are funny that way, ain't they? Let me taste.'

What happened to my plan to join the revolution in Poland and Hungary?

*

IN THE NEWS IN THE SIX MONTHS SINCE I LEFT AMERICA
Grace Kelly weds Monaco's Prince Rainier III. John Osborne's *Look Back in Anger* opens at the Royal Court Theatre. Russian premier Khrushchev denounces Stalin then sends tanks driven by Mongolian soldiers to crush the Hungarian revolt, killing thousands of civilians. Britain, France and Israel attack Egypt over the Suez Canal.

The ship's loudspeaker crackles with static as it relays news of the Soviet invasion of Hungary. '*This is Budapest. Budapest Radio. Budapest Radio. Help us! Help! Help...*' Hungarian workers and students fighting their secret police are rapidly outgunned by the Soviet war machine.

Slowly the passenger freighter *Heraklion* swings into the Hudson river. After driving almost non-stop across America's blue highways to join it, being at sea is just another way for me to *keep going*. Can't stop. Cannot. Staying still makes you a target.

'*Budapest Radio. Help us!*'

My mess-room tablemate, an English police inspector taking his new American wife back to their Sussex home, says, 'You there, Yank – why are you talking back to that radio? If we don't watch out, your bloody Hungarians will finish us all off in another war.' He's angry. 'I did my bit in the last show and my father did his before me. That's enough for one family.' He steers his bride away from me, the weird American. Then comes back for a parting shot. 'It has nothing to do with us. Best stay out of it!'

He's right. If President Eisenhower deploys the 101st Airborne, I'll arrive in a nuclear-incinerated Europe. But trust good old Republican Ike for whom I'd voted, hence my Hollywood girlfriend throwing a drink in my face at my own party. She was an ACLU member – all for civil liberties except when it came to mine.

Budapest Radio sends out a last, forlorn plea.

'*Help us. Help! Help ...*'

Age thirty, no published work, five foot eleven and a half – don't forget the half-inch, solidly built from lifting weights and distance running, horn-rim glasses, all my own teeth, no visible scars, prone to impulsive acts diagnosed as resulting from an 'anxiety disorder'. Never been psychoanalyzed. Heterosexual. My coping mechanisms have worked beautifully up to now.

Bad-tempered Thomas Paine is my inspiration. Like me, 'corset-making' Tom fled to a new country to escape his political and women troubles.

And, oh, yes, I can type eighty w.p.m.

End of profile.

*

I spend most of my time on Jean's number 88 bus. On her next rest day she's off to see her dad – would I like to come along? Dad is an 'old lag' at Pentonville prison on the number 17 bus route. It's like a family picnic, traveling there with Jean's mum and a couple of brothers who live on the Isle of Dogs in the East End. Jean is vague about the nature of her dad's crime: 'This an' that, mosly fiddles, nuffin' serious.' This isn't a big-time crime family, but getting 'banged up' is part of the price they pay for having lived by their wits since the war. Dad himself is a handsome fella whose only grudge is against the Irish. 'This place … I've seen worse, a bit cramped maybe. But I don't care for the Micks. Political they are, hold themselves above us.' I'm translating here, because to an American their working-class English is like *Tibetan For Beginners*.

Then it's back to my day job, riding Jean's Routemaster magic carpet. I could do this forever, except that she wakes me up one morning to announce, 'Me dad's been released a bit early and 'e's comin' for a visit. Catholic, you see, and funny about certain things. Unless you're going to marry me, best bugger off.'

She's terrific to me as usual, sacrificing wages by changing shifts to a number 49 to World's End, where she puts me down on the sidewalk outside a coffee bar, a poky-looking place called Fantasie. 'Here's your stop, luv. Look at 'em, sunning themselves for all the world like royals. They don't do a stitch of work all day – the Chelsea Set's just the place for you.' (Jean pegs me as a natural 'artist' because I correct her grammar.)

She pushes me off the back platform with a kiss. 'Where can I find you?' I shout. But, in a puff of exhaust fumes, my only London friend is gone.

RICHARD HILLARY IS MY CO-PILOT

Over coffee outside the Fantasie Café I catch the eye of this Pretty Young Thing, a long-haired blonde all dressed in black: Capri pants, long sweater with cowl neck, no jewellery. She looks away, indifferent and blasé. Across the street a Gaumont cinema is showing *The Prince and the Showgirl* with Marilyn Monroe and Laurence Olivier. I offer, 'I'm just in from Hollywood. I met Marilyn there.' No response. Frosty expression. Then, in a plummier accent than Jean's, the blonde asks: 'Did you ever meet Stewart Granger then?' *King Solomon's Mines* is my favorite picture, I lie. That does it. She says: 'Like to come with me for the ride of your life?'

And they say Englishwomen are cold!

Except that isn't quite what she has in mind.

Philippa, who works nights as a dancer at a Piccadilly club, stuffs me into her yellow Austin-Healey sports car and zips through the West London suburbs then south to the Sussex Downs and a disused RAF/US Eighth Air Force base in the middle of farm country. As the wind whips her untied hair into a Medusa tangle, she shouts, 'Manston, Biggin Hill, Battle of Britain, all that. Airfield's gone to rack and ruin now, of course, like the rest of this bloody country.'

A small truck idles on the rutted runway, attached by a rope to a glider tipped over on one wing. 'I'm a trainee pilot,' Philippa says brightly, 'so come along.' Then, lapsing into mock-Cockney, 'Yer tykes yer chances if you do, mate.'

I've never been in a glider before and scarcely in an airplane, except for a trip in my drunken friend Ray's Piper Cub, tossing leaflets over Los Angeles. I scrunch down in the rear cockpit space behind Philippa, wearing a pair of sunglasses she's lent me, dual controls at my feet, and before I know it the truck on the field, driven by her pal, jerks us aloft, sky-borne, weightless.

'I have control,' Philippa announces. Does she ever! I'm so afraid of passing out or vomiting that I keep my eyes shut tight, which only makes the vertigo worse.

'Warm air is with us,' she informs me over her shoulder, 'so I'm going to buzz my village!' And we swoop down thousands of feet, pulling up practically at roof-level, sure to stall, before she loops round and round a tiny hamlet, which then all of a sudden seems to be thousands of miles below. I fix my by now wide-open eyes on a picture-perfect rural landscape dating back several millennia. If only I knew how to decode this Monopoly board of neatly hedged and walled fields, green patchwork and bramble borders, grey stone walls marking boundary lines clearly visible from up here. I see country churches like turreted mini-castles holding sway over their graveyards, single-lane roads, turnstiles, gently rolling hills crowned by darkly foliaged copses ... all stretching away before me as far as Dover and the Channel I'd illegally crossed a fortnight ago. On a late-spring afternoon it looks so peaceful and welcoming, nothing untamed or unpredictable about this terrain, though quite probably it is the scene of murder, mayhem and all sorts of sullen mysteries – I've read my Agatha Christie and *Cold Comfort Farm*.

As the glider lurches between air currents Philippa points out more airfields. Both her father and her uncle had served in the Royal Air Force. Hornchurch, Northolt, Kenley, Debden ... the places down there are written into her family history. 'Eleven Group, 610 Squadron,' she says. 'My uncle got through the war, but Dad didn't. End of story.' What makes her come back to the spot where her father was killed? I yell over her shoulder. 'You don't have to shout,' she says. 'Listen. No sound.' It's true. The quiet up here is unearthly.

'Why do I come back? Because I'm an air-cheologist,' she puns. 'I help to dig up crashed planes. A whole team of us do. It's the least we can do. Mum hates it. Says it's morbid. She's right.'

As an American child fed on wartime newsreels, I spent hours gluing together balsawood Spitfire models and blotting up anything I could find out about the RAF's 'Few' in Fighter Command: airborne knights of the Round Table, who rose above London on their 12-cylinder Rolls-Royce Merlin engines to confront Hitler's swarm of killer-bombers head-on. Those eight Browning .303 machine-guns in the outer wing panels dogfighting the Nazis' Messerschmitt 109s. 'Scramble! Scramble!' Prince Valiant spiraling down in smoke and flames …

Philippa loves to throw jargon about, like 'sink rate' and 'slope lift', but when I ask 'What is that?' she says, 'Not sure I understand either.' I finally force myself to stop punching my heel down on a non-existent brake and surrender to the skies, gazing out of the Plexiglas window beside me as if I were safely on the top deck of Jean's bus. Down there, far below, the whole of the Battle of Britain is memorialized in now-defunct air bases and radar stations, strung out like a cement girdle between London and the Dover cliffs. The ants below had saved my life.

I could go on gliding forever, I think. Until Philippa says, 'You have control.' Panic. Until she adds, 'Only kidding.'

That's when a bloody, mangled face appears on the other side of the window beside me, gazing in. 'Who's that?' I shout.

'Who's who?'

There's a scarred and wounded man in smart grey RAF battledress standing on the wing, staring right into my eyes. He's trying to claw his way in with mutilated fingers. Lacking eyelids and much of his burned lips, his face is horribly disfigured. My very first, authentic vision, I recognize him from his book-jacket photo: Richard Hillary of 603 Squadron, author of *The Last Enemy*, which

I'd read over and over again back in Los Angeles. Hillary, an extraordinarily handsome Oxford college boy who had rowed for his college Trinity, became a fighter ace after shooting down five Messerschmitt 109Es, but was himself later shot down over the Channel, suffering horrific burns to his hands and face. The Americans later invited him on a propaganda speaking tour but cancelled the invitation when they realised how bad for the war effort witnessing such injuries might be. Semi-repaired by surgery, he talked himself back into active service and was killed in a crash, having used his pain as a rite of passage … a means of self-identification … in the conviction that intellect alone could conquer fear. It was a belief with which I totally identified.

I blink and shake my head, but the phantom – no, it really *is* him – keeps staring back at me. We must be over Hornchurch, his home field. I reach out and hold on to Philippa's shoulders for dear life.

The gargoyle face and clawed hands vanish. I look for a smear of blood on the Plexiglas to prove that they were really there. 'Let me out of here,' I plead, 'I'm going to throw up.'

Without a word she banks the glider, giving me a view of the wide flood plain of the Greater London splodge to north and west, a beast of a city.

'How do we get down?' I whine.

'It's a little tricky,' she calls back over her shoulder. 'Remember, I'm just a trainee pilot. No license yet. We'll go bumpety-bump a bit, but not to worry! They didn't.' She means her father and uncle, and she's already told me how that turned out for her dad.

Her London flat, round the corner from the Fantasie, is pure luxury compared to Jean's tiny room. How can Philippa afford it? She says, 'I've a gentleman caller. Businessman type. Generous. Twice a week down from Manchester. Nice chap, no trouble.'

I ask if, um, er, she wouldn't like a cup of tea … first? Native custom and all that.

Are all Englishwomen going to be like Jean and Philippa? Or is it my good luck that so many men never came back from the war?

Richard Hillary will remain a presence in my life for years to come.

THE SUM TOTAL OF WHAT I KNEW ABOUT ENGLAND BEFORE SNEAKING IN …

… was a children's cartoon mish-mash of Hal Foster's Prince Valiant comic strip set in fifth-century Camelot and blood-stirring movies like *Gunga Din*, *The Lives of a Bengal Lancer* and *The Four Feathers* ('Stand fast, lads!'). Child star Shirley Temple, quoting Kipling, spoke for my imaginary England in *Wee Willie Winkie*: 'Fear God, honour the Queen, shoot straight and keep clean.' Talk about indoctrination! Movie houses were my prep schools. I studied *Mrs Miniver* ('We, in this quiet corner of England … This is the people's war! It is our war!'), *One of Our Aircraft is Missing*, and war-inflected without mentioning the war *Brief Encounter* ('This misery can't last. I must remember that and try to control myself'), *Great Expectations*,

Odd Man Out, *The Third Man*, *The Red Shoes*, *Whisky Galore*, *Kind Hearts and Coronets* and *Passport to Pimlico*. Thus, long before skulking ashore at Dover, I'd designed for myself a 'civilized' battle-weary England, emotionally restrained, perpetually one step behind and two drinks under. Because that was how I wanted it to be.

Somewhere to slow me down.

KING TUT AT GOODGE STREET

I'm homeless again after Philippa shoos me out, sleeping in the Underground and hardly ever venturing into daylight. My system is to buy a ticket on the Central or Piccadilly Line and go far out to, say, Cockfosters or Ongar, then curl up on a station bench using my GI jacket as a pillow until the morning trains resume service. Typhoo tea, almost-inedible cheese sandwiches (where's the cheese?) and public 'conveniences' keep me going.

On various park benches I pick up scraps of a personal library, discarded copies of 'the Sundays', everything from *News of the World*, the *People* and *Sunday Mirror* to the *Observer*, *Sunday Times* and *Telegraph*. After reading them, I use the newspapers to line my boots and keep my feet warm. My eye catches on the screaming crime headlines (GANG BOSS IN SICK JAIL SEX ORGY WITH STRIPPERS!), but also the back pages of the 'qualities': book reviews by George Orwell, V. S. Pritchett and Philip Toynbee. They seem so confident of the intimate writer-to-reader connection, as if speaking to an equally well-educated next-door neighbor. How do I set about finding such neighbors?

The London Tube is childishly simple to navigate. Unlike Jean's buses where chatter was part of the service on offer, on the Underground nobody talks. They remain silent as the grave. It's like sitting opposite Tutankhamun from Tooting and Imhotep from Islington: serried ranks of Egyptian mummies. All the passengers are so profoundly, deeply self-contained that's probably how they made it through the war: zoning out the bomb blasts. Eye contact must be a punishable offense here. Mad, they're all mad.

One day I'm caught in the deep lift shaft at Goodge Street station which, reputedly, once housed one of Winston Churchill's air-raid shelters. Our sardine-packed cage abruptly jerks to a halt, imprisoning us all shoulder to shoulder for ten, fifteen minutes. The single dim overhead bulb flickers. *Nobody speaks.* Our collective plight provokes only utter silence. Then, after an eon of muteness, a lazy drawl slices through the barely suppressed anxiety. 'I say, are we the Lost Patrol down here? Somebody be a good fella and press that red alarm thingamajig.' Nobody stirs. A woman's voice replies, at hysteria pitch: 'No need to panic, is there?' The drawl's owner – a gent with furled umbrella, upcurled mustache and trilby hat – pushes forward and thumbs the red button, saying crisply, 'Panic is permissible in certain circumstances, madam.' Whereupon most of the lift's other passengers, instead of drawing a collective sigh of relief, fix their gaze on him in silent contempt and mutter under their breath about the pushy gentleman with the umbrella. What a bounder and rule-breaker! No team player he!

How did these people ever survive each other?

I'm streetwalking, sick of subsisting on eel pies and sleeping on my boots in Rowton House refuges so they don't get stolen.

'Come and join us, mate. You look buggered an' all,' a friendly voice bellows from the pavement outside a Camden High Street shopfront. 'Buggered and all' is too right. Sleeping overnight in parks or on station benches, money now down to zero, and thinking: There must be *another,* different England from the one I'm adrift in.

Sprawled around a table outside this small North London commercial pottery, several workers in paint-and-clay-spattered overalls are enjoying a break in the rare spring sunshine. The voice that addressed me belongs to a big, bouncy young woman wearing a denim apron. She holds up a mug of tea. 'Sorry, no coffee, but this should fix you up.'

'Amanda Sunshine' is the type of woman I will later recognize in John Betjeman poems: one of his muscular girls in tennis shorts, with hearty voices and bags of self-confidence. She owns the pottery, which specializes in funny little ceramic men made for the American market. 'Nothing artistic or William Morris – strictly Josiah Wedgwood knockoffs. I'm a single mum and need cash flow.'

She lets me stash my typewriter and duffel – I've compressed my London life into its familiar outline, it's never torn, gaped or let me down – in her shop and do little chores in the clay-scented basement, where the small figures are baked in a permanently fired-up kiln before being tin-glazed and decorated. She has four employees, three young male apprentices and a journeyman female potter, and spends most of her day signing invoices or throwing at her kick-wheel. Sometimes she lets me whirl a ghastly-looking pot of my own, sending the pleasantly strong scent of wet earth up my nose. Mainly I earn my keep by lifting and carrying and, just once, making tea. Strong back, weak brew.

'Blegghh!' says Jeremy, one of the apprentices, spitting it out. He tells me it takes a thousand years of tea-drinking history and scientific precision to be able to steep tea properly.

My first weekend at the pottery Amanda tosses me a key and commands, more than invites, me to sleep over on her houseboat. What a woman! She practically exhales good cheer.

For the next fortnight I camp out in a brightly painted houseboat anchored at Cookham, a small and sleepy Berkshire town, a time out of time. A false spring comes early – a routine English phenomenon, I'm told – and leaves and flowers are already in bud, uncommon warmth descending along with swarms of bees and horseflies. Amanda comes down that first Friday night, and as soon as she's unpacked she climbs into the boat's skiff to row me alongside the towpath. It's warm, damp and pretty; she does all the work, gracefully pulling on the oars. Great life.

A born Betjeman girl she's not, I discover. Amanda reveals she's a *kindertransport* child – a German Jew, one of 10,000 children whisked out of central Europe as war broke out in 1939, who came to Britain in a government-backed emergency rescue mission. One morning the BBC broke into the News to ask for volunteers willing to take one or more German or Austrian children, between the ages of eight and seventeen, and the applications poured in.

(This, when President Roosevelt refused to accept refugee kids.) Amanda's mother and father had vanished into the death camps but she found safety with a well-off, childless English couple in the countryside who did not, as happened in many such homes, force her into involuntary service as a housemaid or farm laborer. She grew up much loved and indulged, un-Jewish and High Anglican – and very English. 'And why shouldn't I?' she demands of me. 'They saved my life. Least I could do, right?'

Amanda is into full-on maternal sex, smothering me in her large breasts and gripping my body with hands that are strong as iron from her potter's work. She takes forever to 'come off' and practically drowns me in her: 'Wait! Wait! Wait! Wait! Uh … yes.' Yet though she tries to disguise it with her exertion and sensuous cries, I do not satisfy her. She'll smile up at me afterwards as if to say: This is it? All there is?

Theorizing about English women after only three interludes is premature, except for a certain discernible fragrance they have in common. My Los Angeles girlfriends had what's rare in the UK: access to proper showers and plenty of hot water. In a land of medieval plumbing, Jean, Philippa and Amanda bring a tangy, provocative sweat-scent with them. The fact is, it's hard to stay properly clean in post-Blitz England.

Living, and having warm humid hearty sex, on a houseboat in a strangely summery spring, with nothing to do but wander around Cookham village when Amanda is away at her London pottery, I happen upon a strange man with stringy disheveled hair, strolling resolutely down High Street by Odney Lane bridge. He looks like the photos I've seen of the American poet Robert Frost, and is trailed by a gaggle of laughing children as he trundles an old pram chassis holding an easel and canvas. Are those pyjamas I can see under his work trousers?

Since he's unshaven and rumpled I assume he's a hobo like me, and fall in step with the children who trail the man, chattering, not badgering but using him as a sort of moving maypole to cavort around. Finally, the disheveled man chooses to turn down the lane by the church leading to the graveyard. The children trail him as far as the gate.

'Who is that guy?' I ask.

'Mr Spencer,' one of them chirps.

'Does he have a place to stay?'

A kid says, 'His family's been here for *centuries*.'

And off they go. Leaning on the graveyard wall, I watch the old guy at work as he sets up the easel from the pram, unrolls and nails sketch paper to it, and uses charcoal to rough out an outline. Though he seems not to mind having an observer, I leave him alone to work: a decision I've since come to regret. At a local pub, the King's Arms, I learn the scruffy little man is Stanley Spencer, a painter I'd not then heard of. From comments made by the patrons it's clear Spencer is mildly liked and tolerated in equal measure. 'He's no bother except to his housekeeper and whichever wife he's on or off with these days,' says a drinker. 'Randy little goat,' another customer smirks. No malice in the comments, just amused affection.

I like spying on Mr Spencer when I see him next. He is closely observing workmen on the High Street, this time using oils while he quickly sketches them at work laying pipes in a ditch. Years later, I learn that I witnessed one of England's greatest painters, Sir Stanley Spencer, outlining a scene for one of his visionary masterpieces: *Christ Preaching at Cookham Regatta*. Finding the holy in the ordinary. I wish I had pestered him more because he died soon afterwards. Since then I've become slightly obsessed by his religious pictures, how he put his neighbors into scenes of the Crucifixion and Annunciation, and my favorite, *Christ Overturning the Money Changers' Table.*

The Cookham interlude ends abruptly when Amanda's adoptive mother storms onto the houseboat and, finding us lying in the bunk, screams: 'Did I bring you up to behave like this, Amanda? Thank God your daughter can't see you! What are you doing with this … this …'

I realise I don't wish to be referred to as *this* ever again.

A ROOM OF ONE'S OWN

> The mirror is doubtless defective, the outlines
> will sometimes be disturbed, the reflection faint
> or confused; but I feel as much bound to tell you
> as precisely as I can what that reflection is, as if
> I were in the witness-box, narrating my experi-
> ence on oath.
>
> George Eliot, *Adam Bede*

On a Brompton Cemetery bench where I'd been sleeping someone left a crumpled flyer for a 'huge' anti-fascist rally to be held outside Earl's Court Tube station, within walking distance of the cemetery. Yes, finally, a job for Johnny Storm!

Flashback to Paris, a few weeks ago. Scene: the American Hospital in Neuilly.

'*Mais, j'espère pour vous que vous plaisantez*! You're kidding, M. Sigal,' says the nice young English-speaking French doctor when I explain that the other doctors' big brown pills ('*pour les maladies chroniques du foie*') only make me sicker. 'Your symptoms are classic: *une dépression nerveuse*. These *bagarres* you provoke are *épisodes maniaques … vous êtes un toxicomane au conflit.*'

He thinks I'm addicted to violence? Doesn't he get that being at the centre of the action is the only thing that helps to reduce my state of perpetual terror? Hemingway advised expelling emotional pain by writing. I do it the French way: by rioting.

God, doctors are stupid! I reach across the desk and hit him.

Rage works for me. I *love* Parisian street violence. Always a drama, a *crise*, operatic scuffles that erupt so predictably on Boul' Mich', I factor them into my daily routine of typing pages that are blank because I pulled out the ribbon. *Algérie Française! À bas les fascistes!* In a mob I'm invulnerable, shrieking the battle cry of my favorite comic book super-hero, Johnny Storm aka The Torch. 'Flame on!' he yells as he launches himself at the Evil Ones.

Back to the present moment outside Earl's Court Tube station …

A ramshackle wooden platform is manned, provocatively, by the British Union of Fascists. The flyer called for a mass protest, but where are the masses? Around me is a fair-sized turn-out of a dozen or so clean-shaven fellows in black pants and black T-shirts or else square-shouldered business suits worn like uniforms. Hair cut short back and sides military-style; some even affect Hitler-style mustaches. But where are the anti-fascists?

There he is, up on the platform, the Great Man of British Nazism, retitled the British League of Ex-Servicemen and Women. He's wearing Bertie Wooster-esque hunting tweeds and flannel trousers, more college professor than screaming ideologue, spouting about 'Jewish finance' and 'negroid influences'. The Union Jack draped over the platform has a superimposed swastika-like lightning bolt, with BRITAIN FOR THE BRITISH printed on it. Where does that leave me?

Darkness falls, and the incurious home-bound Tube passengers shoulder past. 'Bullshit!' yells Johnny Storm the Torch. (Later, I'll learn to scream 'Rubbish!') The two helmeted constables lounging in a nearby police box couldn't care less, so I steal a scene from Cary Grant in *North by Northwest* – all my best and worst ideas come from movies. 'Bullshit!' I repeat. A ton of flesh crashes into me. Ah, bliss. 'FLAME ON!' Mosleyite punches are an ecstasy of unfelt pain.

Even though I'm backed up against the police box, the constables give the fascists plenty of leisure to do what they do best. Momentarily driven to my knees by a hammer blow to the head, I tell myself I must get up and fight ... Like hell! These guys are serious. I'm chased down Hogarth Road, randomly duck up some stone steps and run down a hallway at the top of some carpeted stairs. A woman backed up by a man – he, too, has a trim little mustache – holds up a large cooking pot by its handles and threatens me with it. 'It's boiling!' she shouts. Oh, no. I hug the side of the hallway as several pursuers tumble in after me, and the woman hurls down a deluge of hot water. Over cries of pain and outrage she calls to me, 'Come quick, comrade.'

Comrade?! Pure dumb luck. My saviour turns out to be Gina Harrison, former Yugoslav Red Army partisan, and her guy is Stanley Harrison, foreign editor of the *Daily Worker*, the Communist rag. They've seen the fascist turn-out from their window. I've hit the jackpot here.

Except, sorry, they have no spare room, though a friend has a friend who …

*

> Yes, I do believe in something. I believe in being
> warm-hearted. I believe especially in being
> warm-hearted in love, in fucking with a warm
> heart. I believe if men could fuck with warm
> hearts, and the women take it warm-heartedly,
> everything would come all right. It's all this
> cold-hearted fucking that is death and idiocy.
> D. H. Lawrence, *Lady Chatterley's Lover*

*

See me now the way she probably does the first time.

Standing on her doorstep – woollen watch cap pulled down over my wind-frozen ears, threadbare army field jacket with collar hiked up over a roll-neck cableknit docker's sweater, dirty jeans with thumb in waistband and fingers pointing unmistakably to crotch – I am the reincarnation of James Dean, feet planted firmly in an old pair of newspaper-stuffed GI combat boots: a working-class beauty in distress.

'They say you have a room for rent.' I cough harshly, fog-induced bronchitis setting in again. 'Well, do you?' I stand shivering on her doorstep. 'Have a room, I mean.'

It's her! My Mononucleosis Dream Woman!

She replies sharply, 'Americans like their comfort. The room is too squalid,' and starts to shut the door, just like Lana Turner does on John Garfield in *The Postman Always Rings Twice*. I stick my foot in the door, the way Garfield does. 'I'll take it!'

*

> He was examining me. I have never in my life
> been subjected to as brutal a sexual inspection as
> that one.
>> Doris Lessing, *The Golden Notebook*

PREVIEW OF A COMING ATTRACTION

High cheekbones, astigmatic green eyes, Pendleton blouse, a cricket bat and boy's school cap in the hallway ... In dreams begin responsibilities.

Fade in: Ext. An African savannah of rolling grassland. Day. A sixteen-year-old GIRL races through the tall bush. She loves being on the open veldt, laughing and playing a secret game by assigning names to the flat-topped monkey bread trees. A sense of a prisoner escaping. In b.g. a plantation farm with African laborers bent picking crops. The girl sprints until she is exhausted and flings herself on the ground, flips over on her back and holds her hands up to the burning sun, in celebration or plea we cannot tell.

Fade in: Ext. Chicago busy street corner. Night. Freezing cold. Dirty snow banked up on curb. Adolescent boys, shivering in topcoats and team jackets, hang out in front of a hot-dog joint. Much machismo: hitting, punching, joshing. Leader of the pack is a fifteen-year-old would-be tough guy in a then-fashionable 'zoot suit', all wide shoulders, narrow-ankled pants, topped off with outrageous two-tone shoes. A covey of local girls passes by, noses in the air but wanting to be noticed. The zoot suiter leads a chorus of obscene insults and sexual innuendo. 'Hey, Phyllis! Phyllis!' She pretends to pay no notice. He sidles up to her, calling out: 'Syph ... Syph ... Sy-phyllis!' She turns and slaps him in the face. He and the other boys love the attention and laugh at themselves and her.

*

For a Californian used to modern kitchen appliances, Doris's place at 58 Warwick Road, SW5, might as well be Tobacco Road. The split-level maisonette has a midget-sized un-American refrigerator, no washing machine, car or TV, and a draughty toilet with a pull-chain in the back, an outhouse in all but name. Not even a toaster which, Doris claims, is an American abomination. On the other hand, there are those marvelous cheekbones.

Home safe. Thank you, Jesus.

For the next couple of years, my escape route from Immigration officers attempting to track down an American on the loose is to squirrel out through the narrow window in my top-floor back room (rent £2 per week) overlooking Nevern Square and hide behind one of 'London's fantastic forest of chimney pots', as Ed Murrow described them in his wartime broadcasts. Climbing in and out, the sashes moving smoothly under a liberal application of Imperial Leather soap, I feel like a master criminal. 'Made it, Ma, top of the world!' God, but it's always freezing cold, inside or out. How can she stand living like this? When the coast is clear, I climb back through the window like a jewel thief, sit myself back down at her sewing table, now my improvised writing desk, and madly scribble, scribble on a yellow pad. Can't write, cannot! *Must* keep going. Must!

WHEN EDMUND WILSON'S DAUGHTER PUT A GUN TO MY HEAD AND PULLED THE TRIGGER

Last year in Boston: my foot hard down on the gas pedal of a DeSoto Fireflite convertible, racing 2,983.7 miles of blue highway via 1-80E and 1-90E, I arrive, high on White Horse scotch, Dexedrine, Miltown tranks and myself, on the Beacon Hill doorstep of a publisher's office, drawn by their ad I found in a magazine in a dentist's office. Unsteady on my feet, in my head still following those double yellow road lines, I bloviate to an editor at prestigious 125-year-old publishing firm Houghton Mifflin that I'm the new F. Scott Fitzgerald or maybe Norman Mailer ... or some other famous writer, except that Houghton's chief editor, Dorothy de Santillana, actually *knew* Fitzgerald and I have no manuscript in hand because I haven't written anything yet. Not one single published word. But, channelling my Hollywood agent song-and-dance, I snow-job de Santillana and her young assistant, Rosalind Wilson, with a book proposal pitched straight off the top of my inflamed brain. Spiel, gabble, sell, sell! It worked for Selznick, why not for me with the original publishers of Hawthorne and Thoreau?

A study in disbelief, this bulky beautiful woman looks me up and down, unimpressed. She's about to throw me out when Wilson, daughter of the literary critic Edmund, whose *To the Finland Station* changed my life, nods affirmatively. The goddess Clio, bursting from the clouds, sighs, 'All right, how much will you need for the coming year?'

Good golly molly, they bought it! What now? Except spend the next years in hysterical deafness, blinding headaches, vertigo and whatnot. So this is what it's like being a writer.

'It's only a matter of time before you crack up,' the Paris doctor had predicted just before I hit him. I guess he had his revenge.

FASHION IS SPINACH

'Don't try to change me,' Doris warns on our very first night in bed together, the same day that I arrive at 58 Warwick Road. Her Valor paraffin heater with its woozy gasoline scent sends shadows dancing over the ceiling.

Don't try to change me. Is she kidding? Too late.

You can't imagine how difficult it is to shop for women's clothes in post-war, austerity England. The material is there at long last – clothes rationing just ended – but the clumsy cut and drab lack of style! Almost my first action on entering Doris's life is to drag her out to the shops, Harrods and Harvey Nichols, Marshall & Snelgrove and Swan & Edgar, to get her kitted out as befits her lush figure and sensuality. She stumbles at the first hurdle and never quite recovers. 'It's my shoulders, don't you see?' she moans, holding up a Norman Hartnell abomination. 'Impossible!'

I do my best with the human and textile materials to hand. Supervise a chic, off-the-eye haircut. Personally pumice her tobacco-stained teeth (she's a serial Silk Cut smoker). Apply a touch of eye shadow, remove unnecessary shoulder pads from her new silk blouses, and look for skirts with that extra little flair. There now, my creation is not bad at all.

Except, of course, what I believed I owned, I was only leasing.

YOU CAN'T DO THIS TO ME! OH, CAN'T I?

WHEN: A year later. A rainy day in spring.

WHERE: outside Earl's Court Tube station, this time without Mosleyites.

She and I strolling home in a light drizzle at dusk.

SHE: 'A West End theatre is putting on my play.'

CLANCY: 'Oh, yes? What's it about?'

SHE: 'You. Us.'

I stop and turn her around to face me by the shoulders I've dressed.

CLANCY (WITH RISING ANGER): 'You're kidding? How dare you?'

SHE (CALMLY, A SMILE): 'How dare I not? I am a writer. It's what writers do. We write.'

CLANCY (THINKING, I'LL KICK HER ASS): 'You can't do this to me!'

SHE: 'Oh, can't I? It's already cast.'

CLANCY: 'What's it called?'

SHE: *Play with a Tiger.*

CLANCY: 'I'm the tiger?'

SHE (WITH A FELINE SMILE): 'No, I am.'

CLANCY (SEETHING): 'Next you'll be talking about my orgasm.'

SHE, EYELIDS FLICKERING: 'What a very good idea.'

*

Clancy Sigal told (Samuel) Beckett one day how

Doris Lessing, with whom Sigal was living …
had introduced him as an identifiable character
'Saul Green', a macho kind of American, into
several of her books. He explained to Beckett
what a disturbing experience this had been.
Beckett shook his magnificent head. 'Identity
is so fragile – how did you ever survive?' He
looked at Sigal more closely. 'Or did you?'
> James R. Knowlson, *Damned to Fame:*
> *The Life of Samuel Beckett*

PS Beckett is rehearsing *End Game* in a Chelsea pub with his two favorite Irish-born actors, Patrick Magee and Jack MacGowran. Both Magee and MacGowran, in anguish, plead with 'Sam' to explain their roles to them. 'Sam, I don't understand this character. What does it mean?' To which Beckett replies, 'Boys, just say the lines on the page and don't worry about the meaning.'

PPS When Beckett learns about my work with schizophrenics he speaks with some difficulty of his mentor James Joyce's daughter Lucia whom Beckett dated and then over the years had to watch going mad. Uncharacteristically, he reaches over the drinks to grip my hand. 'Don't play with it,' he warns. 'It's incurable.'

A LITERARY DEBATE

Doris and I educate each other. She tutors me in the knotty dynamics of London literary life, and I instruct her in playing stud poker for matchsticks and listening to American blues and jazz on her ancient radio, tuning in to Willis Conover's

US Armed Forces station. By now an avid fan, she knows about Bessie Smith and Billie Holiday but not Delta blues geniuses like 'Son' House and the great Robert Johnson, said to have sold his soul to the Devil at a Mississippi crossroads in exchange for upgrading his talent on the Gibson L-1 guitar.

She, sleepily: 'Darling, would you ever sell your soul to the Devil?'

Me, without thinking twice: 'All the time, every day.'

These quiet moments are the best.

In all this time we have only a single literary disagreement. One morning, relaxing in the kitchen, I don't know how we get around to discussing the Russians, Gogol and Turgenev and our mutual fondness for Tolstoy. I'm re-reading *Anna Karenina*, one of Doris's favorite novels. She thinks Anna is a fool for love but also admires her for dying at the end rather than living in disgrace, without the love of the man who abandons her. Feeling lazy and irresponsible, I suggest that the novel's real victims are Anna's two men, her stuffy husband Alexei Karenin and her lover Count Vronsky.

'What?' Doris can't believe I'm serious.

'Look at it this way: Anna can't stand her boring husband so she leeches onto this dashing, not very bright officer. She's actually a predator, destroying her husband's reputation and taking over poor dumb Vronsky who never knows what hit him. Anna is the villain, they're the victims of her reckless lust!' There, now.

Doris looks across the table at me. Eyes agleam, teeth slightly bared. 'Ah, so it's war to the death, is it, my friend?' And then laughs to indicate that she's not seriously declaring war on me. I think.

Being 'Red', formerly (me) and still (her), is a strong bond between us, the symbiosis of defiance and disillusionment; we temporarily complete each other. It helps that we've both had secret services surveilling us, she in Africa, me all over the States. They're such a fixture in our lives we feel there's no point in worrying.

Once a week Doris 'has in' a cleaning lady, 'Miss Hogan', whom she loathes but masochistically refuses to fire, if only because half-mad Miss Hogan actively, vocally, loudly, despises her and snarls curses that in some odd way seem to satisfy Doris. Broom in hand, Miss Hogan savagely swipes at the dust-covered stairs while uttering, 'Communist slut … cunt … dirty whore … fucks niggers … sucking off her Yankee pimp …' And so on, sometimes under her breath, occasionally so loudly they can probably hear her across the road. Doris and I joke that Miss Hogan is a government spy. After all, who would ever suspect a mentally disturbed, alcoholic skivvy?

PS We know that all this time MI5 and MI6 were watching the house from across the road because Doris 'kept an international Communist brothel'. See Lessing's MI5 file P.F.97,471: '… attractive, forceful, dangerous women, ruthless if need be.'

TWO TIGERS IN A CAGE

Of course, she's had previous guys. One night, in a relaxed torpor, she mentions whips and chains, revealing a wearily nonchalant attitude to her old lovers' sado-masochistic quirks. Where's the harm if it pleases them? She's sympathetic to what they endured as child victims of the English ritual of packing off middle-class kids at a vulnerable age to single-sex, 'muscular Christian' boarding schools where they get a taste for pain; it's one of those things an amiable sex partner puts up with, yes? It seems to make little difference to her if the men are hetero, homo, in between or all three; she merely accepts whatever permutation it is as the natural condition of the artists and politicals she's been with. Her cosmopolitan attitude is something I'll have to learn to copy if I don't want to look like a hayseed.

And she speaks about how hard it is to be a woman, a single woman, a woman raising a child, a woman writer earning a living by her work. Most of all she complains bitterly about the attitude of the 'comrades' towards her and her writing.

Incident: as a London couple we go to dinner with friends – Communists – he a businessman, she a nurse. Afterwards, when I think we've had a perfectly fine time, Doris grips my arm on the stroll back through the smog to Warwick Road and mutters, 'Did you see that? *Did* you?'

'What?'

'How they patronized me,' she spits. 'They *hate* me. Hate the fact I'm a writer. Hate writers! Hate *women* who write!'

'But … they're comrades!'

'They're the worst,' she snarls. Nobody can snarl like Doris, with curled lips, bared teeth, followed by a super-expressive 'Ha!'

'Don't you see, darling. The left is just like the right: they talk culture but they hate us. We're wayward and unpredictable and that's dangerous to deal with. Better anything than danger!'

I love that 'we', as if I too am a published writer. I'm thrilled she accepts me as a London Literary Villager even if I have nothing to show for it. I view it as a real gesture of friendship offered amidst the storms and stresses between us. Were George Sand and Chopin like us? In the euphoria of ardour and comradeship, the Really Momentous Issues are deferred in favor of 'What's for lunch?' I chow down to stifle terror, so that meals are often a prelude to the erotic. She is a fabulous improvisational cook, dashing from her writing table to the kitchen to please her man, producing stews and homebaked bread on demand. She's a genius at making do with very little; food rationing (an egg a week, two ounces of cheese, a few of butter) ended just recently. After cooking and serving she becomes a different woman in the easy languor: lazy, affectionate, sluttish. There are moments of deep rapport – so much in common, so much to talk about – until the stone wall of incomprehension rears up between us.

What she isn't is a natural nurse. If I moan and groan, fall over and blank out, race around the house hyper-anxiously, Doris will not play Florence Nightingale. The unstated position is: you, Clancy, have to take the consequences of what you are. She's one tough farm girl.

Other times she gives generously in our stolen moments, but in the next breath seems to fight for the right to exist. She frankly desires a masculine keeper. 'I'll untie my fallopian tubes and we can have a child together. I'm so fertile, it's guaranteed.' Her fertility isn't just gynaecological either. Sometimes, in the middle of the night, she'll leap out from under the covers to scratch a note next to her ever-present bedside typewriter. I'm lying spreadeagled, drained, and she's on her literary toes? She's showing me how religiously writers budget their time.

Love is the forbidden word. We've spoken of it only once, Doris turning to me and saying, 'You don't know the first thing about real, true, deep love, do you, my friend?' We stare at each other blankly.

There's that stone wall again.

A PASSIONATE AFFAIR WITH IRIS MURDOCH

Doris's writer friends often pass through to socialize in our kitchen, all of them male, almost all young and present-able. I call them the 'four Johns' (Osborne, Amis, Braine, Wain), with occasional appearances by Chris Logue, John Berger, and any other eligible guy – married or not, sexually ambiguous or not. They come calling in the hope I won't be home, but I've got antennae and make myself obnoxiously visible while they're around. Most of them, especially if they went to public school, are clueless about dealing with a coarse, know-nothing American. Anyone too Oxbridge is a non-starter; only the leather-jacketed art theorist Berger on his big black motorcycle, and the poet Logue who had served military prison time for theft (a man after my own heart), felt like any threat to my ... well, I can't call it domi-nation, let's say ascendancy.

I wish Doris could be as cool about my 'doxies', as she calls them, as I am about her swains. Every time I go out of the house and return in the early-morning hours she's sure I'm having it off with one of the girls along Bayswater

Road or some other lowlife female. I've given up explaining that I just aimlessly wander where the feeling takes me, which she doesn't believe for a moment since in her eyes London's streets are mean and ugly whereas to me they're wonderful accidents waiting to happen. Writing is her job, mooching with no destination is mine. How else would I survive?

Emotional crises erupt all too easily at 58 Warwick Road. To wit: sometimes I'm invited to speak – as a foreigner, an American or, worse still, a 'victim of McCarthyism' – at your normal protest meeting. One night at Red Lion Hall I'm on a speakers' platform at a packed meeting about apartheid. Why am I even here? I wonder. Senator McCarthy and J. Edgar Hoover are sweethearts compared to South Africa's policemen. And I'm currently in a phase of suffering dizzy spells – Doris calls the frequent falling-about my 'condition'.

On the dais I glance over at the next speaker, the author Iris Murdoch, thinking, Hmm, some dish. Moments later, as is my habit, I pass out … onto Murdoch's lap. In front of 200 people. Blank out. Wake up staring up into her baby blues (or brown or whatever), noting her boyish cropped haircut. Will she push me off in disgust? Not a bit. It's like waking up in my mum's lap. She smiles down at me and says quietly, 'That happens to me too. Do you need help?' So sweet and gracious. Is it my turn to speak? Upsydaisy, on my feet. Murdoch whispers, 'You're not on quite yet.' And the evening proceeds without further incident.

But later, at home, Doris has heard about it and accuses me of deliberately making a crude pass at Murdoch. (An ongoing accusation.) I plead *nolo contendere*, and we're off to the races again. Thus, with her sixth sense, Doris gets it 100 per cent right that I've sized up Murdoch as a woman and 100 per cent wrong that I fainted on purpose. And she wasn't even present in the hall that night!

The next morning over breakfast all she says is, 'Well, my dear, I suppose there's some consolation in the fact that you're doing it with a better class of tootsie.'

Iris Murdoch a tootsie???

THE GREEN HILLS OF AFRICA

Doris really is an African girl – with African suitors.

'What are you doing here with the missus, white boy?' Big Joshua Nkomo demands one day in Doris's kitchen. 'You have no business being with her. We are her friends. You are an upstart. What do you Americans say? Skiddoo.'

Her black Nationalist African friends are martyrs of the liberation struggles in Rhodesia, South Africa, Nyasaland and Mozambique. They couldn't be more straightforward about viewing Doris, the London left's Rita Hayworth, as their property. All have suffered the rite of passage in white men's prisons, and are socialist in outlook except when it comes to women. Harry Nkumbula, co-chief of the Northern Rhodesia African Congress, is a hearty, blunt-spoken man. 'When I walk in the door of Mrs Lessing, you walk out, boy. Understand?'

Boy?

I offer them tea, linger over it, and in the end the winner is whoever can outsit the competition in a kitchen chair: always me. I'm not going to leave her alone with this bunch.

Only Kenneth Kaunda, later Zambia's first president, treats me kindly. 'You must forgive us, Clancy. Detention with hard labor is not the best place to learn how to capture a woman's heart.'

LOVE'S WAR WOUNDS

Doris's white male friends are almost all war veterans, distinguished on the battlefield but shy in the sex stakes. Their wives, however, are something else.

The women of the war generation have had five long years waiting at home for their men while coping with the drudgery of child-care and the terrors of living in England under siege or else seizing their newfound freedom to step in as ambulance driver, munitions worker, social worker, ship builder, air raid warden. Almost overnight on VE Day, the war as motor for social change seems to go into reverse. No sooner have the husbands been demobbed than they are going AWOL, to resume careers or wrestle with ideological demons, and these newly liberated women must resume the role of wife again. The result is that, occasionally, apparently perfectly proper women will fondle my knee under the table, not always pretending it isn't happening but openly wanting to be paid attention to. Their men, obsessed with politics, don't notice, or, worse, do notice and don't care. But Doris has eyes in the back of her head. 'They may want to sleep with you ... Don't you dare!'

The women's despair, defiance, anger and disappointment are temporarily directed at me.

A wife confronts me on a street corner one night in the snow.

'Please. I want to.'

Me, sputtering: 'But Jack is a comrade!'

She stands there waiting. Snow falls lightly. 'I'm not pretty enough, is that it?'

'Of course not.'

'You've been to our house. With that damn oil heater of yours! Our kids taught you cricket. I want to.'

'I can't. I'm sorry.'

'Doris says you're a hypocrite. She's right.'

Sexual tension prevails at 58 Warwick Road. In front of her portable typewriter, Doris will be lounging in a wicker chair, (great) legs crossed, smoking, brainstorming, eyes gazing into space, leaning forward a little, showing tan bosom in the V of the silk blouse I got her, and I'll say 'I'm hungry!' and she'll type a few last words and then strip off and the afternoon is gone and for the moment so are my fears. But I am more circumspect when her son Peter is home, which makes her furious. 'WHY DO YOU HATE SEX SO MUCH? I'M NOT YOUR BLOODY MOTHER! YOU'RE SUCH A PURITAN!'

Writing is her oxygen. Mine is bolting from the house to discover my own metropolis.

*

London at this time is still pitted with bomb craters, each telling a story, now the haunt of crabgrass, 'bombweeds', and little indescribable animals running wild. The scenes of devastation all around remind me of Depression-hit Chicago. Smashed and set ablaze by thousand-plane Luftwaffe waves, St Swithin, London Stone, St Stephen Walbrook, large pockets of medieval London ... all are gone.

I crave to learn more about the private lives of the Londoners who existed and worked where now only voids remain. (Twenty thousand died in air raids, including the victims of 'blast lung'.) Wartime signs still point to air-raid shelters. Did veterans of Ypres and the Somme shrug off the WW2 Blitz or suffer from it worse than others did? What had they felt while cowering in flimsy Anderson shelters or anxiously scanning the sky for Hitler's pilot-less buzz bombs? Clerks, housewives, bowler-hatted City stockbrokers, taxi drivers, thieves and spivs ... I make up stories for each forsaken address: 5 Christchurch Lane, 16 Prince Albert Road, 23 Maiden Close, Wren's St Andrew-by-the-Wardrobe.

With no way of verifying this, I'm told that London in the Blitz was a more egalitarian place than it ever was or would be again. That the Nazis' rain of death had made possible a different kind of England. That the electrified fence of class dissolved, temporarily at least. That England was experimenting with a new kind of history.

I'd arrived in an interregnum, after the doodlebugs but before there was money to rebuild: stability of a sort. There are plenty of unexploded bombs still scattered around the scarred city. A bleak, otherworldly serenity has settled on the streetscape. It suits my mood perfectly. The cleared but still-wrecked streets seem to mirror my own 'condition'.

How had the living survived the day-to-day scrimping, skiving, scheming? When they were bombed out or just couldn't take the shriek of sirens anymore or having to smuggle off-ration bacon from the local butcher in return for God knows what favor. Here and there, while picking my way through the side streets, I eavesdrop on tales of loneliness, husbands, sons and fathers who never came back from Tobruk or Singapore, marriages broken under the stress of continual bombing, the sheer inedibility of whale meat, children who've never seen an orange and rescue workers looting from corpses. I am struck by the prevailing stoical acceptance of wartime life and death, though some stories I hear are starkly different from the 'London Can Take It' propaganda films, all stiff-upper-lipped together.

Slowly, slowly, it sinks in. Holding on, that's the thing.

So what's the trick to managing that?

THE DALAI LAMA OF WELBECK STREET

'The "trick", my friend, is something alien to you. Insight,' Doris tells me without rancor. Calling me a 'monster of deceit', she persuades me to see a faith healer in Tottenham whose queue of patients, including Druids in full costume, stretches all the way down the road. I enjoy eavesdropping on the sick and lame gossiping about ley lines, the Cerne Abbas chalk giant and the man up ahead who, apparently, is in daily contact with the ancient English gods. When it's my turn I give the healer a pound note, kneel and let this old guy – scruffy, dandruff, bad breath – rub my scalp.

Nothing happens.

'Of course not. You're still looking for a magic cure,' says Doris, as if she hadn't suggested I go to him.

So she sends me to my first-ever legitimate shrink instead, a former lover of hers, a solidly built, phlegmatic Central

European, relaxing in a chair in his office at Maudsley Hospital, Denmark Hill. He has amused eyes, and a frown that resembles a thin smile. After hearing my list of symptoms, he diagnoses: 'You are definitely an unbalanced person. Manic depressive most probably. Why don't you come into my hospital?'

'Oh, yes, what for?'

He shrugs. 'A little ECT,' he says. Electroconvulsive therapy for stomach ache? 'Like many similar patients, you are in denial. Verging on psychosis, in my professional opinion. A touch of ECT and you will be right as rain.'

I sprint for my life down the hospital stairs and out into the (comparatively) fresh air of Denmark Hill.

Next batter up: 'Mother Sugar'! Dr 'Helena Ziperstein', Jungian Catholic and Doris's current analyst, is an elderly lady with an attic consulting room in the West End. She resembles an ancient Dalai Lama, a small wizened creature who sits almost doubled up in a high-backed chair on a raised dais as the grey afternoon light filters down on her through a skylight. Will she take me on? I ask.

She shakes her grizzled head in resignation. 'No, dear,' she tells me. 'I am too old. You are *der Sprengstoff*, too raw and dangerous. It would kill me. So sorry. I feel selfish telling you this.'

But am I crazy? I beg to know.

'Ach, crazy. Don't worry about it too much. You have so many trees to chop down, what means this?' Her head lolls on to her breast as if she sleeps, and I tiptoe out. She doesn't charge me.

Oh, joy. Mother Sugar has reprieved me from the burden of insight.

His tenth rule for writers is: 'Try to leave out the part that readers tend to skip.'

*

> Call us drab and dismal, if you like. And tell us
> we don't know how to cook our food or wear
> our clothes – but, for heaven's sake, recognize
> that we're trying to do something ... extraordi-
> nary and difficult – to have a revolution for once
> without the Terror ...
>
> J. B. Priestley, *The Linden Tree*

*

'Fair Shares For All': on bomb-site billboards you can still see slogans from a time when everyone – well, almost every-one – 'pulled together'. The war-induced impetus to create a more generous society was there, briefly.

Yet, even as I arrive in London, it's slipping away. There's a widespread belief – I hear it expressed in pubs, offices, on building sites – that something good was recently within people's grasp but now is leaching away, and nobody knows exactly why. Labour militants speak of 'betrayal', doctors and teachers of 'lost opportunities'. The 'socialist experi-ment' is closing down. But there was a moment ...

If Tom Paine were me he'd want to bring back to America this adventure of living through Britain's experiment with democratic socialism. Clippie Jean got me into the welfare system whose small print I've since doggedly set myself to read. So, gritting my teeth, I slog through masses of bone-dry government papers like the Beveridge Report's *Social Insurance and Allied Services*; *Income Distribution and Social Change* by Richard Titmuss; John Vaizey's *Education in a Class Society*, and Brian Abel-Smith's *The Cost of the National Health Service in England and Wales*. With my own eyes I've seen how the innovations suggested by these works can improve my immediate circumstances: a free consultation with a doctor, emergency cash, a sense that if I fall there's a safety net to catch me.

It's only a sixpenny ride on the number 9 bus and I can stroll into the London School of Economics and say hello to the authors of the government reports. 'Hi, I'm an American and ...'

(They've put railroads and electricity under public ownership. Can sex also be nationalized?)

Doubts about the 'welfare revolution' occur to me only when I compare the visionary speech-making with the pressing needs of real people I meet on London buses and streets. For example, many bombed-out families were hurriedly rehoused in flimsy-looking temporary structures, the unhandsome 'prefabs' that are expected to last only ten years. Labour's urban planners, obsessively into 'slum clearance', sweeping away the past willy-nilly, are keen to bulldoze these temporary dwellings quickly and move people into the new concrete Le Corbusier-style high-rise 'ghettos in the sky' where the lifts unfailingly fail. But the prefab families I speak to *like* their ground-level, easy-build homes that have indoor plumbing, a fireplace and a boiler for central heating (unknown to them until now) plus a patch of grass outside where the kids can play.

I want to believe. But I also like to listen.

YOU CAN RUN AND YOU CAN HIDE

Bursting with the urge to write, but not writing, a cyclone of emotional energy gathers in Warwick Road. There's only so much walking in the rain you can do, so many Odeon afternoon matinees you can face, so much effort you can expend on trying to remember 'permitted' licensing hours (pubs shut from 2.30 to 6 p.m., just when you most need a drink), and nobody to play with when Peter is away at boarding school. Doris just wants peace and quiet to get on with her work; peace and quiet drive me half-insane.

Running away works. It really does.

'Destination, please?'

Where other men's domestic storms drive them to cosy refuges in Boodle's and White's, my clubs are the railway termini of King's Cross, St Pancras, Euston, Paddington, Victoria and Waterloo, armed with a paperback volume of Pevsner's *The Buildings of England* in one hand and a Bradshaw's rail timetable in the other. I'm used to wide-open American spaces so England – only 300-plus miles north to south and east to west – takes some adjusting to on my part.

'How far will this money take me, ma'am?' I'll ask the lady at the ticket window on my way to Glasgow, Cardiff, Newcastle, Manchester, Liverpool ... anywhere far from the psychological war zone in SW5. I sleep in station forecourts, shuttered tea rooms, guards' vans – and usually, at the end of the line, there's a smile and a cuppa for me. 'You a Yank then? My sister married one of your blokes. Know where Schenectady is?' Or, 'Yes, I suppose you can sleep here till the ganger comes. American, I see. Wouldn't know Ernie Kubalek, would you? Ninetieth Infantry chappie. Our left flank outside St Lo. We met up behind a hedge, exchanged fags and addresses. Have to be honest, my regiment could've had better support from your blokes. Untried, were they?' 'Ooooh, you're cute, aren't you? When do I get off work? Cheeky!'

I'm learning a people's history from those busy making it, but Doris isn't convinced. 'Ha! As if you're going to find out all about the native working class by sleeping with their women!'

Well, it's certainly one way.

Wonderfully, aimless travel takes me into the rarefied universe of teenage train-spotters. Once these platform-haunting kids, the spiritual sons (rarely daughters) of Blitz-era enemy-aircraft spotters, see that I share their passion for the still gorgeously functioning A4 steam locos, wreathed around with smoke from their coal-fired engines and tooting their steam whistles, they're only too happy to share their coded secrets. Like them I carry a small notebook in which I jot down the numbers of the snorting iron horses thundering past. The advent of diesel is rapidly making coal-fired engines obsolete so when the locos pull into the station the steam drivers and their helpers climb down and readily impart their arcane secrets, with pride, nostalgia and sadness, to an interested American stranger. It's a terrific honour to be invited into a loco's cab and shown the firebox and controls and ... ecstasy! ... how to pull the cord for the train's whistle and to learn its codes. What unadulterated pleasure! And how bitterly the kids on the platform envy me!

In each and every town I wander there's always a WW1 monument in the main square or street, listing names and units, with shorter lists of the dead from WW2. Standing in the rain, gazing at the honour rolls of the Leeds and Accrington Pals and Grimsby Chums – the Great War generation, many of them still rotting in Flanders shellholes – I imagine blood rather than water dripping off the granite rifles and helmets and winged angels of the public memorials.

And in these towns there is a constituency of spinsters – Miss Carmichael the primary school teacher, Miss Plunkett the district nurse, Miss Owens the recluse who lives with her cat up on the hill (and who some suspect is a witch) – the widows and girlfriends of the three-quarters of a million British soldiers who died in WW1. These women are disproportionately middle-class because their officer boyfriends, fiancés and husbands were mown down percentage-wise in greater numbers than private soldiers. There were often no funerals because the mutilated dead had to be buried in foreign military cemeteries, so the women left behind never even had the consolation of saying goodbye. They were left forever wondering if the Unknown Soldier was their Frank with whom they'd had an 'understanding' before he enlisted. These female solitaries, suffering their own form of shell shock, without men or physical contact or sex in their lives, now in their sixties and seventies, are instantly recognizable in any town or village, though none of the younger people I speak to even realise why these women live alone. God knows how many such there are scattered all over the United Kingdom, ignored or taken for granted or, simply, invisible.

So this is what the famous British 'restraint' and stiff upper lip are all about: the lonely pain of thousands of grief-stricken women isolated in their unexpressed rage. It's as if after the Armistice a law was passed: keep it to yourself.

Hitchiking back to London one day, I'm picked up by an elderly miner in his Berkeley three-wheeled motor, just outside Eastwood, Nottingham, birthplace of D. H. Lawrence. He chats about serving with his 45th Foot–Sherwood Foresters regiment in 1916. 'Oh, aye, hardly anyone from my lot got back. I was gassed. The mustard. After, went back down to t'pit. Imagine, with my lungs! You know, they killed us all, even ones like me who made it back … we survived but we felt dead. Don't let anyone tell you different. My wife knew. Daft kid I was. For a long time, I couldn't stop shitting myself – like I did before a Hun attack. Not a bit ashamed to say it. It's what I remember most. The bloody embarrassment of it.'

Back in Whitehall it's hard to miss the equestrian statue of the man who sacrificed them all, Sir Douglas Haig the lunatic general, never under fire himself, who master-minded the 141-day Somme butchery by sending Tommies forward at a walking pace into German barbed wire and sniper fire. I couldn't have advanced like that to near-certain death but would have cowered in a shellhole or played dead and prayed, but my Sherwood Forester friend, old pals falling to both sides of him, kept walking right into the Kaiser's *Maschinengewehre*. The Russian Army mutinied, thirty French divisions rebelled, why not the British with near to half a million killed in just one needless assault? And why hasn't anyone dynamited Haig's arrogant memorial in protest? I think about it every time I pass by, because I'm qualified to blow up things with C4 plastic. It would take less than a pound and a makeshift detonator, but I think twice because of the innocent pedestrians who might be harmed. To my surprise a deep sadness, like the Sherwood Forester's despair, disables my anger, because on Poppy Day the survivors of the worst massacre in world history until the Holocaust hobble past the Cenotaph with undisguised pride, shouldering umbrellas like rifles with soldierly bearing. How can they? Truly, there is something about English people I will never understand.

Now for the other, domestic, war.

THE INVISIBLE MAN IS CONCEIVED

In Warwick Road, predictably, a problem with multiple identities surfaces, hers and mine. As days go by Doris will refer to herself as 'she' while gazing at me astigmatically as though from afar. For her I'm there but not there. Quarrels and tight silences escalate and take on a weird cast. I've done something wrong, but what? She'll say: 'You're trapping me as a person I don't want to be.' Or, 'Why do you take such pleasure in torturing me?' Except it's torturing 'her'. Tiny slips, telling lapses. Is it any wonder I roam the house humming 'Don't Fence Me In'.

She's starting to relate to me as this fictional character building in her head for the Big Book on which she claims to be 'blocked'. (I should be so blocked!) We don't talk about it much except that I keep catching her looking at me in this funny way; she claims it's merely my imagination, 'All part of your breakdown – your sickness,' she concludes. At a house party with her friends – of all people Henry Kissinger, sucking up to London's intelligentsia, is there too – she wraps an arm around my neck, almost in a choke-hold, and proudly announces, 'Clancy is my doing. I *created* him!'

To be the object of someone else's writerly scrutiny is dreadful beyond death. I've become *him*. But hold on a sec. By closely observing how her imagination systematically constructs a *him thing*, a pebble drops into the still pond of my mind. After all, who knows what *he* is capable of? Think, Sigal.

GOONS IN THE RAIN

But the thought of someone appropriating my identity gives me a headache. Relief comes only by wandering north with the train-spotters or, blissfully, at half-term when Peter and his pals are home from school and I spend the days with them.

Thwack!

'Not fair! S-s-s-simply isn't cricket! Out, out!' protests Woodjie the ventriloquist's dummy after I swing the flat-sided bat and send the hard, seamed leather ball sailing high over the bronze head of Peter Pan in Kensington Gardens on a rare gorgeous day. Woodjie, the fifth member of our little gang, with his red wig, lipsticked mouth and floppy hands, is the property and voice of fourteen-year-old Occy. At the far end of the makeshift crease stands Ernest, grave and loose-limbed, tipped for an England try out. He frowns at the way I violate cricketing protocol by swinging the bat, whammo, like the St Louis Cardinals slugger Stan Musial. Graceful Ernest, who might have come out of an A. E. Housman poem, is too chivalrous to censure the American immigrant who has overstayed his welcome.

Being 'Doris's children', Peter Lessing and I are especially close and spend a lot of time together in his school hols, lying around in his room reading *Beano* and the *Eagle*'s Dan Dare to each other when not engaging in pillow fights. There are moments I fantasize about us being a real settled family. Aged eleven, Peter is more father to me than child; at home we frequently wrestle and knock each other about – he's a big boy for his age – but he's the mature one who calms things down and sets certain boundaries, with a stern look that says: enough.

In the park my cricket ball pings off the statue and plops into the Round Pond. Peter tilts his beautiful blond head to one side and mourns, 'Clankety has messed up again. Sad ... oh, so very sad,' in the voice of BBC Radio *The Goon Show*'s Neddie Seagoon, followed by Woodjie leading us in shrieking: '*Whatwhatwhatwhatwhatwhatwhatwhatwhatwhat?*'

To hell with native customs. Another mighty Musial swipe of my bat and the cricket ball almost decapitates Peter Pan. Thwack!

*

> Doris's voiceover, Hyde Park scene: 'Why won't you grow up, Clancy? I'm not your mother. You can't keep escaping forever into Neverland.'

She is wrong.

Doris teases me about hanging out with kids, even the older college-age youths like the *Universities & Left Review* boys and girls (Oxbridge, naturally) at their not-quite-ready-for-customers-yet Partisan coffee house, 7 Carlisle Street in Soho, which she calls my new 'playground', which it is. To understand why I seek their company, you need to bear in mind the tumult in the British Left in the late fifties.

*

The British New Left is born of the synchronicity of the British, French and Israeli Armies attempting to wrest control of the Suez Canal from Egypt within days of Russia mercilessly crushing a Hungarian workers' uprising. Youthful disgust and anger create a fresh new UK movement that mingles war-veteran Communists (represented by the *New Reasoner* magazine and thinkers) with untainted-by-war student rebels (*Universities & Left Review*), who include Young Conservatives and many Young Liberals, sickened by the unmasking of the 'underlying violence and aggression latent in the two systems that dominate[d] political life at the time – Western Imperialism and Stalinism', to quote the 2010 *New Left Review* account of the 'Life and Times of the First New Left' by Stuart Hall (see below). The movement marks a cultural adjustment rather than a popular cause, and does not draw much working-class support. Its signature movie, almost a romantic rallying cry, is the Polish-made *Ashes and Diamonds*, patterned on Brando's *The Wild One* but adapted to Eastern Europe's killer ironies.

Sweating off the anxious blues, I paint the Partisan's walls, scrape off wallpaper and scrub floors, which also provides me with my first lesson in the 'dont's' of what later will be called Women's Liberation. 'Don't' No. 1: flirt openly. At an upstairs meeting of the *ULR*'s editorial board I glance at a young St Anne's woman who – she must have been a head prefect in a previous life – immediately reports me to Stuart Hall, our pre-eminent public intellectual for whom the New Left women go ga-ga, though they are driven mad by his apparent indifference. Jamaica-born and unbearably handsome, Stuart has a more flexible view of these things. 'Clancy, remember, we're like the army: keep your eyes front and centre if you want to stay out of trouble with left-wing women. Puritanism is alive and well among us.'

Doris is hugely sceptical of my plunging into London's 'youf culture' that puts me in touch with kids half my age. 'You and your need to "belong". Belongingness is what betrayed us Communists in the first place, can't you see?'

What she doesn't see is how happy I am in the company of kids.

*

It's pure bliss when Peter and his pals are back from school and free to open up for me a whole new child's-eye view of London. I can't see Hemingway following the lead of three *Goons*-spouting kids and a lipsticked mannequin, hunkering on the East India Docks, dangling their legs over the looping, biologically dead Thames, singing 'Row, Row, Row Your Boat' to the bargemen passing by on their way down to Tilbury.

Our Thames playground is still a working river. All around us the tall brick chimneys of East End factories that survived the Blitz rise like ships' masts, though equally visible are the gaps where the Luftwaffe relentlessly blasted the Docklands. On rainy days we'll splosh about in wellies, cutting through bomb sites and back gardens along Regent's Canal down to Limehouse. The canalside is a wonderful jungle gym, a secret world of goldfinches, ducks, dragonflies, gudgeon and chub that elderly anglers fish for all day amidst an L. S. Lowry landscape of gasometers and the backs of tanneries and breweries that give off a boy-delicious smell: a reeky oily stench. If you held a lighted match to it you would blow up half of London. We especially like exploring the unguarded intestines of derelict wharves in Docklands from Bow to Wapping. And, of course, riding a number 25 bus to Whitechapel to solve the Jack the Ripper case while pretending to carve each other up with screams and dead faints. Thus I know that it is perfectly possible to reverse time. All you need is the company of adolescent boys.

If it rains too hard – this is London – we repair to Doris's place or to Ernest's mum's flat for a muscular (read, hysterical) game of Pit, with cries of 'Wheat! Barley! Oats!' as we pound on each other, emerging – to Ernest's mother's horror – bruised and bleeding from our card game as if we've been in a war zone, which emotionally we have. Or, best of all, we just lounge around together sharing tattered copies of *Roy of the Rovers*.

When Peter is home I take him to a Bertram Mills Circus, or – he can't stop laughing! – a show by the Harlem Globetrotters and their star clown-genius Meadowlark Lemon, or in especially quiet moments I'll spin him tales from my former life in Hollywood while he claps his chubby hands in delight at the farce of it. 'You lie!' he'll scream, and slug me with a pillow. Somehow this solid little boy has crept into my heart even if I have not yet made it into his. If by chance a mental fugue knocks me sideways, the boys will gather round in solidarity. 'Clankety's sad again,' Peter croons, with Woodjie the dummy chiming in as the voice of the Goons' Neddie Seagoon, 'Enough of these funny jocular bits,' and I'm healed for the moment.

In that long drizzly steamy summer we create our own miniature London. Because Occy and Peter have been raised in bohemian free-wheeling circles, they affect poses of unshockability while solemn, conventional Ernest has to be dragged protesting to the movies at the Kensington Odeon where the other boys and I love best the 'Carry On' series, with their punning titles like *Carry On up the Khyber* (think about it in Cockney rhyming slang), full of rear-entry jokes and ghastly humor. (Like gay Kenneth Williams as Caesar in *Carry On, Cleo*: 'Infamy, infamy – they've all got it infamy. Coo!' Accompanied by trombone 'wah-wahs'.) When we deign to include Doris in our movie jaunts she falls about with helpless giggles. She loves laughing.

What she doesn't find funny are my manners in bed. If I can choose her clothes, surely I can command her orgasm. Think again.

AMONG THE GROWN-UPS

When the boys' holiday is over and they go back to school I must pretend to be a grown-up again. You don't know what an inferiority complex is until, reining in your vertigo, you sit cross-legged on Doris's cashmere-blanket-covered broken-sprung low divan at editorial meetings of the *New Reasoner*, Anglo-Saxon nerve centre of the twentieth century's great democratic revolution in the tradition of Garibaldi, Paine, Kościuszko, Byron and Shelley. Even before *Man of La Mancha* we dream the impossible dream of a continent-wide mutiny from the Urals to Lyme Regis, an uprising of workers and intellectuals uniting to smash the mind-forged manacles of Stalinist regimes, men and women daring once again to imagine socialism without torture chambers.

Except for me, the New Reasoners are the crème de la crème of Britain's intelligentsia, teachers and poets and writers, superbly educated and preposterously articulate, a circle of ex- and soon-to-be-former Reds, dedicated to cleansing the Stalinist stable of horse shit – although this isn't how the group's charismatic leader, historian Edward (E. P.) Thompson, eloquently puts it:

> ... simultaneously in a hundred places, and on ten thousand lips ... [It's] voiced by poets in Poland, Russia, Hungary, Czechoslavakia, by factory delegates in Budapest; by communist militants at the eighth plenum of the Polish Party; by a communist premier [Imre Nagy] who was murdered for his pains. It was on the lips of women and men coming out of jail ...
>
> E. P. Thompson, *The Moral Economy of the English Crowd in the Eighteenth Century*

Craggily handsome, Edward carries on his broad shoulders the ghostly weight of 'history from below' – Levellers and Lollards and Wat Tyler and Luddite machine-breakers in whose direct descent we are or feel we are. His rich talent as poet and archivist is to retrieve a working-class 'oral tradition' all but lost if not for his tenacious digging like a miner at the coal face. Some of Edward's 'positions' I must take on trust, if only because, like me, he is fond of quoting the London poet William Blake. I only wish Doris also took Blake to her accusatory heart:

> *Mutual Forgiveness of each Vice*
> *Such are the Gates of Paradise …*

Fat chance.

I feel like such a fraud in this company because I can't write and they all produce books, pamphlets and essays almost without conscious thought. At the same time I feel a bit senior because I've struggled through the same ideological battles and come through at the other end while they're still agonizing over should we/shouldn't we? (Leave the Party.) Yet how can I not admire men (Doris is the only woman present) who are writers and warriors too? Edward Thompson commanded battle tanks in North Africa and at Italy's Monte Cassino siege and lost a brother to Nazi torture; Basil Davidson parachuted behind enemy lines to fight alongside Yugoslav partisans and took the German surrender in Italy; Alex Baron was a Pioneer Corps first responder at D-Day; John Saville was a regimental sergeant major and ack-ack gunner; Mervyn Jones served on D-Day in anti-tanks and was a prisoner–of–war; Ralph Miliband served in the Royal Navy and also took part in the D-Day landing; Eric Hobsbawm in the Royal Engineers, and so on. These guys fought to protect me, the little Chicago Jew, while I was still collecting tin foil from backyard Victory gardens. How can I even dream of comparing myself to these guardians of my liberty?

'Don't you worry about it, my lamb,' Doris consoles me as we lie in her bed watching the stove's shadows dancing above. 'Even if you had published a hundred novels and a thousand poems they would still see you as my gigolo.' Gigolo? Stud, rake, lothario, fancy man? Sleazy scoundrel Zachary Scott in *Mildred Pierce*? I *love* this categorization and suspect she does too. Even the corner tobacconist, where I run down in the mornings to get her ciggies and newspapers, whispers dirty stuff about me to his wife behind the counter.

Several of the Reasoners are keen on Doris, but only Belgian-born Ralph Miliband makes a move, maybe because he's an ex-sailor and used to making the most of every chance he gets to talk to a beautiful woman. How Old School he is! Even asks my permission. Ralph: 'May I take Doris out for a drink?' Me: 'No.' Ralph: 'No?' Me: 'No.'

Word quickly spreads that I am uncouth.

But, being American, I want only to be liked. Alas, they tend to blame me for everything from McCarthyism to Norman Mailer's sex life. Edward Thompson in particular is infuriated by my impudent (as he sees it) lectures to the comrades. Then there's my habit of fainting dead away on the floor or the nearest lap, even Edward's. He grouches on one of our walks through freezing Earl's Court fog during meeting breaks: 'Clancy, you never stop complaining about our English weather, our food, our telephones and the sheer bloody gloom of London winters. You missed the war and haven't published anything. If you hate it so much here, why don't you go back to your own bloody country?' Edward delights in striding along dressed only in shirtsleeves, chest bared to the cold air. I am bundled up like Bunny Bear in layers of clothing, and earmuffs too. 'Cough … cough … this IS my country now,' I wheeze, shocking myself. Where did that come from?

Partly from the Bomb.

TONY HANCOCK ON THE MARCH

On this wintry night the Goon Boys (Peter, Ernest, Occy and Woodjie) drag me to the overspill balcony of a crowded Methodist Central Hall meeting a stone's throw (in this case, not a cliché) from the prime minister's residence at number 10 Downing Street. Downstairs on the stage your standard ho-hummers, pacifists, priests and do-gooders jaw away. Yawn! We five 'political children' (including Woodjie) are platitude-averse.

But then a slightly hunched, bespectacled professor, A. J. P. Taylor, Fellow of Magdalen College, Oxford, your classic don, rises, pauses for dramatic effect, peers at us over his specs as if to examine each and every person in the vast hall, and dryly summarizes nuclear-blast statistics before suddenly bellowing: *'Would any of you do that to your fellow man?'*

This is met by a shocked silence.

Taylor howls: *'THEN WHY ARE WE MAKING THE DAMNED THING?'*

The crowd quivers under a shockwave of emotion and a surprising roar of agreement goes up. The floor of Methodist Central Hall shakes as if struck by an earthquake. So much for the unemotional English. On this cold February night

the Campaign for Nuclear Disarmament is born and catches
me in its flash flood.

> *I will not cease from mental fight*
> *Nor shall my sword sleep in my hand*
> *Till we have built Jerusalem*
> *In England's green and pleasant land.*

As the great meeting-hall organ thunders, lifting me practically out of my boots, I silently vow that *my* sword shall
not sleep either.

Naturally, after this there's a riot outside number 10
Downing Street where the police horses prance impatiently,
waiting for us. In the melee steel ball bearings are tossed
under the horses' hooves, to objectors' cries of 'Don't
hurt the animals!' – very English, this. I, Johnny Storm the
Torch, jump on the bobbies and am pulled off by Mervyn
Jones, the only New Reasoner actually to like Americans,
who wrestles the police while I scuttle away between their
legs; Mervyn gets dragged off to Cannon Street Magistrates'
Court where I go to be his character witness. He smiles at
me wanly from inside his cell. 'They'll take one look at you
and lengthen my sentence, comrade. Wipe your nose, it's
bleeding.'

Essentially young, studentish, vicarish, middle-class
and contagious, CND's slogan 'Let Britain Lead' is absurd
and poignant. At Britain's weakest moment, its industries failing and a revalued pound worth nothing, CND
is taking up the cry of imperial leadership. 'Let Britain
lead – ban the bomb!' Such liberal arrogance is immensely
appealing.

*

A US B-47's crew member pulls the wrong lever and drops an atom bomb on the beautifully named Mars Bluff, South Carolina, which injures people but fails to explode. Elvis Presley is inducted to the army as Private #53310761. Russia launches the Space Age with Sputnik. Trunk calls (long-distance dialing) are introduced in the UK.

*

CND's first march on Easter weekend 1958 is a fifty-two-mile trek from Trafalgar Square to the bomb-making factory at Aldermaston, Hertfordshire. It starts disastrously in a flurry of snowflakes. We look exactly what we are: a bedraggled Children's Crusade together with a sprinkling of vintage suffragettes flaunting their ancient purple, white and green flags, tortured by force-feeding in prison as young women, now toddling along with walking sticks or being pushed in wheelchairs. Then God speaks, more rain and sleet bucket down – and, weirdly, duffel-coated strangers straggle in from all parts of Southern England to join us. It's a peculiarly English phenomenon: the worse the weather becomes, the more pity and support there is for our sodden cause. Oh, those poor dears!

And what a poor-dear crew we are: priests, sixth-formers, Quakers, trade unionists with their colorful Diego Rivera-like banners (*Labor Omnia Vincit* – Work Conquers All), and geeky Goons fans. Above all, Aldermaston is the political expression of the wildly popular, off-key comedy show *Hancock's Half Hour*, about glum and luckless Anthony Aloysius St John Hancock of 23 Railway Cuttings, East

Cheam, whose monologues send young fans into fits of screaming laughter.

Striding amidst these unhip, uncool CND trudgers a Eureka! moment almost knocks me off my feet. This march, attended by these dowdy earnest unstylish people, is what I've been looking for all along, my potential readers because I'm one of them. But how to do it?

Of course, I vomit, and fall out from time to time to dump it in a paper bag in a trash bin. 'Don't litter, don't litter!' command the lady marshals through bullhorns, like regimental sergeants. By the time our straggling columns reach Knightsbridge the heavens open up in such a classically miserable day that we marchers go crazy. And the worse the weather, the greater the number of the strangers who pour out from the side streets to join the stragglers. Drenched to the skin, perhaps 5,000 strong, we thread through Hammersmith, past a derelict church on the corner of Bute Gardens across from the huge Lyons Swiss Roll factory. A gang of sharply dressed teenagers appears to watch us pass: boys getting their Cecil Gee jackets wet to stare at us, girls folding their arms across their chests and hoping the rain won't ruin their over-one-eye bouffants, all gaping at us marchers as if we're visitors from Mars, which, given the social gulf that divides us from them, we might as well be. CND men in their Ramblers' Association anoraks, and women in safe, serious and sensible long skirts and hiking shoes, look incredibly frumpy compared to this bunch in their Italian-cut suits, winklepicker shoes and razored hair styles for the boys, Marks & Spencer two-tone cardigans and stiletto heels for the girls.

The CND-ers' cheerful cries of 'Come join us!' are met with catcalls of 'Up yer fuckin' arseholes, ya pooftas.' So much for working-class outreach. Little did I know these corner kids were to prove my future.

And away we go... o... o...

PART TWO

The People's War, the People's Land

> This is the people's war, the people's land, and
> what we save we rule …
>   Elizabeth Bowen, *People, Places, Things: Essays*

You won't find my London in an A to Z map or an app. Its heart is the point where the Piccadilly and Circle Tube lines were attacked on 7 July 2005 by home-grown Islamists who also blew up a number 30 double-decker bus in Tavistock Square, in total killing fifty-two and badly injuring 700 Londoners. So much for non-violent England. On my very first night in London, sleeping rough in Trafalgar Square, yobbos in thick-soled boots kicked the crap out of me, a penniless stranger. As I'll soon learn, aggression is always there under the mild English surface.

My own London uncoils like a vast, anonymous and shadowy beast, extending from the East India Docks and Isle of Dogs to the Hammersmith Palais, just before the Thames loops into the leafier parts of Richmond, and north from Brixton up to Parliament Hill Fields and Highgate's bad-tempered Karl Marx bust. It all belongs to me by right of trespass where I left my anxious spoor and sometimes my actual blood on its flagstones.

And down into the smoggy lamplit streets I'll flee, night walking past other vagrants and vagabonds, wondering where we're all going. And then strolling home at dawn, only to see her in a pink chenille robe, cinched so tight she'll strangle herself, waiting up for me at the top of the stairs, arms folded, eyes incandescent with outrage. 'Out with your popsies again, I see!'

Doris is bugged less by sexual jealousy than feminine vulnerability. The night city that is a release for me, fills her with a primal fear. Her shrieking at me – so seductively amused in down register, so snarly in rage, clipped South African mixed with standard BBC – stems from envy at my freedom to wander London's streets alone while she cannot. 'If only you knew what it's like to be a woman on her own in this dreary city! I can't even walk into a pub alone without some hooligan thinking I'm on the game. Damn men!'

Popsies indeed. The truth about my night-time absences is much simpler and duller.

Hammersmith.

For the next two years its grotty streets and restless children will be my real home.

IN THE CITY AFTER DARK

> Deprivation is to me what daffodils were to Wordsworth.
>
> > Philip Larkin, in an interview with the
> > *Observer*, 1979

Every place looks like Chicago in the rain, and it always seems to be raining in Bute Gardens, Hammersmith, West London.

My man, the great god himself Big Joe Turner, is blasting out lyrics from inside the Bute Gardens Youth Club. It's based in a decaying church that must have been abandoned around the time of the Crimean War and even in daylight lies in the perpetual shadow of the vast Lyons factory across the way. Before slipping through a side door, I note a police car outside and its two occupants frisking me with their eyes, which just about tells me all I need to know about my new life.

Swinging open the door, I'm met by a surge of pure energy that almost knocks me off my feet. None of the thirty or so boys and girls in the big, dusty all-purpose room with dirty windows pays a blind bit of notice to the stranger on their premises. Opposite sexes line up across the room from each other, like honey bees sending off pollen signals. They gyrate and shadow-walk to Joe Turner and Lonnie Donegan's 'Rock Island Line'. The girls, I guess none over sixteen, wear tight long skirts and acrylic or fake mohair sweaters over their bony-but-just-filling-out frames; the boys choose evenly between drainpipe trousers worn with Victorian-inspired drape jackets or cooler Slim Jim outfits. Nobody, thank you Lord, recognizes me as a dowdy, drenched CND-er.

The organizer, a weary-looking middle-aged man dressed in a blazer, threads his way through to talk to me. 'You from the police then? Who's done what now?'

'Um, I'm … an American.' He turns to clap his hands for attention, interrupting Adam Faith's 'What Do You Want?'

'Boys and girls!' How that didn't fit these kids! 'We have a friend from overseas amongst us.' That stops them in their tracks. A tall, acne-scarred boy bumps hard up against my chest and for openers growls, 'You know James Dean then?'

Damn right I knew James Dean. It's as if a lightning bolt strikes the dilapidated church building. The Yank knows the Rebel! A crowd swamps me, demanding particulars. I may not have an American passport anymore but James Dean is my visa here. (My back to the wall, it's too complicated to explain how as a Hollywood agent I met with Dean on the set of *Rebel Without a Cause*.)

Trevor, sixteen, on the cutting edge of fashion in an Italian-cut Cecil Gee suit and Dolcis winklepickers, does his chest-slam thing again. 'Whaz he like then? Same as in the fillums? Could 'e pull the birds or was he a poofta like they say?' His chum Len, Ivor, Phil-the-Shooter, Baz and the others push into me aggressively. Some of the girls seem as young as twelve or thirteen under their carefully teased Mafia-wife bouffants. They watch, big-eyed. There's the clear expectation of a fight to come. Phil-the-Shooter shows off his shoulder holster, and some Teds proudly finger fish hooks concealed under the lapels of their drape jackets. They hope I'm a wanker so they can hit me. *I know* these scuzzy kids, they're me, fifteen years ago, on the corner of 16th & Kedzie. Scare me? Sure. Fear is my tranquillizer.

'See,' I say authoritatively, 'Jimmy was in love with this bird Pier Angeli but when she married another guy, he revved up his motorbike outside the church to spoil their wedding.'

Phil says, ''E shoulda carved 'er up so's the other bloke wun't want 'er is wha' 'e shoulda done.'

Feeling trapped, I squeeze myself over to a dust-covered upright piano, which I don't know how to play, but – ever the show off – in a Jerry Lee Lewis crouch, bang down my fists on the bass keys and enthusiastically, if far from perfectly, belt out Pat Boone's 'Chains of Love' with lots of Bobby Darin finger-snapping.

That stops them in their tracks. They don't know I'm already a showbiz sensation.

*

I came to England just in time for the 'second battle of Waterloo', the rapturous reception at Waterloo station given to Bill Haley & His Comets, six already aging Country & Western musicians blasting out their sensational hit single, 'Rock Around the Clock', a London teenager's intro to American rock 'n' roll. Little Richard and Fats Domino are way superior musicians, but Haley's timing is perfect for a whole generation of sixteen- and seventeen-year-olds hungry for primal sex simulated by a shrieking saxophone and a loud bass line. Haley's tour coincides with the meteoric rise and fall of skiffle, a peculiarly English version of Mississippi Delta twelve-bar blues, played crudely with a driving bambamplunkplunk rhythm. Skiffle is made for someone talentless like me because any fool can toot a kazoo and thimble-slap a washboard or stringed broom.

A cut above Bute Gardens Youth Clubbers, skiffle audiences are coffee-bar-haunting, suburban sixth-formers in shaggy knee-length sweaters, the shock troops of the Campaign for Nuclear Disarmament. I'm a born finger-snapper, wailing blues in public to expel my own, and soon

I front my own traveling jug band, the KC Krazy Kats, an ad hoc collection of Home Counties art college and grammar-school boys who all live at home, as, come to think of it, do I, on Warwick Road.

And skiffle even served as my entrée to the Royal Family.

*

While down and out in London, I earn a few shillings as a skiffle-shouter and washboard player in coffee bars. One night, there's a gig going on in a Fulham Road venue when Princess Margaret, the Queen's 'bohemian' sister, then in her slumming-it phase, strolls in with some friends. At the time, Margaret is popular with the masses for her allegedly broken heart after the ending of her romance with the divorced RAF war hero Peter Townsend.

Because we're sitting at adjoining tables Margaret and I chat each other up while swaying in time to the trad jazz group on the podium. Our shoulders touch, our eyes meet, I catch her eye and put a hand on her knee. For a moment she leaves it there. Then, as if electrocuted, she sits bolt upright and her eyes turn to diamond-cold slits. Within seconds her chinless Brigade of Guards escorts – equerries? boyfriends? – loom over me threateningly. Thoughtlessly, I've committed lèse-majesté, disrespect towards a royal goddess. Until that moment she's been advertising herself as the People's Princess. Who knew?

RIOT

The lurid, violent fantasies of the Bute Gardens boys and girls enable me to enter a side of London recognizable to a

Chicagoan bred on ethnic border disputes. Trevor, Len, Ivor, Phil-the-Shooter and 'Vera' become my guides through an underworld of incipient fascism and the so-called teenage revolution that the media terms the 'youthquake'. I haven't yet puzzled out their complicated system of respect, exactly who is a hard man and who a big girl's blouse (candy ass, I would say). The Bute kids, unlike my home team of middle-class Goon Boys, are mostly failures at the eleven-plus, the odious test given in all English state schools to cream off a thin layer of kids with brains and let the others rot; having myself been IQ-tested as 'low–normal' and warehoused in my school's Subnormal (i.e. retarded, or Special Ed) Class, I find common ground with these disaffected teens. Their idea of the 'politics of youth' boils down to frequent street fighting in which I, Johnny Storm the Torch, am perfectly willing to participate.

All it will take is an initiating incident, which duly arrives when the Swedish wife of a West Indian immigrant is attacked by a white mob and the blacks fight back. The resulting melee goes down in London history as the Notting Hill Riots, a turning point in civic life.

And I'm on the wrong side of the fight.

On a late-August night a firestorm of emotion sweeps through the club, sparked by a false rumour that a black man has raped a white girl, which is all that Len and Trevor, Phil, Vera and Ivor need to take off, gathering other youths and adults as they go. A frenzied mob convenes in Elgin Crescent a few streets away. One minute I'm plunking the club piano and the next running towards the excitement of a major riot, Paris redux. Why do I feel so at ease in an out-of-control crowd? The Bute Gardens boys, among hundreds of others, fling empty milk bottles over the helmets of a cordon of policemen guarding a house in Elgin Crescent, and a black man tumbles to the ground with a gash in his head. The mob scents blood. I try to drag away Len and the others once I see their targets are any and all blacks, but they're too enraged to give up. I remind Len and Trevor that they're on probation, but Ivor shouts exultantly, 'Yeah, but it's fun, ain't it?'

Scenting fresh prey, Oswald Mosley's fascist goons mix with the thousand-strong mob who go off on a police-bashing, window-smashing rampage, shouting 'Kill the blacks', inciting gangs from all over London to turn up and join in, torching cars, petrol-bombing houses and attacking random blacks. Crews of Jamaicans from Brixton arrive to protect their brothers and sisters. I come to my senses when I am hailed by Raphael (at the time Ralph) Samuel, an editor with the youthful *Universities & Left Review* and co-founder of the Partisan coffee house, who has appeared with some friends like the Seventh Cavalry to try and shield the black community.

'Welcome, comrade,' Raphael salutes me in the brick-throwing chaos, 'I knew I'd find you here.'

In the confusion, he doesn't notice I'm with the enemy.

AFTER THE RIOTS

Some days after the riots I'm due to appear in court because two nineteen-year-old Bute Gardens boys are up on charges. Sharp-dressed Trevor, with only one lung after childhood

TB, is accused of 'affray' for kicking a policeman in the head in Elgin Crescent. He's pressuring his best friend Len to lie for him in the witness box and swear that he, Trevor, was nowhere around.

But now Len wants to recant his perjured statement to the police.

They've locked themselves in the youth club's loo while the accused works on his reluctant friend. They want me with them in court too, to make it 'look good', so I'm allowed in on this conversation.

Trevor gives Len, his fickle witness, a humorless smile. 'OK, what's the trouble?'

Ashen-faced, Len stares at the floor and clears his throat. 'Dunno really, Trevor.'

'No need to be scared, Len. Just say your piece, that's all.'

'I can't stand up to a prosecutor in court, Trevor. They'll all see I'm lying.'

'Not if you tell it straight, Len. Don't let them rattle you. Just answer yes or no.' Trevor's voice is hard. 'If you get confused, ask to have the question repeated. Don't talk in long sentences. They've got you if you do. None of your long sentences, Len. That's how they sent you down on that car nickin'. Bloody hell, Len! I've got a good job now, and a girl. It was *you* got me into that other trouble.' (Trevor was previously caught and convicted for wielding a brass-studded belt that Len had given him.)

Now Trevor pleads with his friend. 'It was chaos that night. It'll be your word against theirs. Just don't say nuffin' in long sentences.' His voice rises. 'Listen, you got a hundred quid? 'Cos that's what it'll cost to square me. You got a ton?'

'No,' says Len, 'you know I ain't got that kind of money.' He frowns when he sees how serious Trevor is. Several other boys try to come in and use the lavatory. Trevor snarls at them, 'Stay out!' One look at his face and they scarper.

Trevor studies Len closely then says, with scorn in his voice: 'Listen, you want to bottle out, then OK. Nobody's forcing you.'

'But, Trevor, if they get me on perjury it's two years minimum. I'm already on probation ...'

'Yeah, OK, so that's two for you and four for me. At least we go down together.'

'I'm worried, Trevor.'

'What do you think I am? You think I'll be dancing in the fucking dock? I got a job. And a bird. The last thing I want is to go down for four years.'

'I'm scared,' Len admits plaintively.

'What you scared for? Nobody's forcin' you!' Trevor's mouth tightens and he flips his cigarette into the toilet bowl, goes to the mirror and straightens his tie. He is furious but determined not to lose his cool – or his witness. He says slowly, 'It's not as though I was sayin', Len, that you'll get a knockin' if you rat out on me. Got that? Nobody's forcin' you.'

A long, bitter silence stretches between the two boys. I'm not sure if I just heard a threat or Trevor's inept attempt at reassuring his friend.

Finally he says, 'It's simple. We stick together in court and neither of us goes down. If you wanna bottle out now, that's your affair. I'm going to see my girl while I got the chance.' He walks out.

One of the boys from the club comes in and says, 'Hey, Len, you don't look so good.'

I intervene. 'Len, why don't you go have a talk with Trevor's lawyer?'

He looks at me with a faint, forlorn smile.

'Don't get it, do you?' he says. 'No lawyer can settle this kind of thing. Not even God can.'

*

At the Old Bailey Len makes a hash of his alibi testimony and he and Trevor are sent down for three years by Mr Justice Salmon. At their trial, as agreed with their barristers, I 'stand character' for them. Salmon is Jewish so when I return to the club the kids give me stick about 'Jew judges'. They see themselves as victims of a conspiracy against them conducted by all police officers, most teachers, all politicians, journalists, prison warders, probation officers and, now, Jewish judges.

'You one uv them or one uv us?' Trevor asks me before going off to jail.

Good question, Trev.

SIREN

'Vera' is a storm warning of trouble ahead. An extraordinarily pretty sixteen-year-old with a mesmerizing gap between her top front teeth, a dead ringer for the notorious Christine Keeler who later will bring down a government, she makes it hard not to notice her at the youth club. Normally, Trevor, Phil and Len give a kicking to sexual rivals, I've seen their bloody work, but they laugh off the idea of any such threat from me as I'm ancient and feeble.

Trev and Ivor and Phil and their satellite males are ensnared in a complicated web of desire centred on Vera, who is 'one of us' while remaining impossibly out of reach. She's taller than most of the other girls and better dressed; no stiletto heels or beehive for her. She'll even show up in Katherine Hepburn-style wide-legged slacks, a shocking insult to the prevailing female costume of smart Marks & Spencer cardigan worn with a knee-length A-line skirt and paper nylon petticoats beneath. (Other, younger girls try to emulate Vera's perfect figure by dipping their bras in sugar water to stiffen them.) The boys fear and want – and desire to protect – Vera who is brazenly careless with their affections. 'Come get it, Trev – but you'll have to fight Len for me, won't he, Phil?' She drives them wild.

Truth is, she's a semi-pro under the thumb of her pimp Nikos the Cypriot who also runs a filthy caff opposite the derelict church. Both coveted and exploited by Nikos, Vera hangs out at Bute Gardens as often as he lets her because: 'It reminds me of me school days.' All the girls and most of the boys know she's on the game and earns far more than they can, working at Boots the Chemist or on the assembly line at Lyons across the road. Phil-the-Shooter vaguely threatens to kill Nikos, but since Cypriot Greeks are feared even more than the newly arrived black Caribbeans, nothing comes of it.

Late at night when the club shuts we cross the street for a cup of foul-tasting char and some chips at Nikos's steamy hole-in-the-wall caff. With a gracious smile on his fat unshaven face, he'll sit with us and chat up the girls. He's always looking for new recruits, and besides that he likes yanking the boys' chain. Baz swears under his breath: 'I'll do 'im, promise! I'll do 'im. Even if they top me, fuckin' evil-minded wog!'

Nikos sizes me up on the spot. Class, accent, priors. 'Vera, she's a nice bit of stuff, in't she? Tell you what. You take her up West, to the posh people round Piccadilly, and I give you thirty-three per cent, OK? Good business opportunity for both of us.'

Though planets apart, it's only a short walk from the youth club to 58 Warwick Road.

Tonight, in the middle of an intense New Reasoner discussion, the downstairs buzzer sounds: I find Vera, slumped on the steps, bleeding and bruised. 'I've nowhere else to go,' she moans. 'Nikos, 'e's gone out of his mind. The club won't take me in 'cos Mr Griggs the caretaker is afraid Nikos'll bust up the place.' She repeats faintly, 'Nowhere else to go.' What a mess she's in, her blouse ripped off one shoulder and only just wearing what will later be called a mini-skirt, one shoe off and the other clutched in her hand. How did she find my address? I ask. 'Len 'n' I trailed you home once … make sure you wasn't a copper, like.'

Warning her to be quiet, I bundle her up the stairs to the maisonette, but the door is wide open and everybody including Doris gets an eyeful of the new arrival. They all exchange knowing glances except for Doris, who bares her teeth at me. Just you wait.

Later that night, she finds Vera, Peter and me on his bed, laughing over a game of jumping jacks. We've cleaned up Vera's bloody nose and thrown a blanket over her skimpy torn clothes. All cosy and safe, she loves being a child again, being looked after. She glances up at Doris with a bold, brazen gaze. 'Hullo, missus … is it awrigh' for me to stay with you for a bit then?'

Oh, God, here it comes. Peter whispers to me, 'You've gone and done it again, haven't you, Clankety?'

Doris purses her mouth but doesn't kick out her unwelcome guest. All the time Vera is with us, Doris wanders the maisonette furiously brushing non-existent dust from the furniture – normally she hates housework – or simply slouches in a doorway, arms folded and tight lips almost white with disapproval. Meanwhile Vera basks in the safety of Warwick Road. She sleeps in, comes down expecting breakfast, teases Peter, glances slyly at Doris and shows plenty of leg at the table. (How could she not with a pinned-together skirt that measures a millimetre from hip to crotch?) Towards me Vera maintains an amused distance. 'That your woman then?' she asks, in apparent innocence.

Vera manages plenty of opportunities for me to compare-and-contrast her with Doris, twenty years her senior. But the longer Vera stays with us, the more Doris surprises me by primping and priming herself. Once, passing her in the bathroom applying (rarely used) eye makeup, Vera casually asks, 'You sure tha's the right color for you, missus?' (I'm with Peter, spying from the top of the stairs.) Doris's first impulse is to whirl on the girl in a rage, but she checks herself.

'What do you suggest, my dear?' The ice in Doris's tone is lost on Vera who joins her in the bathroom and studies her face from different angles, even running a finger over her brow. 'Not so much,' she finally pronounces. 'In fact, take off all tha' rubbish, it don't suit you. Let's pop down the chemist an' I'll show you what might look proper.'

Is murder in the offing? Not bloody likely. Off the sixteen-year-old hooker and the thirty-nine-year-old novelist jaunt down the road to Earl's Court, to find a Boots that sells 'proper' Maybelline.

But of course it ends in tears when Vera pinches housekeeping money and nicks one of Doris's dresses too, though God knows why since the pink-and-peach number would look absurd on her, whereupon my lovely landlady throws her out. Right on schedule Doris and I have an almighty row, I heft my duffel and (unused) typewriter and move out to a small bedsit in Swiss Cottage. Peter refuses to cry, he never does, but punches my arm for a goodbye wrestle as he sing-songs his goodbye in Neddy Seagoon's trademark *'Needle nardlo noo!'* Children together forever. My heart is his in perpetuity.

'Come give me a real hug,' I demand. A bridge too far for him. He lurches forward as if to embrace me, thinks better of it, and we lightly exchange love punches. My son who never was.

On the doorstep Doris and I kiss. The last thing she says is, 'I have to protect myself from you.'

*

As soon as I move into my new basement room at 15a Fitzjohn's Avenue, I head straight to the Bute Gardens club to announce – ta da! – what I had not until then consciously known I wanted to do. I intend to write about us all.

''Course you do,' Phil tells me, 'why else you 'ere?' All this time they have known. 'Jus' so long,' Ivor adds, 'as you don' poke Vera in the furry cup.' No chance of that, since she and Nikos have gone off to Cyprus on holiday together.

After Trevor and Len are sentenced at the Old Bailey, I lock myself in a courtroom toilet and puke my guts out. Sometimes I'll sit for an hour on the seat, disoriented and straining to expel the black shit of anxiety.

Yet ... *something very odd is happening.* I feel as if my wet finger got stuck in a live socket. (Don't get me started about English wiring!) Permission granted by the Bute kids, and my change of address, seem to have shocked my inert typing fingers into action. I've become '*he*', fictionalized even to myself. Who is this new person?

In my Swiss Cottage basement room, *he* extracts the Corona from its case for the first time in a year. Where is this coming from? Watching Doris madly type, and hanging around as a fifth wheel when the Four Johns and other published writers floated through our kitchen, was like standing next to the vibrations of a huge whirring literary turbine. It seems to have energized me too.

Whoosh! Plop! A short piece about the Bute riot boys drops into a street-corner pillar box, and ... *sacré bleu*! Almost by return post the venerable *New Statesman* offers to feature it under my very first byline and a cheque duly arrives, paid not in pounds but guineas as befits a 'professional gentleman' like a barrister or doctor. Almost overnight, it seems, doors swing open on oiled hinges, editors call me on the shared phone in the hall, more cheques drop through the letterbox. 'Please can you ...?' Please!

Except *he* is the one who is doing it. Who *is* this person? Not me. I am the blocked and tormented one, in pain, cramped up, but *his* fingers fly over the keys, seemingly with an independent life of their own, like the detached hands playing Brahms in *The Beast With Five Fingers*.

IF I DIE IN A COMBAT ZONE

He's still on a roll when Phil-the-Shooter suggests, 'Go and see my cousin up Islington way.'

Based in Seven Sisters Road – I hop a 9 then a 73 bus – this mob, in their early twenties, shows me what the Bute Gardens boys and girls will soon become: thugs, alley fighters, small-time thieves, Wormwood Scrubbers. Or else dead, of course. Family ties don't seem to count for much to these kids. As toddlers they were caught up in the wartime evacuation scheme that tore children away from their mums while their dads were away fighting for their country.

In an Upper Street caff my contact, Phil-the-Shooter's cousin, surrounded by his mates, pulls out an American-style folding hunter's knife and asks if he can stab me. I say, fair exchange. He can if I can return the favor. He slashes at my wrist drawing blood, then offers the knife to me. I hold it against his heart. He doesn't flinch when I press hard until, finally, he sits back in the booth with a nervous laugh. 'Bottle is wot you got,' he judges.

Then his Hulk-huge pal Mick wants a go. As usual, I'm euphoric with fear. 'Go ahead, Mick.'

'My grandmother can hit harder than that,' I taunt Mick, after he sticks his own bone-handled switchblade in my side. The four-inch blade penetrates my GI field jacket. I can feel the warm trickle of blood inside my shirt.

He withdraws it, sees only a trace of blood and demands, 'Gimme your hand.' Palm up, I do as instructed. He drills in the point, drawing a gush of blood, and pushes hard until my hand is a mess. 'Now you,' he says. With my good hand I aim the weapon at his naked throat and press, hard. This is nuts. I stand up in the booth and firmly wrap both my hands round the bone handle and dig deeper at Mick's neck.

His pals murmur 'Hey, now' and 'Hold on' and 'Mick, fer fuck's sake!' Neither he nor I will give way. To my eternal gratitude, a beat policeman on Upper Street passes the caff and glances in the window. I hand the knife back to Mick. 'One of us is a lucky bastard,' he says.

The Punchers are a different class of trouble from the Bute Garden boys and light years away from Peter and the Goon Boys. Each of the seven or eight Punchers has form, almost all have done time in juvenile or adult prison, they're small-time losers with a big-time appetite for bollocking (fighting), codified into an honor system based on jail-time served and the ability to take punishment. Their vocabulary is newly foreign – terms like boob, blag, jammer, raze up and drum were, I assume, learned in Pentonville or the Scrubs. Aside from Phil's cousin, my other intro to the gang comes from Don McCullin, a local kid with a cheap camera and no school qualifications but whose photographs the *Observer* newspaper used to illustrate my Bute Gardens articles. Don says, 'Those kids over in Hammersmith are just a bunch of ponces. I'll take you to where you can *really* get killed.'

Protecting the manor from bubble and squeaks (Cypriot Greeks) and spades (blacks) is their noble cause; weapons of choice are choppers (axes), knives and cars. And, unlike the

Hammersmith boys, the Punchers are avant-garde in their fashion tastes, preferring short haircuts *à la* St Germain-des-Prés and favoring the Modern Jazz Quartet over rock 'n' roll or blues. Mods before there are mods.

A fight is on. We speed across several manors to Wood Green in five cars, the Punchers tooled up with knives, iron bars and, I believe, a gun or two. The Wood Green dance hall echoes to 'Let's Twist Again' by Chubby Checker. All the Punchers keep their coats on as they stroll in. The girls are very young, fourteen plus or minus. Across the floor four boys cha-cha with four other boys, which makes the Punchers laugh derisively as they sip Pepsi and wine from paper cups. Then, of course, it happens. Feet scuffle, girls scream as Little Richard gives way to The Platters, 'Smoke Gets in Your Eyes'. A Wood Green boy is swarmed by Mick, Princie, George and Vic from our side. The boy stumbles backwards over a bench, and the Punchers are on him like savage dogs. Some of the girls are crying. Big Mick, his eyes narrow and alert, jumps up on the bench before crashing down on the boy's exposed head. The Punchers do not seem angry, it's more as if they take a professional pride in what they're doing. Ceasing the attack as smartly as it began, they calmly adjust their clothes, regroup and take their own sweet time over leaving, daring anyone to retaliate. Later, back on Seven Sisters Road, I join Mick, who is walking away through the fog.

He says, 'Fun, wasn't it?' Adding, 'Wouldn't 'ave 'appened if not for you.' He explains that the fight was laid on for my benefit so I'll have something to write about.

'You'd half kill a guy to get your name in the paper?' I ask.

He says, 'Can you think of a better reason?' A few weeks later the Wood Green boys retaliate by invading the Islington manor and a Puncher is knifed to death. A chain of events precipitated because I was there.

PS The article I write about this incident provokes angry letters to the editor. I defend myself but, later, concede I was so eager to 'get the story', I hadn't thought through the human consequences.

THE MAGIC HOSPICE OF TUDOR STREET, EC1

Some words of mine printed in a weekly newspaper read by what George Orwell jeered at as '... every fruit-juice drinker, nudist, sandal-wearer, sex-maniac, Quaker, "Nature Cure" quack, pacifist, and feminist ...' offer me the keys to a new kingdom.

Socially, I've jumped up a notch. I'm now an '*Observer* man'.

*

The most boring part of a life is success. England is so small that word seems to get out telepathically that this new American may NRBOOU, not really be one of us, a curiosity like Le Pétomane or the Powhatan exotic Pocohontas, forever an outsider but admissible on approval. The terrific upside of this is that when I phone a cinema for show times the strange lady in the booth replies, 'Oh, I know that voice. You're Clancy Sigal. Heard you on Home Service last night, talking about Sinatra or Sartre or somebody beginning with an S. Smashing.' At last I have a Voice.

Does accomplishment cancel out anxiety? Like hell. At any moment I expect someone to grab me by my collar and arrest me for false pretences. In fact, nobody calls my bluff except me.

*

The *Observer*, with its stately masthead and roll call of patrician literary journalists, Pritchett and Toynbee and Connolly, with whom I used to stuff my boots, is then at the peak of its influence as a highbrow gazette, though its in-house 'culture of breakdown' has turned the newspaper into a Mayo mental clinic in all but name. The paper's tolerance of its staff's nervous collapses is shaped by the personality of owner and editor David Astor, scion of an almost royal family. His father, Waldorf, 2nd Viscount Astor, is obscenely rich; Waldorf's American-born wife Nancy was the first woman Member of Parliament, a crusader for nursery places for every child, and the domineering hostess of the family's Cliveden estate, reputedly a pre-war centre for Nazi sympathizers (and later the setting for the Profumo sex scandal). My boss, David, served in wartime Special Operations where he'd been wounded fighting with the French *Maquis* and saved by my immediate editor, Terry Kilmartin (also ex-SOE). Winston Churchill called Special Operations the 'Ministry of Ungentlemanly Warfare', an amateurish, messy, brilliant, catch-as-catch-can wartime resistance web that still informs the *Observer*'s try-it-and-see-if-it-works ethos.

My name is being splashed as a BOLD LETTER BYLINE on newsagents' placards, except that *he*, not me, is the real deal. I've named him Bruce, after the stand-up comic Lenny

Bruce, a prince in this new kingdom I've somehow managed to infiltrate.

David Astor is a living, breathing 'Richard Hillary': shy, outwardly hesitant while inwardly hard as nails, heir to a grand title and champion of liberal views. He had a breakdown at Oxford and was psychoanalyzed by the master's daughter herself, Anna Freud. (Who else?) With a mother like the ferocious Nancy, who calls the *Observer*'s staff 'all those niggers and Communists', who wouldn't have problems? David believes in good writing, placing commas where they belong, and rigorous psychoanalysis. The paper's writers and editors are equal number 'conchies' and veterans (Philip Toynbee, Welsh Guards; Michael Davie, RN; Alan Ross, RN; Patrick O'Donovan, Irish Guards, etc.) and all deadly serious drinkers in the office, on their own, or in nearby pubs like the Mucky Duck and El Vino. Alcoholism as a concept is alien to the Fleet Street mind; you may fall down a lift shaft or collapse over your typewriter with impunity so long as you bang out good copy to deadline. An *Observer* reporter who shares an office next to mine (a Tobruk veteran of the Western desert) went so loony that he jumped into a limo carrying a wedding party that included, coincidentally, he insists, his ex-girlfriend and her new husband, and began serenading the bride with the tenor's lament from Verdi's *La Forza del Destino* – no mere pop songs for *Observer* scribes. David Astor paid his hospital bills.

The paper's editors know, but don't care, about my shadowy existence as an illegal – until two Scotland Yard detectives, fake names 'Brown' and 'Smith', show up in the office to haul me down for an interview in a small windowless interrogation room off the Embankment, just like in a spy movie. David Astor protests, 'What? They're going to deport one of my star reporters? [I'm a star!] Let's see about that,' and insists on coming along.

*

DETECTIVE HUNT: 'You've been a very naughty boy, Mr Sigal.'

CLANCY: (glum silence)

DETECTIVE BROWN: 'You have violated our trust and broken a number of Her Majesty's rules, designed to protect this country from intruders who mean her harm.'

CLANCY: 'Oh, but …'

The detectives keep glancing at David Astor all the time they question me.

Half an hour later I'm released and the next day the Home Office mails me an almost-impossible-to-obtain permit to remain in the UK.

Sometimes class does tell.

*

I've never had a patron before nor been so charmingly co-opted. David Astor's personal history is written all over his eczema-troubled, handsome face which reveals the chronic anxiety he takes great pains to conceal. There's plenty of time to study him closely since we talk for hours across the old oak desk in his office. This is large and Dickensian with mullioned windows overlooking the Thames. He likes Americans!

One evening Astor calls me into his editor's lair. Gently, as if it is of no importance, he enquires: 'Have you suffered a loss recently?' My immediate thought is of my mother Jennie in Los Angeles, but we write to each other regularly. I know she's fine.

'No, I'm breaking even.' I'm referring to Kempton Park race course where I like to bet with the bookies. He gives a little cough. 'Perhaps now might be … a good time for you … um, well … you might consider …' He offers to pay for psychoanalysis. My troubles show then? He laughs when I enquire about this. 'You're a mild case compared to some around here.'

Even though Astor is shelling out for Freudian sessions with Dr Augusta Bonnard, a benign grey-haired lady with a kindly face whom I see in her creeper-covered St John's Wood house, the analysis fails dismally because she insists I lie in a dark alcove and free associate to the ceiling. I squirm, yawn, snooze, until finally she judges, 'Mr Sigal, I'm sorry to say this but you're unanalyzable,' a verdict that will be repeated over and over again in various other consulting rooms. What a relief! I'd begun to fall into comas on her couch while my hands crept protectively over my balls.

*

On Dr Bonnard's couch I weaselled out of proper psychoanalysis by drifting off into reveries about my Hollywood days and how I actually came to be here.

I blame it on Humphrey Bogart.

I'm a talent agent in Cold War Hollywood. Making deals and pushing open doors for Donna Reed, Peter Lorre, David Niven, Jack Palance, Richard Burton and Barbara Stanwyck plus platoons of screenwriters and directors. Bogie, our biggest client, is dying aged fifty-eight. I should have seen it coming from his last couple of pictures. My boss Mary Baker, his long-time friend and agent, says, 'He's under the knife. Betty says he won't make it. It's the end of the business as we know it. I'm getting out. And so are you.'

I've just been fired.

That last night, when I go out on my balcony all is strangely quiet at the Andalusia Apartments, West Hollywood. The evening smells of jasmine and burned cinders from back-yard incinerators. For once the downstairs driveway is empty of federal agents' cars. Night sounds echo around the neighborhood.

When I answer it my telephone is surprisingly clear of wire-tap static. The FBI has given up on me, it seems. A big letdown. I needed villains in my life, and now they're gone the only villain left is myself.

PITCHING OFF THE PITCH

Though cowards flinch and traitors sneer,
We'll keep the red flag flying here.
> – 'The Red Flag' by Jim Connell,
> anthem of the British Labour Party

Being co-opted is oddly pleasant if you're embraced by rich bored open-minded gentry who flaunt their wealth by dressing down in pig-shit-covered Wellington boots and old cords. I hate camping in the fresh air but find I am pleased to be invited to yomp in the mud on weekends spent in Palladian country houses, familar to most people only from *Brideshead Revisited* and *Downton Abbey* – except that TV omits the brutal truth that the stately bedrooms are so freezing, I tote my Valor paraffin heater wherever I go, which my amiable hosts think 'too, too American'. (Let them freeze their bums off!)

Everyone in this new milieu is devastatingly charming, in contrast to the notable lack of charm in my other Left-oriented world. But enter a country house and you are instantly offered drinks, can run your admiring eyes over walls hung with fine paintings, help yourself to food served from silver chafing dishes, take a bed and sometimes a daughter on temporary loan ... all the courtesies are offered, especially if you share your hosts' taste for slaughtering small animals and birds to the sound-effects of guns detonating and reels whirring. By contrast, if you happen into any old-style Labour Club, you're liable to be greeted with suspicious glares and a total absence of hospitality. One of England's open secrets is how liberal and flexible its aristos can be if they remain unthreatened, and how deeply, deeply conservative the Labour movement is at heart.

In the civilized setting of a country house it seems I can do no wrong, make no misstep, nor even say the wrong thing – even if I do get my titles mixed up so that it's easier to call the host by his first name, which they take as further proof of American informality. My clumsiness with a shotgun and lack of evening dress at dinner are viewed as harmless exoticism. Actually it's all quite relaxing. (Social note: the Very Old Rich I meet are much more casual and unfussy than the Newly Rich who insist, ridiculously, on black tie and cigars in the billiard room.)

Being taken up by the ruling classes is bad for my politics, but it's fun to be served on fine Spode china, to pat their Golden Labrador gun dogs, be lent a prized Purdey shotgun, and asked to sing for my supper only by predicting that their class is doomed, which they love because they've been hearing such talk since 1381 and they still own half the land in the country.

Sample conversation:

Clancy: 'You know, Henry, your class is doomed. The tide of history is against you.'

Sir Henry: 'Yes, yes, you're so right. We've had it, no doubt about it. Been that way for donkey's years. Can't tell you what a relief it will be to offload all this and sell it to some rich American. Imagine the cost of the upkeep! He can have the lot – except for my wife and daughter. Ha-ha! And, of course, the dogs.'

(Update: many of these handsome estates are now owned by Russian, Saudi and Malaysian oligarchs via untraceable shell companies based in Bermuda or the Caymans.)

I would become a convert to the patrician world were it not for the obligation I feel to keep up the grind of leafleting and doorknocking and circuit-riding on the Workers Education–Ruskin College–Miners Institute rounds of trade-union jamborees, Fabian Society weekends and Victory For Socialism picnics. I speak at seaside CND rallies and New Left clubs, even at Eton College whose juveniles can't care less that I sweat, grow pale and sometimes clutch at the table for support. 'Comrades!' I exhort even the Etonians in their absurd morning coats, top hats and ties, without a clue how to follow up except to let my tongue loose and see what happens, skiffling the optimistic Marxist blues. My dance card is crammed, what with a Friday to Sunday at a country estate one weekend, then the next the Durham Miners' Gala where I speak, even tell jokes, from a makeshift wooden stage in front of massed pit-village bands and thousands of spectators on the Old Racecourse, backed by a glorious colliery banner proclaiming PRODUCTION FOR USE NOT PROFIT and … oh, sorry, faint dead away to laughing cries of: 'Whoops, the Yank's drunk!' 'Someone 'elp him up or he'll 'urt a babby!'

On that wooden platform, despite my exuberant body language, I don't actually feel much at all but, responding to their hunger for Yankee optimism, I harangue them as if I'm at a Hollywood pitch meeting. Keep them awake at all costs!

Talk talk talk will blow the blues away.

Not bloody likely. Sheer terror still makes me crap my pants.

What is it Doris is always telling me: 'Darling, how sad. You'd rather perform than feel.'

'You stand up straight, my friend,' she commands back in London. 'There you go. Don't you dare fall again. Did you hear me? I said, STAND UP!'

To a passing stranger it looks as if a female mugger is attacking me in Great Portland Street instead of propping me up against the broken brick wall of a bomb-site while I recover from one of my serial fainting fits. I continue to pitch face forward in living rooms, meeting halls, from speakers' platforms, and off my second home: the open rear platform of Big Red buses. Dizzy spells strike without warning, rooms spin, so do I, and … boom! I'm flat on my back again, staring up at a low grey sky. (Fans of the epileptic Ian Curtis of Joy Division will get the idea.) The response of passersby to my twitching body laid out on the pavement is class-specific; Chelsea and Kensington householders dash out with blankets and Thermoses of hot tea; in Hackney or Whitechapel, locals step over my supine form with barely a glance, though one or two kick me to see if I'm still alive. Good old proletarian solidarity.

A 'LONDON MARRIAGE'

Doris and I are now acclimatized to our amiable, quarrel-free 'London marriage', so open you can hear the wind howling through the cracks. Indeed, compared to literati past and present, we're practically Ozzie and Harriet – see H. G. Wells's serial womanizing despite his marriages; Vera Brittain, her husband and Winifred Holtby; Katherine Mansfield; Clive and Vanessa Bell; Ottoline and Philip Morrell; Rebecca West; Kingsley Amis; Beryl Bainbridge; the sainted Keir Hardie and Sylvia Pankhurst. A 'London marriage' is a venerable institution.

Doris and I lead separate, independent lives while she keeps a room reserved for me in her new digs on Langham Street, round the corner from BBC Broadcasting House whose Art Deco lobby is my private priest-hole before I go upstairs to the same studio George Orwell used to broadcast from. Free to seek relationships elsewhere, we're like an old married couple with an 'understanding', except what each of us understands may be a little different. She blames me for forcing her into other men's arms. ('You made me do it. I'm really a one-man woman. Why did you make me your slut?') Hypocrite that she is, she never confesses to the randy pleasure she freely takes. All I ask is that she bathe afterwards. Eew, the unwashed look of that leather-jacketed biker poet!

One part of me thinks: there's nothing wrong with this arrangement because it's how it's done in sophisticated circles. The other wonders: really?

On Parents' Day at Peter's Quaker boarding school I'm his father-for-a-day, watching over the chubby little boy with the deep gravelly voice acting Toad in *Toad of Toad Hall* and aching to hug him till he screams for mercy, which at home we do a lot. But instead there I sit, slouched in a camping chair, surrounded by the cream of London's *bien-pensant* lawyers and poets and novelists and wine merchants and pretty ladies in big floppy hats, with their messy, bohemian sexual arrangements of which I'm now a part, as a London husband and pseudo-dad. Illegitimate myself, I sometimes worry I'm illegitimizing Peter. But this is the life I've chosen for now even if sometimes I wonder: what is it like to live straight?

LEN, ON HIS KNEES

Don't go down in the mine, Dad,
Dreams very often come true;
Daddy, you know it would break my heart
If anything happened to you …
— 'Don't Go Down in the Mine, Dad',
commemorating the 1907 South
Wales mining disaster

When London becomes unbearable British Railways' incredibly cheap fares help me escape to the North: the Yorkshire dales and moors, the Pennine Way, and former industrial valleys where breathing comes easier nowadays.

The Yorkshire moors smoulder with a barren beauty, elemental and alive. Blessedly, my troubles can be shrugged off and left behind as I stride the peat and heather. Pocked with slag heaps and the gallows frames of working collieries, this isn't the Brontës' romantic Yorkshire. I travel further north, through smoky, smelly Tyneside and the South Shields shipyards where the propellers of half-built ships stand as tall as Nelson's Column and dwarf their surroundings. Catherine Cookson country. I'm amazed that nobody I know in literary London has even heard of Cookson, Tyneside's most popular writer, except to put her down as a 'romance novelist'. Why haven't they read *Rooney* or *The Fifteen Streets*? Her stories are like a map of the North.

And then, the North comes to me.

I ache for human contact. Most of the donnish men in my orbit recoil from physical intimacy outside the bedroom. Back in Los Angeles my best friend Ray Kovacs and I wrestled and punched each other all the time as a measure of our love. It's a *muzhik* peasant thing: if you don't hit, you don't care. But London writers and artists seem to regard even the slightest brush of bodies as a brutal assault on their privacy. 'We don't do that in England,' snarled the historian Eric Hobsbawm when I first approached him with outstretched hand. I grabbed his anyway and shook it like the Liberty Bell; the tall and gawky Marxist looked ready to faint with surprise.

Inevitably, Len Doherty enters my life.

Below the upland moors my habit is to explore what's not yet industrial archaeology but fully working mills and factories. I find I enjoy the ear-ringing sounds of stroking hammers and steam whistles from early-Victorian machines still blasting the manufactories' harsh music. I talk to steel foundrymen at Sheffield's Tinsley and River Don works, glass grinders at St Helen's Pilkington works, cold rolled metal handlers at Parkgate Steel in Rotherham – good for a friendly "ow do', a Mackeson's and often an invitation back to their homes. Northern warmth is a cliché based on fact. Up here, I can shake hands and barge straight in with, 'I'm Clancy Sigal from California,' and be more or less accepted; unthinkable behavior among London's literati.

The exceptions to this cordiality are the insular, tight-knit little coal-mining communities dotted all over the northern hills. There, frosty stares from the miners and their wives make me feel like a black man getting off a bus in Mississippi.

That's until a magazine asks me to cover, ho-hum, a conference on working-class literature at London's University College ... yawn. Except that up on the stage there's an actual live-specimen coal miner/author. In a break I stalk him to the nearest pub for an interview. This strange, skinny guy, handsome to the bone, seems permanently exhausted. Surely he can't be strong enough to pick up a shovel. He stares me up and down. 'You a journalist?' It's not a question, more of an accusation. 'Newspapermen are all whores and liars,' he tells me. Unprofessionally, I say, 'Well, fuck you too,' and start to walk away, which is when he smiles broadly. 'Eh, up. Jus' faffin'.' I barely understand his broad Yorkshire accent, but the warmth of his teasing – I understand that. He puts his arm around me, which makes this the first real physical contact I've had with another man since coming to this country. Outside on the sidewalk we're like two chimpanzees inspecting each other, finding excuses to touch and compare. At a Cypriot-run strip club in Soho where I take him, Len gets belligerently drunk, swipes at the bouncer, and he and I bond by getting tossed out on our ears on Frith Street. God, I've missed nights like this.

*

Thurcroft, Len's thousand-year-old Yorkshire pit village, lies in a West Riding valley between Rotherham and Laughton-en-le-Morthen. It is an area of undulating moors over rich veins of bituminous coal that has been mined in the area since Roman times. I'm a guest in Len's National Coal Board-leased house, enjoying playing with his kids and scarfing down his wife's cooking. Although Len is a Communist, as are many of Thurcroft's miners, we ignore politics and instead share strategies on how to subdue our separate anxieties. Len, having published a couple of novels that never made him enough money to escape the mine, is only in his early thirties but already scrawny from black-lung and silicosis, with the miner's typical cough and stoop and blue scars running over his naked body from working in three-foot-high seams. A third-generation collier, he knows no other life but feels he'll die buried underground if he doesn't get out.

Above ground, calling in favors, he pushes me into a lift cage with his mates. It drops like a stone, so fast I don't have time to be dizzy. Then, off to do his daily stint, Len leaves me on my own in a side tunnel where I'm soon lost in the darkness. Two thousand feet straight down and almost a mile in, where two rich coal seams meet, confident that somewhere in the darkness nearby men are trained in mine rescue, I'm struck by an almost supernatural clarity and peace of mind, broken only by the distant chink-chink of colliers at work in the distance. An occasional dim head-lamp passes by, illuminating men I've come to know by name. They're skilled as surgeons, work with comparable precision, digging, chipping, shoveling, advancing coal walls by hand and with exquisite intuition placing wooden pit props to combat the groaning and shifting in the earth that surrounds them. Miners are artists at work on a carbon canvas.

Idealize them? Of course I do. 'Shock troops of the class struggle' and all that. But I'm not blind. They're hard, often brutal, sometimes vicious to their wives, their 'drabbletails' (girlfriends), and one another. Imprisoned by coal, they take extravagant pride in tradition, technique, and in exhibiting a blank defensiveness to outsiders. No quarter given to the weak or the quitters.

While I'm in the Miners' Club one day, Len's branch chairman, Brad, turns on him because he's taken time off sick. Len defends himself: 'Ah, Brad, that's unfair. Tha knows why Ah'm not at t'pit now. Ah'm not fit enough.' Brad snipes back, 'Tha'rt nobbut a young lad, tha'rt fit enough. Look at me! Fifty-three and still shifting at the face.' And so on. Len takes this criticism painfully to heart. He wants his fellow miners' approval – but also doesn't want to die down in the dark.

A MINER'S WOMAN

It's almost impossible for a London alien like me to speak privately with a miner's woman without her husband glaring daggers, not at me but at her. When Len is at work on day shift, I, the visitor from Mars, wander around Thurcroft taking in its permanent acidic odour of sulphur and looking for someone, anyone, to chat me up. I'm hailed by a wife hanging up washing in her back yard.

Courageously, she doesn't care who spies on her. 'Don't let those union boys shoot you a line,' she tells me over the washing line. 'I've been married fourteen years and haven't had a week's kissing since. My man's all right, I don't hate him the way some women here hate their husbands. But he's so tired, all the time. Can't even play with the kids. What kind of kissing can there be then? The days he doesn't work, we fight. They say money doesn't bring happiness. Let me find out for myself!

'So, like I was saying, we get our kissing where we can. How long you staying in the village? Only joking! But it's not natural, is it? For a woman to go without kissing. So everybody gets it from somebody else: in the front door, out the back. Women get tired of being married to husbands who come up from pit too dead to know black from white. Hardly a woman I know isn't going with another man or hasn't done. Preferably a surface man but anyone at a pinch. How long did you say you were visiting for?'

A dilemma. Should I or shouldn't I? On top of a slag heap of all places.

PS A quarter of a century later, in the failed miners' strike that destroys the National Union of Mineworkers and seals the doom of most British pits, village women like this one come into their own, not only acting as a nation-wide support group but taking the initiative: organizing, consciousness-raising, letting the country know what it means to live as a miner's wife.

The last thing Len says as he puts me aboard a Sheffield-to-London bus is, 'Oop the guttersnipes!' That's what Doris calls us.

Oop the guttersnipes.

Neither of us mentions what we both know: at this moment funeral services are being held for forty-five miners killed at Six Bells colliery in South Wales, the second major mining tragedy in under a year. Nine months ago forty-seven Scottish miners had burned to death underground at the Auchengeich Colliery Disaster.

HE LIVES!

Strange are *his* ways. *Bruce,* my Typing Self, unloads *his* feelings for miners in an off-the-cuff rambling note to the Houghton Mifflin editors in Boston who'd risked their money on me but so far hadn't seen a word. I guess in some kind of despair they send my muddled scribble to George Orwell's publisher Fred Warburg, who phones me.

'Dear boy, come for a drink and write us a book about these miners of yours.' Dear boy? A whole book? Way past *his* comfort zone. It took everything I had just to crank out a short article. I may be keeping classy company over at the *Observer*, but let's face it, I'm not a *real* writer.

How many words are there in a book? Off I go back North.

What is it Doris is always telling me? 'Stop your bloody whining about working-class boys finding it so hard to see themselves as artists. What do you think it's like for women, you fool?'

Oop the guttersnipes.

In Thurcroft, dog-tired from pit work, Len is in an ugly-pugnacious mood, and we're both so fed up with ourselves that one night, on waste ground behind the Miners' Club, we viciously fight it out with fists and boots, as if to the death. I must be crazy because he's the South Yorkshire Coalfields' Amateur boxing champion. Mindless rage, spilled blood. I lose a tooth, but since he's drunker, I 'win'. That is, we finally end up on the ground, reluctant to trade any more blows, and I'm on top. We feel undignified, but spent. Why does physical violence calm us so?

After our fight, Len agrees I should have a go at writing about miners from Thurcroft and other local pits that I've gone down, like Maltby, Dinnington and Barnsley. After glancing at my rough after-action notes drawn from memory, he says, 'Be raht. Best y'do addle brass for it, mind.' (Translated: it's OK. Be sure to get money for your work, though.)

Procrastination, talent's evil sister, diverts me to the wool-making town of Halifax where the *New Reasoner*'s Edward Thompson and his historian wife Dorothy share Holly Bank, a beautiful gritstone house on a hill. They, too, snigger at my travel companion, the Valor paraffin heater.

Long-distance telephone calls are still rare in England so when the operator rings the Thompsons' house in search of me I know this must be bad news. My mother Jennie Persily has died of a sudden heart attack in Los Angeles, a friend reports. How could she abandon me so far from home?

I must have suspected something was up because recently we'd begun writing to each other more frequently. I'd felt the need to know more about her 'scandalous' history, but now she's abandoning me before we reach the punchline. Impossible for her to die. In shock, I stumble downstairs, muttering, 'My mum is gone.' Nil response from assembled politicals in the living room, where nobody rises to their feet to put an arm around me. What's wrong with these humanitarians – so humane except to their own? I remember Kollontai's plea for a more humane approach by the political classes:

> We call ourselves Communists, but are we
> really that? Do we not rather draw the life
> essence from those who come to us, and when
> they are no longer of use, do we not let them
> fall by the wayside, neglected and forgotten?
> Our Communism and our comradeship are
> dead letters if we do not give of ourselves to
> those who need us. Let us beware of such
> Communism. It slays the best in our ranks.
> – Alexandra Kollontai, Russian revolutionary

Afterwards, Mervyn Jones, who rescued me at CND's Downing Street riot only to be jailed in my place, takes me outside for a walk. 'Forgive us, son. It's the English thing. The war. We don't mourn. Keep our emotions in check. Otherwise there's too much pain. But trust me, it's felt.'

Jews bury their dead fast and, as I'm not there, the California friend on the phone has to do the honours at the Workmen's Circle cemetery in the San Fernando Valley alongside Jennie's union chums in the *schmatte* trade. I debate whether to return and visit the grave. At the US Embassy in Grosvenor Square, the chargé d'affaires, one of those tall slim well-bred creatures with a New Orleans accent, coolly decrees that if I return home with an invalid passport he will *personally* see to it that I never leave the US again: 'Because we don't need people like you running around the world bringing our country down.'

KADDISH

Having moved out of Doris's, in my Swiss Cottage room I've felt chilled to the bone since Jennie died and left me. What are you supposed to feel when the woman who gave you life is gone? Her legacy to me was love and catastrophe, it's up to me how I orchestrate them. The last time we saw each other was on the dance floor at a salsa club where her 'Cuban hip movement' embarrassed me but drew loud applause from the young crowd; on factory wages she kept a dozen pairs of red-spangled dancing shoes. Every time I remember her, I feel freezing.

Do Jews believe in Heaven? So much for atheism. Weirdly, from out of nowhere, awkwardly I sit shiva for Jennie – a mourning ritual of which I'm largely ignorant. How does one perform this barbaric custom? As if directed by an unseen hand – the same one that types my copy? – I shroud the wall mirror with a towel, stop shaving, and for several days eat only dry bread while rocking back and forth in a Buddha pose – can this be right? – muttering: '*Ha'makom yenahem etkhem betokh she'ar avelei Tziyonvi'Yerushalayim* ...'

What is this and where is it coming from? '*Oy vey iz mir, oy vey iz mir …*' Over and over again, from somewhere deep inside me I never knew existed.

Jennie was my fixation and now my fix is gone. I'm completely alone.

Without warning the sun in my brain bursts through the clouds. *He* is unleashed once more. Such a cold, cold heart. So it's true what they say: a loved parent's death splits a writer open like an atom exploding in a chain reaction. Writers are monsters. In a single sleepless weekend *he* hits those keys and produces a first book, *Weekend in Dinlock*. Sorry, Ma.

Sex helps, again. An athletic blonde taking a secretarial class in Kensington has a bedsit down the hall from me. She's the broad-shouldered captain of the All England Women's Field Hockey team, and I'm her first Jew, she claims. She calls me 'darling', comes like a locomotive, and eases herself into my room by asking if I need my typewriter oiled. 'Heather' has many such euphemisms for instant sex. 'Machine fixed.' 'Tea time!' 'Keep your clock ticking?' The thing is, she always finds excuses to slip into my room while wearing her hockey uniform of white Aertex short-sleeved shirt tucked into a navy blue knee-length wool skirt, long woollen socks and hockey boots that she insists on wearing to bed.

*

Another bus ride up to Thurcroft to show Len Doherty my hotly typed manuscript. Sitting at a table in the Miners' Club, I nervously watch him flip the newborn pages with his licked thumb and read every single fucking word, studying, judging. He lays the last page atop the pile, and has the power right there to stop my writing career dead. Instead he sighs, 'It will be the making of thee.' The implication is, I'm using him and the village to advance myself.

The next morning he takes me to the bus, unpins the hammer-and-sickle badge from his coat that a delegation of Russian Don Basin miners had gifted to their Yorkshire counterparts, and fastens it to my sweater. He follows this up with a swift punch to the arm as I board the coach. His last words to me are: 'Guttersnipes of the world, unite!'

AVE ATQUE VALE

Len, suffering from lung ailments and reeling from exhaustion, at last finds work outside the mine as a part-time scribbler on the local rag, the *Sheffield Star*, which evolves into full-time, award-winning reporting. Returning from assignment in Vietnam, he is passing through Munich airport in 1970 when masked Arabs toss a grenade among the passengers on his airport bus. Len lunges at the grenade to kick it away from children, saving their lives, but it explodes, killing a husband and wife and leaving Len with painful neck and spine wounds from which he never quite recovers. Overwhelmed by guilt, and feeling responsible for the couple's death, in 1963 he commits suicide. Today nobody knows his name. The Thurcroft library doesn't carry his novels, *The Man Beneath*, *A Miner's Sons* and *The Good Lion*, and the village's website fails to mention him. When I make enquiries of his London publisher, the gentleman can't recall him either except for saying, 'Oh, you mean that drunken miner?'

I owe him a life, too.

CHANGING SIDES

First-book euphoria. Debut! *Bruce* is now a real writer. Jacket photo! Reviews, royalties ('Best y'do addle brass for it, mind'), change of lifestyle. The fledgling author leaves behind the dusty dank meeting halls he formerly patronized in favor of the warm welcome he receives from a surprising quarter: the wine-and-cheese circuit in postcodes NW3 (Hampstead) and W11 (Holland Park), where *his* new friends are conservative – with a small 'c' – Labour Party bright young technology-mad pro-American brainiacs, on the wrong side of the issues *he* (and I) care most about.

These people love the Bomb, are snotty about my rain-drenched CND marchers, hate trade unions, and bask in the conviction that they're the logical heirs to Britain's Tory 'natural rulers'. 'What school did you go to?' is frequently asked, openly or by inference. They may have begun life as socialists but what really counts is: did you attend a top fee-paying school like Harrow, Dulwich or St Paul's and then go on to Oxford, because being the product of a state-run grammar school ('grammar grub') doesn't quite cut it. 'Clancy, where did you go?' 'UCLA.' 'Surely you jest. It's a sweater, not a college.'

These chatty get-togethers are recruiting grounds for outsiders like me, 'outsider' in this case being defined as anyone who does not have an Oxford (and ideally Balliol) degree in PPE. You needn't be an Enigma code-breaker to grasp the importance of Philosophy, Politics and Economics as an entrance qualification for eventual admission to the British establishment. Cabinet ministers from both parties, BBC apparatchiks, opinion-forming Fleet Street journalists – top people, in other words – more often than not read PPE. It's a class insignia so taken for granted by its bearers they'll invariably respond to a question with, 'Whyever are you interested in anything so uninteresting?' Always a dead giveaway you've stumbled on something worth pursuing, I find.

I have a big mouth but a torpid mind, which just barely gets me by at New Reasoner or New Left meetings but helps keep me on my toes coping with this NW3/W11 bunch who seem able to spin concepts at warp speed. At first I freeze, intimidated, then catch on. There's a trick to it, the very opposite of Hollywood agentry. The key thing is: no boasting or bragging; self-deprecation is the hallmark of a first-class mind.

They're all as self-confident as if they're already cabinet ministers: people like Shirley Williams, A. J. (Freddie) Ayer, Bill Rodgers, David Marquand, Anthony Crosland, Dr David Owen, and Susan Sontag's Chicago-born husband Phil Rieff the sociologist. Naturally they're at the uncontaminated end of the scale from dirt-smeared, horny-handed men of toil like Len Doherty and the guys at Pilkington's Glass, Ford Dagenham or Forgemasters Sheffield. This new breed of social democrat despises the 'romance of socialism', rooted in fusty Utopian ideals, and promoted by not very bright or interesting people. In other words, my sort. But that I go to conferences, organize ginger groups and leaflet like mad *for the wrong side of the Labour Party* bothers them not in the slightest. It's an urbane broad-mindedness I'll encounter time and again, in Oxford colleges and aristocratic country houses alike, because they have an infallible instinct for who's on top and so can afford to practice tolerance.

What's not to like about these alert modernizers? Once I was covering a play at the Lyric Hammersmith when an audience member collapsed. While the rest of us dithered, a modernizer, Dr David Owen, leaped smartly over the seats to do CPR and save the victim. I crawled over to hold the man's hand. 'What the hell are you doing?' Owen cried. 'Helping,' I said. He muttered, 'He doesn't need his hand holding, idiot, just go and call 999!'

You won't see any of the modernizers on grubby, tedious anti-nuclear marches. For example: Secretary of the Fabian Society Shirley Williams (Oxford, Fulbright scholar), daughter of the remarkable and pacifist Vera Brittain, opposes nuclear disarmament, which even the Pope is in favor of. 'Sentimental bosh,' she calls it. For modernizers, displays of naked emotion are politically risky and maybe even a little disgusting.

What do you do when you are embraced by nice people who hate what you are about?

*

In the eleventh century Anselm, Archbishop of Canterbury, proposed a bloodless ontological argument for the existence of God. His adversary, Thomas Aquinas, argued that logic alone proved nothing since it can prove everything. Men fought to the death over this theological gulf between brain and feeling.

I was up to my neck in Labour Party quarrels as a believer in the True Cross of Clause 4's commitment to full-blooded socialism. On conference floors there were fist fights between people like me (called Bevanites) and The Others (called Gaitskellites) over sacred Clause 4. Remembering that medieval dispute, it's clear that what we were fighting for control of was the soul of the party.

*

Sunward I've climbed, and joined the tumbling mirth ...

I have been invited to dine at All Souls High Table – Mecca for brainiacs. It didn't take very much: a well-reviewed book; jawing into a BBC microphone. How lucky I am that the BBC is a cultural dictatorship and not a democracy! And even if you are only a C+ college dropout, All Souls takes you in as a blood brother (no sisters admitted!), for friendly conversational weekends. Vintage port from the cellar ceremonially passes clockwise and I have my own personal elderly scout to draw the drapes and call me 'sir'. This is the life! I even browse their wonderful library, amassed on the broken bodies of Caribbean sugar-estate slaves owned by an All Souls benefactor. Alas, the disgustingly sweet Portuguese wine loosens my tongue, which gets me quarrelling with my neighbor at table, a distinguished Foreign Office mandarin, about why his department always backs fascists. I am not asked back to All Souls.

To add insult to injury, a short time after the All Souls debacle, I am invited to join the Savile Club on Brook Street in Mayfair whose members have included Thomas Hardy and my almost-favorite London writer Patrick Hamilton as well as my all-time favorite Evelyn Waugh.

The offer is withdrawn because, to take a clear shot on its venerable billiards table, I sprawl on its hundred-year-old green baize and, to the horror of the members, accidentally rip it.

THE REVOLUTIONARY INITIALS

Don't try to follow the initials, but there's another exclusive club that welcomes celebrities, even minor ones like me. Unbelievably the Socialist Labour League (formerly the Revolutionary Communist Party, later the Workers' Revolutionary Party), prophesying a 'revolutionary situation in Britain', switches from recruiting workers to going after well-paid media and theatrical types who, whether from class guilt or conviction, flock to sit at the feet of its charmless Leninist sage-out-of-a-Graham-Greene-novel, Gerry Healy. Even a stylish *Vogue* model attends from time to time. Something strange is going on in my 'set' when ordinarily level-headed professionals can subjugate their minds to an Irish farmer's Trotskyist son. He seems to wield an almost mystical power over successful artists. I'm flattered to be asked, but run for the high ground after listening to Healy lecture on 'the present crisis in the arts'.

Ken Tynan, the *Observer*'s drama critic, catches up with me in the hallway. He can't stop laughing while whispering in my ear, '"*Our doubts are traitors, and make us lose the good we oft might win, by fearing to attempt*" ... darling, don't worry, it's Shakespeare. You bloody coward, come back and suffer with the rest of us!'

New money ...

New friends ...

New status ...

Girls! Girls! Girls!

Oh, yeah?

HANGOVER SQUARE

A bowler hat launches me into my upscale new life. With an amused smile, Susan Sontag's husband, eminent Freud scholar and sociologist Phil Rieff, a charter member of this 'centrist' (Left-loathing) socialist milieu, buys me a Lock & Co. hand-made hat: 'Being as you're not a grubby proletarian anymore, this should help you become that ridiculous thing, an "English gentleman".' How did he know?

So out go the crewneck sweater and GI boots, in with Crockett & Jones handmade shoes and Chukka boots; cavalry twill trousers from Cordings of Piccadilly; scrimshaw and silver hip flask (Walker & Hall); Dunn & Co. 'County' cap; Viyella check shirts; bespoke belted poncho (on my new Harrods charge account; how marvelous to stroll in, choose from their overpriced food counter and not receive a bill for months, merely the manager's fawning letter); Blackthorn tweed jacket with rear vents (Savoy Taylors Guild – not yet Savile Row but I live in hope); and of course a dashing trench coat (Army & Navy Store), like the one Joel McCrea wears as Hitchcock's *Foreign Correspondent*.

An American Englishman is a comic sight except to himself.

There now, all kitted out for a brand new life. Bring on the girls!

Starting with new digs as befits a London gent.

TOMB RAIDER

Farewell squalid basement bedsit, hello my bourgeois, bachelor-friendly flat at 67 Princes Square in a five-storey Edwardian house in Bayswater, W2 with a street view of the key-holders' garden in front and a narrow mews in back. In the 1890s it was a spacious single-family residence, probably for a mid-level manager of the Metropolitan Railway Company that was engaged in tunnelling from Paddington to Hammersmith. Around the outbreak of the Great War the house was broken up into smaller flats for railway clerks and their families, and now me. Number 67 sits between Notting Hill Gate, an odd little half-chic, half-seedy neighborhood with its lively pubs and Embassy Row leading down to Kensington Palace, and Westbourne Grove sliding past the Portobello Road open-air market, with bolt holes in the narrow alleys, serpentine back streets and circular crescents, and the Harrow Road canal a dumping ground for trash and dead bodies.

Unaware, I've built my own tomb, redecorated as Young Smooth Single Guy, with fitted grey carpets and high corniced ceilings, white walls and floor-to-ceiling triple-lined custom-sewed Heal's orange velour drapes to shut out light and noise. No pictures on the walls, no adornments. A Japanese Samurai would feel at home here.

I'll finally kill anxiety in this gladiator's arena or die in the attempt.

As soon as I move in it feels as if a coffin lid closes on me.

Because *he* needs peace and quiet, I muffle street sounds by installing double glazing, lock and bolt the front door, order groceries delivered, tape rags to the rear window overlooking a neighbor's bonsai trees, unplug the phone and TV. There now, blessed silence. Half-suffocated on paraffin fumes from the Valor heaters, mildly blotto on Balvenie single malt delivered to the doorstep by a green-painted, horse-drawn Harrods cart, sprawled in my House of Fraser king-sized bed warmed by two hot water bottles, Corona #3 portable on my lap, a crumpled *National Geographic* map of the United States pinned to the opposite wall, a copy of Kerouac's *On The Road* to hand, typing like crazy, I lie back half dozing and let *him* do all the work. Thanks, Bruce.

Lifted practically to the ceiling by a rush of love for the people I'd left behind, I write about them before I forget. *Going Away*.

It only took five years, then splat! A second book. Last shot. My tank is drained.

How to fill the sudden emptiness? That wrinkled *National Geographic* map of the United States I used for inspiration gives me such a longing for the real thing ...

THE BIG SHUN

Homesick, I reach out for the first time to other London Yankees. I'm sure to find a welcome there, especially from the exiled Hollywood blacklisted types like me who gather every Sunday for the regular Hyde Park softball game (see Glenda Jackson and George Segal in *A Touch of Class*) played by expat film-makers, some of them my former agency clients. When they coldly, deliberately, ignore me, I call on Hollywood exiles like Carl Foreman and Joe Losey, who shut doors in my face. What's up with that? Oh, yes. The penny drops. Émigré politics. Someone anonymous has spread word around that I'm 'untrustworthy' and possibly a CIA 'source' or FBI informer. Who knows how this stuff starts? My countrymen's rejection is painful at first but turns out to be a blessing since it keeps me away from certain kinds of Americans and leaves me no option except to keep connecting with the natives.

PS Eventually the culprit outs himself. 'Fred', a black-listed expat screenwriter, confesses that he invented the rumour about me.

'But we're friends, how could you?' I ask him.

'Yeah, that bothers me too. How could I? But, hey, my analyst is helping me through this.'

*

IN THE NEWS
John F. Kennedy is sworn in as first Catholic President of the USA. The Cuban Bay of Pigs fiasco. The Berlin Wall goes up. Motown signs the Supremes, and Patsy Cline records Willie Nelson's 'Crazy'.

There must be other kinds of Americans around to feed my longing. Thank you, Jesus, for cold-hearted editors with hot deadlines.

Mel Lasky, the fiercely anti-Communist editor of *Encounter* magazine, a not-so-secret CIA front payrolled by the Congress of Cultural Freedom, couldn't care less about exiles' feuds. He's a perfect example of why editors rule my life. Shrewdly reading my mind, he dispatches me to mingle with and report on the home folks: American GIs on Strategic Air Command's nuclear bases scattered across the eastern English counties of Norfolk, Suffolk and Oxfordshire. They are launching pads for American B-47s, each carrying a multi-megaton nuclear device pre-targeted on Moscow and Kiev. In WW2 SAC's boss, General Curtis LeMay, had his bombers cremate Tokyo by fire-storm, and now he's demanding a 'Sunday Punch' first strike so he can drop his 133 A-bombs and blast Russia off the map before the Russians do it to us, which is why his B-47s are airborne round-the-clock, waiting for the green light.

The air bases, insular and strange Little Americas with their PXs and Mayberry-style schools and small-town amenities, are a reporter's dream because, unlike Britain's military, US officers are not gagged by the absurd Official Secrets Act. Americans *love* talking. God, how I miss American blab! At USAF Brize Norton I'm even proudly shown a nuclear bunker where a drunken sergeant fired a bullet from his .45 directly into The Bomb, which failed to explode thus saving an entire Oxfordshire population. You can't beat an open society of motormouths.

> Look, mister. Let's not talk crap. If that whistle
> ever blows for real, do you think I'm coming

back alive?

– Pilot officer, Brize Norton AF base

No, sir, I don't think much about what you call the consequences. No, not very often; in fact, seldom at all. You're too busy up there … it's a routine. Just like carrying this Coke bottle across the room and bringing it back … Well, yes, if someone told me to, I'd press the button … You have to remember, bombing now, it's a lot more efficient than in the last war. We always try, you know, for pin-point bombing, and we get pretty good at it. But this time when we deliver a bomb … it may be five miles off the mark but we know we'll have struck our target anyway. I know it sounds a little, you know, crude, but when you knock out everything, you knock out something.

– B-47 crew member, Burtonwood, Lancashire

These Americans … They're the loneliest people I've ever dealt with. They just don't know how to be alone.

– English community relations officer, Oxfordshire

If I had the time I could do marriage counselling all day, twenty-four hours a day, seven days a week, fifty-two weeks a year.

– USAF chaplain, Burtonwood

If they ask me, I tell them they're on the right side, that there is a just war. But nobody ever comes in to seek guidance on that sort of thing.

– USAF chaplain, Brize Norton

Back in the States they say you can't legislate
a change in men's hearts. Let them take a good
look at the Air Force over here. It may not be all
that I want, but it's a damn good first step.
                    – African American officer, Oxfordshire

Go get 'em, IRA!
                    – American airmen at Fairford AF base
                        on hearing news of a terrorist raid
                            on British military barracks

PS My photographer, the *Observer*'s Peter Keen, has a fractured skull. Each morning, before setting out on a tour of bases, he goes into the bathroom to wrap the top of his head in a fresh antiseptic bandage because as a child he'd been struck by a falling girder during a German air attack. 'How did you get that?' ask some of the airmen. 'In a bombing raid,' Peter replies.

*

The Little Americans on US air bases are frozen in a 1950s time warp. As I am too, until …

THE GIRL HAPPENS

An odd late spring. Things fall out of place. The chalky West London sun slants down in a pale yellow drizzle that makes me feel slightly ill. The four of us are an unlikely little band: Sally Codrington, Mike Cohen, Melville Hardiment and me.

My Swingin' Sixties start to happen when a voice bellows from the public bar: 'JEWS!'

'FUCKIN' ISRAELITES OWN US, RIGHT? Piss in our beer and we drink it up with damn all protest. Dogs lying in our own vomit, we are. BLOODY JEWS!'

Curious, I go around the public-bar partition of my local, the Prince Edward, to see this blowhard nursing his beer. He's husky and ruddy-faced and has ten years and fifty pounds on me. Shut the fuck up, I tell him politely, and he just as nicely tells me to fuck the fuck off, and almost in synchronized motion we nut each other and go crashing down like two of the Three Stooges.

'Jesus,' he mutters, holding his head and rocking back and forth on the ciggie-strewn floor, 'I'm sorry you did that.' My head is bleeding, too. Unwilling to risk further pain, we chat instead.

Melville Hardiment and I turn out to have a lot in common. He, too, is a guttersnipe, 'scum of the earth' as the Duke of Wellington described his own troops at the Battle of Waterloo, your classic anonymous British soldier, call him ranker, dragoon, grenadier, pikeman – Melville's ancestors probably sweated blood at Agincourt. Today, he's a late-fortyish hard face from the madly incestuous Cambridgeshire fens where native Saxon warriors once hid from the Norman invader. Sharing a bench with me in my garden, he describes himself as 'a fairish painter, a goodish poet' who teaches in a Secondary Modern school, where (by his own admission) he guiltlessly seduces his girl pupils, eventually marrying one or two who, he says, insist on calling him 'sir' even in bed. What should I do with this guy? For all his mockery, he 'gets' me as a writer, and I get his (rather excellent) poetry. Well, Ezra Pound and T. S. Eliot didn't like Jews either.

Melville is war's creature. His father gassed at the Somme, his brother Peter killed in a battle not far from Touffreville where Melville almost caught his, and he's ex-Regular Army having enlisted in the Hungry Thirties, fought in India and Burma, escaped the Japanese at Singapore, and with the East Yorkshire Regiment landed with the British Third Division assault on Sword Beach in France on D-Day. Though wounded, he was one of the few survivors of his company.

*

'A Man of Few Words', by Melville Hardiment

Black eyed Corporal Farrell
was a man of few words other

than the usual anglo-saxons
sprinkled around barrackrooms
and camps. He had no words
for the ragged shrapnel slicing
through his kneecaps but
used his morphia and that was that.
We sat side by side in the sun,
for 'lightning never strikes twice
in the same place' I had said.

Side by side wishing the frank
sharp crack and slap of shrapnel
would cease and leave us be.
He might have dreamt of England
and some soft hospital bed. I don't
know, and we just waited. And then
a sniper's bullet holed his head.

He looked at me reproachfully and barked
'Fuck!'

This was first published in the *Salamander* magazine and included this note from the editor: Hardiment was a sergeant in the East Yorkshire Regiment, who took over command of his unit when his officers were killed on landing in Normandy. He fought a campaign through the murderous cornfields south to Caen. By the time he was wounded near Touffreville, east of Caen, some forty-one days later (the event described in this poem), he and his corporal were the only members of his company still intact.

*

In the next pub we crawl to he proudly pulls from his wallet a yellowing photo of himself relaxing atop a heap of German Wehrmacht corpses. 'I ate their fucking ears. Know what a human ear tastes like? It's good.' AWOL in liberated Paris, he met the artist-writer Wyndham Lewis and other expatriate Vorticists who encouraged his evolution into a full-blown, voting, rioting, British Union of Fascists dues-payer. With the soul of a poet, his only flaw is he can't stand Jews – except as friends.

'You shock easy for a Hebe,' Melville says. 'Come on, I married this fourteen-year-old girl once. For fuck's sake, she was of the Israelite persuasion too, and nothing ever shocked her. She was eleven when she first proposed to me. "I'll have you, sir, really I will. I'll wear you down." And too bloody right she was, mate.' Melville is proudly *lumpen*; dispossessed and uprooted, he jeers at my social mobility. 'Oh, yes, you're from the fucking pro-lee-tay-reeat, give me a break, comrade!' He pokes fun at my writing for elite rags like the *Observer*, *New Statesman* and the (former *Manchester*) *Guardian*:

> *The working class can kiss my arse*
> *I can afford the* Guardian *at last.*

He sees life through the eyes of a squaddy, an ARAB (Arrogant Regular Army Bastard), an ear-eating private soldier skilled on the Bren LMG, and someone with a microscopic eye for caste distinctions. 'You haven't a clue about the real upper classes, have you?' The first of his marriages was to a titled lady 'who fell for my uncouthness and my cock. I made it as far as the swells would let me. They can smell the shit we're from. It's their sixth sense. They'll find you out too, eventually.'

The uncomfortable fact is Melville and I complement each other.

He swears he's too old for street fighting, but I'm not. I've signed on with guys assembling a '62 Group' in the image of the fiercely combative 43 Group of WW2 Jewish ex-servicemen, including commandos and a Victoria Cross winner, who fought Jew-hating British Nazis with brass knuckles and steel-toed boots, jumping Mosleyite meetings to hit, slug and maim under slogans like 'out-fascisting the fascists' and 'get them before they get us'. (Vidal Sassoon, then an apprentice hairdresser, was a 43 Grouper.) But native Nazism is a snake that never sleeps. The aging Mosley storm troopers who'd chased me at Earl's Court are being replaced with teenage punks like my friends in Islington and Hammersmith. In a melee with British National Party militants outside Paddington station, I found myself flailing alongside a boy, Mike Cohen, also bike-helmeted and masked, who after the police wade in and all's clear, invites me to speak to his sociology class at the London School of Economics. Mike, who looks like a fragile and obedient *yeshiva bocher*, is in fact a crazy street brawler who speaks almost inaudibly, carries himself hunched like a shtetl scholar, has a fringe of black beard, large watchful eyes and seems always on the verge of apologizing ... but for what? He's as gentle (most of the time) as Melville is rough, a child-man, by trade a tailor's apprentice in his uncle's Whitechapel shop, by night a ferocious brawler screaming the ancient East End cry 'They shall not pass!' As a boy he'd witnessed the Cable Street Riot when Jews and Communists and their neighbors clashed with fascist Blackshirts – '*No pasarán!*' They shall not pass – and Mike never forgot.

Melville sizes him up immediately when he reaches across the beer-spattered pub table to finger Mike's hair. 'Where are the ringlets, then, Rabbi? Jews. Oughta walk around with a sandwich board saying "Kick me".' Because Mike dreads personal confrontations, as opposed to street brawls, he pretends Melville's anti-Semitism is not to be taken seriously. Mike is secretly flattered to be included in the company of such luminaries as a published poet and a BBC voice. His gratitude for this – his 'wetness' – drives Melville into a rage. 'That's what's wrong with you people. What are you so everlastingly grateful for, eh? That Bayswater isn't Belsen?' As a matter of fact, rifleman Melville had liberated the death camp Bergen-Belsen, but this experience instead of softening his racism seems to have deepened it.

'What's the problem,' he demands of Mike and me, 'with strangling a Kraut guard even if you have to die? I would have done.' The sight of all those stacked *Konzentrationslager* corpses had disgusted but also twisted him into this attack-dog snarling mockery. 'You don't *really* mean it. After all, you freed my people,' Mike cries. 'The fuck I did,' retorts Melville, 'we ran across them by accident. Fortunes of bloody war. Damn near gave me a heart attack, those haystacks of dead Jews did.' And so on.

Mike the fighting Jew and Melville the Jew-baiter are bonded to each other as I am attached to them and we three to Sally.

The instant I spotted Sally (Sarah Elizabeth) Codrington, sprawled like a hoyden watching my London School of Economics talk from the back row of Mike's class, I sputtered off into (further) inanities. Of the hundred or so students on banked benches in the lecture hall, the sight of this girl, gypsy-dark, lean as a boy, Greek or Italian or possibly North African, with irregular features and a lopsided grin, struck me dead between the eyes. After class, she slips in with Melville, Mike and me for a drink, and she and I go on to spend most of the summer with each other and Mike and Melville. She fits us all like a glove. I get chills looking at her.

'You have no idea what you fellas saved me from,' she says. 'I do,' pipes up Melville, ''cos I married one of your breed.' Sally's breed, it turns out, is Middle England landed gentry as the youngest daughter of Rutland's Lord Lieutenant – a viscount or baron or ordinary knight, I can never tell the difference, does that make Sal a 'Lady'? – where she's expected, nay encouraged, to have little or no education and to marry 'well'. The Queen stopped formal royal presentations for debutantes at court but in The Season, Ascot races and Henley Regatta and all, tradition demands Sally husband-hunt with the rest of her aristocratic cohort.

She's twenty-one and 'county' to the tips of her Schnieder of London riding boots. Dissimilar to my usual aristocratic hosts, she lacks their easy 'charm' but can be awkward, ungainly, and more emotionally open than the upper middles or lower uppers I've met.

Sally is a study in entrapment who shares with us her dream of escape to a different, undefined-as-yet life, a breakout from her niche in the social pyramid. A keen horsewoman, she adores her family and its riding-and-hunting excitements while convinced that deliverance is not for the likes of her. 'I'm glad I wasn't born a washerwoman or factory worker. I'd like to go into politics or nursing or *do something* with my life. I could become prime minister except for those dreary Tory fêtes. Don't you dare laugh! Nobody in my family is a writer. That's the problem, isn't it? Nobody is stopping me but there it is.' Melville and I tease Sally, which she takes in good part until we trash her family whom she fiercely defends along with its inherited feudal traditions. 'I love working the land with our tenant farmers.' She punches my arm. Their farmers. 'Clancy, you know it only from books – I live it. It works for our people.' Our people? How baronial. If I propagandize to her about the Tolpuddle Martyrs and the Peasants' Revolt, that's usually when, exasperated with each other, we tumble into bed.

Proviso: on our first night together she confessed to virginity, and when I hesitated promptly threw on her clothes and the next thing I heard was a postcard from Morocco: '*You can now – Sal*', meaning she'd gone to Africa to get herself deflowered, and on returning to London insisted I owed it to her – that and the plane fare to Tangiers.

Nothing so far has prepared me for Sally who is fifteen years my junior. Her argument is that she's an 'old soul' while – Doris would love this – I never quite grew up. Sometimes, during sex, she'll look thoughtfully into my eyes, as if enquiring about something, but then the question evaporates and it's all right again. Other times she'll suffer an attack of sadness out of nowhere. 'What's wrong?' I enquire. 'Absolutely nothing.' 'Do you have a guy, a boyfriend, back home?' 'No, not really. Just someone I'm supposed to marry.'

Each of us needs rescuing but Sal's need is urgent because right now she's reluctantly rooming with two other secretarial-school debs in Kensington. Her family insisted on this to immunize her against London's wickedness. First order of business, Melville, Mike and I form a commando raid to kidnap and bring her home to us – that is, mainly, to me.

Like James Dean and Natalie Wood and Sal Mineo in *Rebel Without a Cause*, the four of us create an artificial family on some distant classless science-fiction London planet. We've seen the film naturally and only half-jokingly refer to ourselves by our movie names. I'm James Dean's neurotic rebel 'Jim'; Mike Cohen vulnerable 'Plato'; Sally our 'Judy'; my apartment a kind of grown-up nursery. Only Melville refuses to play his part, calling it 'adolescent horseshit', which it is. But in our hearts we believe it. Sally is even fond of quoting Natalie Wood-as-Judy's line, *'We're not going to be lonely any more – ever.'* Sally is God's gift to us. I say it's a relief having a lady friend who shares none of my values. Melville snorts, 'I hate euphemisms like "lady friend". She's half your age and you're fucking her arse off.'

Mike winces to hear this; arguments except with street fighters make him physically ill. Melville sadistically enjoys working on Mike's – and my – anxiety. He'll say, 'Of course, Mike is a cut above me because I was born of serfs and the Jew will always get one up on you. But he knows I could break his neck with my bare hands.'

At such moments Mike goes into a kind of grey-faced shock. 'Christ,' Melville jeers, 'you two Hebes hate reality, don't you? Maybe that's why you don't have a future in the England that's coming. *My* England.' Is he far-sighted or just nuts?

Sally will take a deep breath and say, 'What am I doing with two Jews and a fascist?' She yearns to be just one of the boys but the girl part of her belongs to me alone, selfishly, like Belmondo and Jean Seberg in Godard's *Breathless*, currently all the rage. Our romance even has the same feel as Godard's unexplained and unexplainable jump cuts, following a logic of its own.

We guys are her shield against fate … and vice versa. 'Oh, I reckon,' she sighs, 'I'll have to marry the boy next door – David is an air chief marshal's son, on a farm near ours – and I'll have lots of babies and slosh around in wellies with a kerchief round my head breeding prize pigs. Mind, I like raising pigs.'

She's a born chancer, helmetless and heedless, barnstorming her two-stroke 98cc Vespa through heavy London traffic, cornering like a TT bike rider, one leg scraping the pavement, weaving reckless patterns around the Minis and Aston Martins, or else balanced upright on the saddle like a trick rodeo rider. From my pillion seat, holding on for dear life, I beg her to slow down, as I did in Philippa's glider, but like Philippa she enjoys scaring me and daring herself.

Unexpectedly, I'm also her publisher. Based on the surprise sales of *Weekend in Dinlock*, Secker & Warburg hires me to commission a series of short books, 'Eye on Britain', which is my excuse to expensively lunch writers I admire (Dennis Potter, Angus Wilson, V. S. Pritchett, Penelope Mortimer, Elaine Dundy, etc.). Nepotistically, I sign up Sally to write *County Girl*. Her writing style is just forming, but she buckles down to it. 'Am I your good girl?' she'll taunt me as I tear apart her sixth-form prose. She is feverishly hungry to experience it all, sights and sounds and sex, and above all everlastingly ravenous for the warmth she says her three men give her. I'm also her tour guide around 'Red' London, showing her Orwell's old bedsit and Chartist pubs ... oh, we have a grand time, and she loves every minute. We walk all over rebel London holding hands. Hers are surprisingly tough and leathery; maybe she really does work in the fields with 'her' peasants.

'Now it's your turn,' I tell her, and ask her to talk about her home county – so small it's easy to bypass on my way to the steel towns of Sheffield and Scunthorpe. 'My father knows only one Jew – something Montagu,' Sally observes. 'As in Capulet and Montague?' 'No, as in the merchant banker.' 'You think he'll mind meeting a second?' I ask. She laughs. 'Only if you owned a bank and were Sir Clancy.'

We compromise by camping out next to the Peter Pan statue in Kensington Park Gardens. Sally, a former Girl Guide, brings a canvas tent and a picnic hamper, and we climb over the iron railings after sundown. The night is warm. We snuggle together around a flashlight, devouring ham and sweet pickles and playing tricks with our fingers to make duck and dog shadows on the inside of the tent, hoping they don't alert the patrolling groundsmen. I tell her how Peter, Ernest, Occy, Woodjie the dummy and I used to play cricket here, and she says, 'You really are Peter Pan. Otherwise you wouldn't be with me. You'd be married to some BBC wallah up on Primrose Hill and running about in an Austin-Healey.' What she doesn't know is that I dream of bringing her to America with me. I'm torn between wanting to possess her and watching her fly free.

'Will you ever marry me?' I ask before I know what I'm saying.

She does a double take, angling her neck, sits back on her haunches, snaps off the flashlight and says, 'Well, aren't you something?'

THE LAST TROUBADOUR

The trouble is that each of the four of us has what Melville calls a hump back – a personal flaw or embarrassment, like Mike's bad luck with women, Melville's inability to publish, Sally's almost suicidal recklessness, and my falling-down fugues. My goal is to build myself up to be at least as suitable for Sal as her air chief marshal's son whom I visualize as uncannily handsome, athletically robust and an all-round good chap – *he* doesn't collapse in the street or crap his pants. I must talk to somebody in authority about my own hump back. Looking for answers, I check into the National Hospital for Nervous Diseases in Queen Square where I've heard that my all-time hero, the four-minute-mile trackster Dr Roger Bannister is a resident physician. Verdict: great runner, bedside manner not so great. Stethoscope in hand, he glances at me in the bed and curtly orders the ward sister, 'Clearly neurotic. Discharge him.'

Brian Inglis, of the 133-year-old *Spectator*, for whom I write, is an authority on 'fringe' paranormal medicine. 'Hey, Brian, here are my symptoms.' Over lunch at The Ivy he listens carefully then points me to Watkins Magick & Occult Bookshop in Cecil Court off Charing Cross Road. The place can't be too weird, I reason, since the *Spectator* is High Tory.

Watkins's hole-in-the-wall shop seems straight out of *Bell, Book and Candle*. It smells like a health food store and is full of browsing customers who look like warlocks in town for the day. I waste an afternoon browsing idly over nonsense tomes on magic ley lines, alternative religions and ancient heresies that soon every God-struck adolescent will be hipped on: John of the Cross, Meister Eckhart ('*If we are to dwell in Him… we should take leave of ourselves and of all things*'), primitive rebirth rituals, St Teresa of Ávila, Lao-Tzu and Zen, the Gospel According to St Thomas, Elijah the Essene, the Tibetan Book of the Dead, Martin Buber and the Baal Shem Tov. And of course Aldous Huxley's *Doors of Perception*, later Jim Morrison's inspiration for The Doors.

Ah, but what have we here? Ping, ping. *Massacre at Montségur: A History of the Albigensian Crusade* by Zoé Oldenbourg. Flip pages. Cathars. Hmm, fascinating. Albigensian 'total liberty and complete obedience' sounds right to me. Slowly, a great mental door swings open. A light flickers. Know what? My idol Tom Paine has it all wrong when he calls religion of any kind wicked; obviously he hasn't yet read his Catharism. These guys, with their blend of martyrdom, nostalgia, violence and defiance, were thirteenth-century cool.

That night, surprising Sal and myself, I break the news that we must stop making love because of my new identity as a Cathar priest and that as soon as I annihilate the material world's tyranny, I'll be able to dissolve my Self into the good God of pure spirit that struggles against the bad Satan-God of the flesh. Only by renunciation of erotic courtly love can I launch myself into the realm of the Perfects, the Cathar *bonhommes*. The what? Sal turns to me in bed and lowers one eyelid, her habit when puzzled or disturbed. Doesn't she see that celibacy is a sign of my improving health?

The Great Door opens wider. I am now *three* people: the former me; and Bruce-the-typist; and Brother William the Unrepentant of Montségur, a sexless thirteenth-century Cathar Perfect troubadour. Bruce does the typing, but Brother William carries the harder load with his faith-based lists of 'Thou Shalt Not', including have sex.

At some point, I feel sure, Sally and I can work this out.

But we don't get the chance. That weekend Sally is killed in an accident while riding in point-to-point. The *Sunday Express*, which carries her picture on its front page, reports that her foot snagged in the horse's stirrup at a hedge jump. I, Brother William, deny her death; after all, what is a single life measured against my 20,000 brothers and sisters massacred by Pope Innocent at Béziers? Jesus and Satan are brothers, the world as I experience it disgusting, the only way out is death, Sal is wiser than I am.

Leave it to tungsten-hearted Melville to *feel* something. He puts his arm around me. 'She was never going to last very long,' he says in his old soldier's voice. Mike weeps.

We put on our Sunday best and take the train from King's Cross to Sally's home village of Uppingham for a country funeral, quite posh, a mix of rural gentry, farm hands and retired military. The Codrington clan, whose line can be traced back to William the Conqueror, turns its back on us. Sally's polished blondwood coffin up by the altar in the small fourteenth-century church is almost hidden under wreaths of blood-red roses. All around the church's interior are memorials to local men killed in foreign wars, from the Rutlandshire Regiment of Foot at Quebec through the WWI trenches, Dunkirk retreat and the Anzio landing south of Rome. 'Bloody fools,' mutters ex-soldier Melville as we kneel in the pews. 'Shut up,' Mike hisses back. Sally's father is Colonel-in-Chief of the local regiment.

In the churchyard after the eulogy Melville lights a cigarette and scans the funeral-goers, especially the women. 'Fine specimens. Haunches like broodmares. Goers.' He gives me his hard grin. 'Pity. You were on your way to being the only Yiddish Lord Lieutenant in British history. This was your big chance and you funked it. I wouldn't have.' I hit him really hard, and hit him again as he goes down like a sack of potatoes. The funeral attendants come running, a small sensation breaks out.

Melville gets up from the ground without striking back. Just shakes his head sadly at me. 'If you hadn't stopped fucking her she'd be alive today, moron.'

> Sarah Elizabeth Codrington
> F,#243504, b. 4 November 1939, d. 15 April 1961
> Sarah Elizabeth Codrington was born on
> 4 November 1939. She was the daughter of

William Melville Codrington and Katherine
Theodosia Sinclair. She died on 15 April aged 21,
following a point-to-point accident.
From *Burke's Peerage, Baronetage & Knightage*,
107th edition, Volume 1, p. 846

*

It's easy to love the dead. Her life force overcame my slogans.

Sally had drawn us together: princess, daughter and wife. This same summer Ernest Hemingway blows out his brains with a Boss double-barrel shotgun in Ketchum, Idaho, and we three grieving survivors in London implode when Mike, in despair, burglarizes the office of *Bulldog*, the National Front magazine, to pour glue over the presses and is locked up for B&E in Pentonville before vanishing into London's pitiless world of radical communes; and Melville, who shrugs off emotion as he did at the Normandy beachhead, moves to a New Town, marries again, and runs for his local council on a right-wing ticket. He and I meet only once again for drinks at the Prince Edward and then he keeps his sergeant's voice down to a whisper. 'It's the new wife,' he murmurs. 'Hates me talking about the past. Says it ages me.' Wisely, I don't ask how old the wife is.

Our summer together is over.

BUBBLE BOY

The *Sunday Express* with Sally's photo on the front page is the last newspaper I'll read for a long time. I refuse to watch

TV news either. Slamming that door on the outside world, I incarcerate myself as a solitary inmate in the monk's cell I've built at Princes Square, to dispose of my Self, toss it on the junk pile, live as if already dead, free from attachment. Killing the Self means disposing of my expensive worldly goods until a grim coldness is achieved, tearing down and rebuilding my flat (see Gene Hackman in *The Conversation*) to resemble my idea of a Cathar cave. Living like a fugitive is second nature to me. Don't answer the phone. Hear footsteps in the hall – crawl under the handmade couch till they go away. Laugh and cry to myself. I listen obsessively to the first movement of Mozart's Jupiter Symphony over and over again, and Ralph Richardson reciting Blake's *Songs of Innocence,* and a Vegas cabaret singer called Frances Faye banging out 'The Man I Love'. Why? Why not? What I'm doing will make me new.

With brushes and bucket I re-paint my walls a deep blue, the color that signifies wisdom, strength and trust in Buddhism. Alone in the bleak apartment, I conduct Yogi feats: holding my breath for four minutes timed by a stopwatch; swallowing a cotton swab and pulling it from my anus by its string. Intoxicated on self-denial like the anorexic Christian mystic Simone Weil, physically wasting away, I feel amazingly clear-headed and all-powerful, The Human Torch as Lord Shiva.

When the blue walls close in and William Blake's imps and demons on the ceiling start to insult me, even Shiva needs a break and I skulk off to the Imperial cinema, Portobello Road. It is pungent with weed. I run screaming from shootouts on the screen, pursued by the movie's Apaches and cowboys down Westbourne Grove where phlegmatic Londoners couldn't care less about the man in a monk's robe dodging imaginary bullets. (The heavy wool garment was sewn by Doris 'to shield you from the Dark Powers'.) Fog-shrouded nights are my preferred time to hide in welcoming bolt holes in Kensington Park Gardens, the Harrow Road canal banks, the railway goods yards of Westbourne Park Road, the doorways of Notting Hill shop-fronts. In no time I drop fifty pounds on a diet of distilled water, cabbage hearts and Brazil nuts.

I will kill my Self to regain my Self or die trying.

I will burn out my impurities by main force of will.

It is a Hitlerite notion if ever there was one.

Hardly aware I'm crossing a line between London-eccentric and just plain nuts, I launch into a final search for help.

OCH, MON

> The schizophrenic is one who is broken-hearted.
> But even broken hearts can mend, if we have the
> heart to let them.
>
> R. D. Laing, *The Politics of Experience*

'Och, mon, it's aw bullshit!' are Dr R. D. Laing's first words to me as I slouch in a cracked leather chair opposite him in the soothingly dark consulting room at 21 Wimpole Street. 'Whyever'n hell you seein' alla these other boozhie doctors for anyway?' he demands. 'All your bleatin' an' moanin' like your standard Jewish neurotic when it's pairfickly plain as th' nose on your face ye've got the makin's of a first-class schizophrenic.'

A what?

*

Scene: that shaded consulting room on the ground floor of 21 Wimpole Street, London. Time: early 1960s.

My first session with the 'celebrity shrink', Ronald David Laing, was recommended by my writer friend Alan Sillitoe, who says, 'Try this guy. He's working-class like us.'

Laing gives me a long, heavy-lidded, penetrating gaze and snorts: 'How in fuck do Ah know what makes ye th' way you are? Gawd knows Ah don't. Ye're alive tae carry out your Mission is why, ye puir fuck.' Mission? He grins slyly. 'It's for me tae know an' ye to find out. Ha-ha!'

Laing is always quotable. 'People get mentally sicker than they have to because they deny the power of their sick experience.' Of course! My puking and fainting have not been in vain, after all.

This is the guy for me.

He's about my age (mid-thirties), with the doomed beauty of a haunted artist, and boasts a colorful slum background; later, it turns out he has been fashionably downgrading his real Presbyterian middle-class origins in Glasgow. He speaks of 'the mad' in different ways. First as if they're members of his own extended Scottish family and therefore to be cherished, but also as an 'oppressed proletariat', like the blacks of Alabama and South Africa, who are driven mad by the impossible 'binds' that society and their 'schizophrenogenic' families put them in and to which their only rational response is descent into a 'hyper-sane' insanity. Wow.

In polite society – he calls it 'their world' – he's the Bob Dylan, maybe the Malcolm X, of 'existential' psychoanalysis.

For all his books' jargon – ontological insecurity, being-for-itself, etc. – the simple message is that doctors should stop treating mental patients as objects to be ministered to and meet them in a more human 'I-thou encounter', whatever that is.

That's his public self. But there's also a secret Laing to be revealed in his own good time. (I love secrets!)

Smoking a thin cigar, he leans forward to look me over intently. 'Tummy aches and faintin' spells is crybaby stuff. Come off it, man! Ye've got bigger fish to fry.' Like me, Laing fancies himself a street brawler and after a couple of sessions suggests we spar around his room, jabbing, hooking, feinting. A bit odd but he's the doctor.

Laing was once a British Army medic, which may be why he calls himself a 'sojer of the mind', a point man reconnoitring the frontiers of mental disturbance, seizing the high ground in order to heal the mentally wounded. By joining in his assault on 'bourgeois' sanity, we will cure ourselves of the insanity of our normal middle-class lives. Sojer rather than patient. Hup-hup. Fighting machine. Makes sense.

*

Laing's ascendancy is perfectly timed. Antonin Artaud's 'madness is truth' is all the rage, with feminists going around chanting, 'We are all mad. If you are a woman then you are mad.' So madness is in the air.

The 'double bind' is the ticking time bomb of normal family love as preached by Laing and his professional partner Aaron Esterson ('Go away but tell me you love me'), a contradictory communication that drives kids literally psychotic. According to them, one must struggle to be free of the double-bind of love in order to find one's true self.

> From the moment of birth ... the baby is
> subjected to these forces of violence, called love,
> as its mother and father have been, and their
> parents and their parents before them. These
> forces are mainly concerned with destroying
> most of its potentialities, and on the whole this
> enterprise is successful.
>
> R. D. Laing, *The Politics of Experience*

Laing takes up a lot of my session time by raging against his own parents, and his medical internship in Scottish mental and British Army hospitals whose therapies included insulin coma, from which some patients never woke, electroshock (ECT) and icepick-through-the-eye transorbital lobotomy. Laing damns himself to a hell of guilt for ever taking part in such 'mind butchery'. The brutal economics behind these procedures disgusts him: it costs thousands of pounds a year to keep a person in a mental hospital; a lobotomy can be performed for only a few quid. Do the math.

Occasionally Laing insists we switch roles and chairs, he becoming the patient and I the therapist, and we celebrate this together in his office or my flat by swilling (then legal) LSD, straight from the Swiss Sandoz lab. Deep in acid, Laing stares moodily into space and is mute about what he experiences because it's too profound to share; my own trip is disappointingly dull, mere out-takes from the birth trauma except when spying on my parents fucking to make me. So *that's* where it went wrong.

Somehow, despite chemical blackouts, by sweat and sheer tenacity we pull together the Philadelphia Assocation – the name derived from the classical Greek for brotherly love – as a registered charity to create, or find, A Radical Place of Healing. Careering by car all over southern England, we stumble on Kingsley Hall, a former Baptist chapel in East London.

Laing is over the moon: 'This is IT!' After months of frustrating, fruitless, sour-tempered, back-breaking, morale-draining car trips to find our Holy Grail of a perfect healing place, it's this disused structure in Bromley-by-Bow that he finally chooses. It has the proper vibes apparently because Mahatma Gandhi once slept here in the upstairs cell that soon will be mine. Nevertheless, when curious local children and their mums wander into the Hall they usually take one look at us and flee as from Satan.

Euphoric and delighted, Laing sends out a call for 'intelligent [i.e. middle-class] incurable schizophrenics' at the end of their mental rope to fill the place up; almost overnight we become a Mecca for movie stars and celebrities like John Lennon as well as a safe haven for the truly desperate on whom conventional medicine has given up.

And ordinary people come too, in slews and droves, at any hour of the day or night, the crazy, lonely, homeless, given-up-on-themselves, psychotic and neurotic, hippies, draft dodgers, mystics, academics and celebrities, maverick doctors, acid fiends and 'victims of family love', the lost and wanting-to-be-found finding a sanctuary here with no locked doors or coercive medical jargon. They are seeking what is absent from their lives: compassion, pity, kindness, decency, mercy and tolerance for their mood swings and odd behaviour. Almost without exception our first guests breathe a sigh of relief that they have found us: 'At last, someone who actually understands.'

*

Exalted by this new comradeship, my first Philadelphia Association meeting is an eye-opener. There is, I'm given to understand, an Outer Circle of supporters, and an Inner Circle of specially selected 'Friends of the PA' donors who have privileged access to the doctors, and an Elect of Inner-inner Circle that includes the three main doctors, Laing, his fellow Glaswegian Esterson, and David Cooper; a social worker, Sid Briskin; a lone woman, Joan Cunnold, formerly chief ward nurse in Dr William Sargent's wing at St Thomas (notorious for Sargent's appetite for electro-shocking patients); and now me.

'Why me?' I ask Laing, who appoints me acting chairman of the Philadephia Association.

'Oh, ye're qualified awright. Ye're on your way ahead o' us all.'

On my way where? He just smiles enigmatically.

One of the first things I learn about is the gallows humor the three psychiatrists share, a sort of group code of practice based on the belief that death is preferable to the soul murder practiced by their contemporaries. It is a form of violence the PA is sworn to resist.

Outside enthusiasts, drawn by Laing's magnetism and the wish to do good, apply constantly to join us. Like High Court judges, we sit in a semi-circle putting to applicants a single poser: 'You're a combat soldier underfire. The enemy is chasing you. You must move fast or die. You stumble on a wounded enemy soldier who needs medical care. Do you slow yourselves down by taking him along ... or shoot him to make your escape?' Anyone who gives the humanitarian reply is blackballed on the spot.

Hey, this stuff is *serious*.

*

Without irony we call ourselves 'a revolutionary community of the elect' (like the early Bolsheviks) where admittance is by damaged heart. Sid Briskin, the group's indispensable worker bee, qualifies for a platinum card because his father murdered his mother then killed himself. Though naturally full of ideas and élan, we suffer badly from charity fatigue, the long painful haul of clashing egos on the rocky route to a halfway house for suffering psychotics. We're irritable with one another, physically slapping each other around, bullying ourselves in ways we'd never do with patients, now called 'guests'.

The group's short fuse is partly due to the strain of the Inner-inner Circle's practice of splitting our attention between our public charitable face and our underlying belief that we are Illuminati, mentally bracing ourselves for our own individual Ecstatic Voyage once certain earthly matters (like wives, mortgages, children, etc.) are dealt with.

Under all the bickering and ill temper, we're passionately bonded by the shared conviction that we have it within our power to begin the world all over again, as Tom Paine might say. Each of us in our turn will leave this old earth and, after overcoming a series of near-death quests, return to a totally virgin reality. It can, it will, happen ... the day after tomorrow.

A fascism of the spirit creeps unnoticed into our little circle.

Feeding off a mutual interest in shamanic rebirth rituals, Laing and I cook up a perfectly reasonable plan to ship me off to Mother America to re-conceive and re-deliver a better infant version of myself now that we've discovered what went wrong in the first place. I was born wrong. Rebirth will be a prelude to the Final Liftoff to … to …?

My secret agenda is to get the hell away from our rancorous Philadelphia get-togethers that are shattering what's left of my nerves. Some nights they're like pub brawls with the two Glaswegians, Esterson and Laing, swinging at each other. I return to America in the wake of the Cuban Missile Crisis and leave days before President John F. Kennedy is shot by a former Marine with a $19.95 rifle.

*

FIRST TRIMESTER

Pregnant in my head and releasing mental endorphins, on a snowy January day, walking off the gangplank at New York's 32nd Street pier after a seven-year absence, I head straight for the Bowery House of Hospitality, an office-cum-soup kitchen run by Dorothy Day, the conscience of Catholic America. She works with the poor and outcast. We chat as she stands, aproned and sweating, behind a large urn dispensing coffee and sandwiches to the down and out. Is my father here among them?

Day and I connect like old lovers. She pauses in the middle of distributing food to look into my eyes and say, 'Anyone who tries to do good usually ends up a troubled soul. God sends us the poor and wretched and then adds the shit we pile on ourselves for good measure. Stay and work with us if you're of a mind.' She laughs then. 'But I can see you must work elsewhere at the moment. How restless you are!' Of course I can't tell her my Secret Plan to deliver the Gnostic Pearl of Wisdom in code to infidel Americans.

Dorothy Day points me to Catholic-funded Monteith College in Detroit, a school for disaffiliated working-class kids. 'That's you,' she remarks. I kiss her and am off in a Greyhound bus along snowy roads, burning with a fever to learn all this strange country has to teach me if I can find a place in it again. I picture my wall map of the whole of the USA. It is like a giant mother, its roads fallopian tubes, each city a stage on the birth canal.

Since I'm drug-free for this journey, I know I'm sane.

*

The blue highways led me away from America; a 'black pipeline' brings me back.

Detroit, Michigan is where the action used to be for me. Where as a United Auto Worker functionary I learned to use a sap, a composition-rubber blackjack, to break a man's wrist but carried a .38 anyway.

Today, as I write, Detroit is a byword for industrial decay. But on this trip the joint is jumping. T-Birds, Plymouths and Impalas are selling at a record rate, factories hiring, the union strong and healthy. At the same time the racial metropolis is exploding yet again. All over town, on pirated tapes, Malcolm X's voice crackles. There's that distinctive double-octave high A sharp of Malcolm's incandescent anger. *That's* the lost musical note I've been searching for.

At Monteith College's 'school for dropouts' most of my students are the sons and daughters of auto workers, towards whom they feel surprisingly tender though they can't themselves envisage a future spent following their fathers into Ford's River Rouge plant or else being the wives of factory workers. Without exception they suffer from post-Cuban Missile Crisis trauma, feeling some part of themselves died in the nuclear exchange that didn't happen, and ragingly suspicious of older people who tried to kill them.

My seven black students shrug off the white kids' Cuban trauma because they were born, they insist, angry. Sprawled defiantly in the back of the classroom, each of them packs a weapon – a knife or Saturday Night Special – that they proudly flaunt. My real trip starts when one of their fathers, a Chrysler factory welder, recommends me to his union brother, James C. Boggs, half of the 'brains' of Detroit's revolutionary black movement. The other half is his wife, the Chinese-American scholar Grace Lee Boggs.

For much of the blustery Detroit winter, no questions asked, I'm taken into the warm bosom of their family, known as the 'Johnson-Forest Tendency', a splinter group from a spin-off from a fragment of an offshoot within a faction of Leon Trotsky's 4th International, itself a deviation from the 3rd International, which sprang from the 2nd International when Karl Marx took exception to anarchist Mikhail Bakunin tearing apart the 1st International. Marxists split more easily than they breathe.

Jimmy and Grace feed me and – remarkably – accept a perfect stranger into their lives with open-hearted friendship.

They are very unlike the Philadelphians. I sleep on a cot in their attic, crank the mimeograph on their newsletter, and bask in the tenderness of something I've missed: good will. Active in Detroit's Black Nationalist upsurge, they hook me up with Wilfred X, Malcolm X's mellower brother, who spreads the word among the Nation of Islam, which sends the word to black communities all across America to take in the inquisitive white boy from London.

The morning I leave Detroit, Grace and Jimmy kiss me goodbye, and then he reaches behind a little alabaster bust of Lenin on the mantelpiece to pull out a .22 and shoves it in his pants pocket. 'I'll walk you to the bus stop. This is a proletarian neighborhood and we're going to organize these suckers. But right now let's not be stupid.' On the corner he gives me a big hug. 'You precious. Come back healthy, hear?'

All this time he knew.

PS Grace and Jimmy have their work cut out. After I leave, Detroit blows up again in a deadly race riot in which forty-three die. Besides the city police and the National Guard, the battle-hardened 82nd and 101st Airborne Divisions are called in to help restore peace to the streets.

SECOND TRIMESTER

> *Chicago, Chicago, your name is in my heart*
> *My heart is in Chicago wherever I may roam ...*
> — school song

Returning to Chicago means learning to love cops. They're the only way I can penetrate my old Lawndale neighborhood on the city's west side. Once 80 per cent Jewish and the centre of my universe, it is now 99 per cent black and a lot of it is burned out. Except for a nervous telephone repairman aloft on a cherry picker, I'm the only white person around. The cops I ride with are both African Americans, contacts of Wilfred X. They're armed. Each conceals a .45 under his clipboard, a hip-holstered .38 and an ankle-strapped .25 as backup to the backup plus two Mossberg 500 riot shotguns in the rack. 'And you know what,' says 'Officer Henderson', 'we're still outgunned by those niggers.' His partner 'Blanton' steers with his knees while rolling through my beloved alleys so that one hand is free to hold his .45, safety off.

Officers Henderson and Blanton enjoy showing off for the British reporter (me) by jumping out of the patrol car to order adolescent black boys to spreadeagle up against the same brick wall of Howland Elementary that I once peed on. That could be *me* up against the wall. Energized by my presence, the two cops burst into a black shebeen on 16th and Kedzie where Henderson hands me his service weapon – 'Here, hold this, and shoot somebody if he even looks at us' – while he muscles the patrons. (See Gene Hackman as 'Popeye Doyle' in *The French Connection*.)

This pattern repeats itself almost every time I attach myself to a Lawndale-district police officer in the execution of his duty. While it allows me to hang around the Old Neighborhood, my cop escorts, itching for a little recognition, feel licensed to provoke and kick the shit out of numbed-up dope addicts asleep in their $5 a night beds. It's good copy, I suppose, when a detective I'm with chases an armed robber down an alley who shoots at us over his shoulder, bullets whizzing past my ears, and my cop pulls him to the ground, stares down his .38 and kicks him in the chest to disarm him. All in a night's work.

London's Islington dance hall brawl that led to a murder should have taught me the mere presence of a reporter can provoke the violence he's supposed to be observing.

Another night, on the Pulaski Road streetcar tracks, we come upon a sixteen-year-old black boy, street-name 'Dragon', dying of an almost-invisible bullet wound in his chest. The white detective I'm with tells his partner, 'Write him up as DOA.' On the ground Dragon twitches. 'He's not dead,' I protest. The detective calmly kicks the body. Dragon sighs and lies still. 'He is now,' the cop says.

The night after that, Henderson and Blanton stumble on the body of a raped and dismembered eleven-year-old girl in a basement. I ask them what working in a high-crime district does to the souls of cops. Henderson laughs, 'Cops have no souls, only time in.' With a mixture of scorn and contempt he follows his own train of thought. 'Sometimes I think desegregation is a bad idea. I'm from the south side [of Chicago] where Negroes have lived since the Civil War. We are acculturated, man. But, you know, these Southern boys come up North with their mamas, looking for work. Down in Alabama and Mississippi they had to toe the line or get lynched. Yassuh, nossuh, sho nuff suh. All that peckerwood crap. Take that train up to Chicago and the chains drop off. They ain't oppressed no more and they run wild. Cuss, shoot dope, murder each other or white folks. They wouldn't dare do that in Yazoo County. Get my drift?'

Sho nuff.

On my last night with the cops the shaman's animal growl erupts within me as a sort of Tourette Syndrome I cover with sneezes and coughs. If outdoors, I make a toilet excuse and wander into bushes where I squat and howl like a castrated beast, trying to expel the horror inside me. Get it out, get it out. Push, push! I force a laugh when Sergeant Henderson catches me at it in the glare of his flashlight. Sardonically he quotes the law, '"No person shall urinate in any public place in such a manner as to expose his or herself …" That's two hundred seventy bucks for a first conviction. Hand it over, Englishman,' and holds out his hand. I give him ten bucks which he gladly pockets.

*

IN FUTURE NEWS

As I write this a white Chicago policeman is under indictment for murdering a black teenager, Laquan McDonald, by pumping sixteen bullets into his prone and curled-up body on the street. In my cherished Lawndale district, across from my favorite Fillmore police station, the cops have renovated Homan Square, an abandoned Sears, Roebuck warehouse, to make their own Abu Ghraib detention centre where thousands of black and Latino Chicagoans are held without charge or access to lawyers or any record being made of their presence. Most recently, a fifteen-year-old Lawndale girl's ongoing gang rape was seen by forty Facebook viewers without anyone calling the police. I remember my black escorts Henderson and Blanton saying cops working daily with death and dismemberment have no souls: 'just time in'.

'Albert Monroe', a black postal-worker Wilfred X sent me to, stands sentry at his second-floor window, holding a telephone in one hand and a double-barrel shotgun in the other, watching my progress down busy 16th Street, waggling his weapon to signal when it's fleetingly safe for me to slide past young black guys on the street corner. He grew up around here when the Jews moved out and blacks moved in. 'Those youngsters on the street, they're all packing. I wish to God it was only rubber guns like you tell me you had. My son is one of them down there. We were angry, but these kids live in another dimension of rage. They scare me nearly to death.'

TWO WHITE GUYS TRY TO SCARE THE
THIRD WHITE GUY

Où sont les neiges d'antan? Because my Old Lawndale corner bunch has moved out to suburbs like Skokie and Buffalo Grove, my only remaining white friends are Chicago's unofficial mayor Studs Terkel and its unacknowledged poet laureate and my former Hollywood client, Nelson Algren. Being implacable Mid-westerners, they're compelled to punish me for abandoning the city that both cradles and strangles them. Scoffing at my 'English gentleman' pose, they take me on one of their sadistic tours, climaxing in the Shamrock Inn on Clark Street which makes Gorky's *The Lower Depths* look like a Hilton. It is packed with weirded-out Menomonie Indians, puking Puerto Ricans, lost Appalachians, drunken soldiers from nearby Fort Sheridan and homeless geriatrics. Studs says to me, 'Well, kid, here it is, Chicago in all its glory.'

*

I like strolling around all-black Lawndale, the object of hostile glares and predatory shadowings, which is when older Negroes approach and advise me to clear out for my personal safety; I smile, thank them, and walk deeper into the chaos. Then one very old, frail black lady on a stone porch on Sawyer Avenue calls down: 'Mister White Gentleman … you down there … tha's right, you. You want to get yourself murdered, why don't you go down to Georgia or Alabama and let some white peckerhead sheriff beat your brains instead of getting our boys in more trouble?' My first thought is, Well, her boys don't *have* to beat me up.

'Thank you, maam,' I call up.

She turns to go inside, shaking her head in disgust. And I stroll away singing,

> *I'm on my way*
> *To freedom land*
> *Great godamighty*
> *I'm on my way*

ON WINGS OF GOSSAMER

I fall upon the body of America like a sexual predator. I board midnight Greyhound and Trailways buses, looking for ghosts, to Baxter Springs, Storm Lake, Cheyenne and Salt Lake City, paying homage to the phantom shrine of the

Ludlow Massacre, and all over the Western prairie states, staying in homeless shelters or $5 motels. My objective is the Deep South that Officers Henderson and Blanton talk about so disparagingly. But an uncontrollable urge first pulls me West, to the sun, through my Mother America's birth canal, her uterus and womb, her paved highways arrowing to the Rockies and Pacific beyond.

Along the way I can't resist slipping into the embrace of my white Old and New Left comrades, which will be as comfortable as into an old shoe, right? Except there's a stone in it. At colleges along my route, Wisconsin, the Dakotas, Colorado – what a rousing reception for my Coded Message from the Mormons at Brigham Young in Utah! – I'm booed offstage, chairs are thrown at me, a young woman at Sioux Falls shrieks: 'Why are you doing this to us?!'

A student radical at the University of Minnesota confides, 'All the initials were there. RCP (Revolutionary Communist Party), PL (Progressive Labour), RYM-1 (Revolutionary Youth Movement) and RYM-2, CP-ML (Communist Party Marxist Leninist), CP (Communist full stop), CWP (Communist Workers' Party), and assorted Maoists. They hate each other but apparently unite in hating you.' Ah, so I was *getting through*.

A BRIEF UNRELIABLE REPORT ON AMERICAN SEX WHILE BROTHER WILLIAM IS TEMPORARILY OFF THE LEASH

The Pill and Helen Gurley Brown's massive-selling *Sex and the Single Girl* urging women to 'zonk a man' happened while I was out of the US. Now women keep Betty Friedan's *The Feminine Mystique*, crusading for contraceptives and abortion, open on their night tables, freely underlined with exclamation marks !!!!!!!! I'm encountering a strange new plus–minus female power that was only starting to bud in unfocused anger in the fifties America I left.

Now that anger has a target. The women I meet have trashed their boned bras and steel girdles for shorter skirts and Rudi Gernreich's 'no bra bra'. 'Janine', a formerly placid flight attendant, thrashes wildly and, on coming, screams at the top of her lungs, 'It's the BIG O!' As if trying to convince herself? In the throes of it she kicks me in the scrotum. The civil rights lawyer 'Verna', a model of decorum in the courtroom, drags me into bed then slaps me in a fury. What's up with that? An NYU professor, 'Marga', picks me up in Washington Square Park and afterwards slams my head against a lamp post for no good reason. The act itself is getting weirder. In Los Angeles a woman flirts with me in a bar and takes me home into the Laurel Canyon hills where she sets lighted candles all around the fourposter and insists that her toddler son and daughter watch. Where is this candle and incense thing coming from? Sex isn't a bloody church service.

At last, the ocean. In LA I reconnect with my ex-girlfriend Terry Allison (née Tovah Abramovich), last seen in her editing cubicle laying in the Laff Track on the Groucho Marx show *You Bet Your Life*. After we sleep together she demands $100. Me: 'You're a hooker now?' Terry: 'It's more honest than faking laughs I steal from *The Red Skelton Show*.' Even after I pay she won't let me stay the night because she's living with another woman. Me: 'You're a lesbian now?' Terry: 'You're a stupid now?'

I'm forced to do sexual research with a restricted data base, but one thing is clear: a new kind of American woman is being born out there. Or else crazy men attract crazy women.

*

You want to know real crazy? In Santa Monica I stay with Anita, my former Hollywood secretary and now wife of a RAND Corporation physicist who helps plot Air Force bombing raids, he won't say where. They and their prosperous friends, who work for IBM, Xerox, etc., are members of Synanon, originally a rehab shelter for dopers and now an 'alternative community' for Southern California's bored affluents.

Anita and her husband are into playing 'The Game' in which, sitting in a closed circle, they verbally brutalize and insult one another to get a target person to reveal their worst weakness, which in turn provokes the insulted person to force you to reveal yours. Reminds me of some Philadelphia Association sessions. Pure purposeless aggression. But my friends are addicted to The Game. Or, as Anita's husband tells me, 'I bullshit all day at work, Synanon lets me work it off by telling the truth for a few hours on a weekend.' In the Synanon Game he's awfully good at telling Anita what a lousy mother and even worse lay she is. I leave before she gets her revenge.

And I'm the nutty one?

*

Thank heaven for a genuinely sane moment before leaving California. In a beach bar I encounter the local Navajo medicine man, a Hatali, Gaagli the Raven or Joe Smith in American, also a jobbing gardener and confirmed drunk. When he learns I'm an apprentice shaman we do medicine together, praying the sunset down at Venice breakwater, touching foreheads and climbing the Tree of Life to the Top of the World. Then, refreshed, I head South, traveling by bus through Arizona, New Mexico, Texas, Mississippi and Alabama, picking up black riders who are still very careful to take a back seat. 'Whoever heard of a revolution where they lock arms, and sing "We Shall Overcome"?' Malcolm X demanded. I'm about to find out.

THIRD AND FINAL TRIMESTER

This little light of mine,
I'm gonna let it shine
> —Traditional

Into the heart of Dixie to pay my respects to Miss Sara Mayfield, a white lady of the Old Confederacy who grew up with F. Scott Fitzgerald's 'crazy' wife, Zelda Sayre. Miss Sara is the epitome of Southern charm and courtesy. I bring her flowers. She has an interesting arrangement in Tuscaloosa, Alabama, working part-time in the days as a university librarian and passing her nights in 'our local loony bin'. From what I gather she's spent much of her adult life in a mental institution as a consequence of a state governor's political revenge for her patrician family's involvement, or not, in a tangled land deal. 'One day there were cotillions at the governor's mansion and a silver tray, the next working in a kitchen with Nigras.'

After she's shared her story, I tell her about my adventures with English schizophrenics. 'My dear,' she declares, 'you have just described the normal situation of any articulate female in a Southern family of my generation. All that mint-juleps-and-magnolias gentility leads straight to the booby hatch if you've got a speck of gumption in you. It's just like all those old fairy tales: the princess gets kidnapped only there isn't a Prince Charming – unless he's like Scott who, if you ask me, made Zelda crazier than she was, out of nothing more nor less than pure creative jealousy. She paid a high price for his love.'

PS A few years later Sara Mayfield recovers or else finds a way to convince her keepers that she is well and publishes well-received memoirs of Zelda Fitzgerald and H. L. Mencken.

*

The final months of a pregnancy are no fun. Oh, my aching back … constipation … eating for two. A black doctor in Odessa, Texas, thinking I'm the father not the mother, reassures me those are normal symptoms. So I'm off to …

… AWL-BANY

> If you're not prepared to die here then you're not facing reality …
> —black teenager, Albany, Georgia

In Albany, Georgia, the lynching state, an elderly black lady and I lean against the brick wall of a Trailways bus station. I just got off and am seeking shade in the hot, humid weather. I'm sweltering, burning up inside. She gently fans herself. 'Sure is hot,' I say. She looks away. All these new white strangers in Albany, what tricks are they up to? 'Phew,' I add sincerely. Finally she murmurs, 'Not for this time of year.' And moves off.

As soon as I step off the bus I'm shadowed by Chief Laurie Pritchett's patrol cars, keeping slow pace with me. As I'll find out all over the South, local cops despise white carpetbaggers who are blamed for all this civil rights nonsense. Actually, they have a point because, as I'll see, if white volunteers stay long enough in Albany, invariably they suffer an extraordinary mental tanning process whereby a pale skin – and identity – turns an imaginary black. Dennis Roberts, the white 'commie nigger-loving Jew lawyer', hired by his mentor King, one of only three black lawyers in Georgia, defends Negroes so often in front of hostile Southern judges that unconsciously, like other volunteer whites, Dennis has begun to shuffle his feet, lower his eyes and 'sho nuff' his speech.

Albaynee, Jawjuh. Red clay banks, Dr Pepper signs, Gulf and Amoco gas stations at country crossroads, designated White and Colored water fountains. The Flint river, where it's rumoured 'insolent' blacks have been thrown in and drowned. Pecan orchards and cotton fields, a hot steamy sun in late June. By the time I arrive, just about everyone who *is* anyone in Awl-bay-nee has been jailed, hosed, roughed up, had bones broken and scalding coffee splashed on them, including most young blacks and a contingent of nawthun white liberal kids. In the hottest weather, black teenagers, subject to mass incarceration, know not to leave home without putting on three sets of underclothes for the days they expect to be in jail.

The Albany white establishment has its own way of retaliating against fussing 'Nee-groes', including taking away federal social security from the elderly. The US Attorney General Bobby Kennedy floods the area with (white, Southern-born, hands-off) FBI agents who do absolutely nothing because Bobby doesn't want to risk his brother JFK's re-election by offending cracker voters.

I'm welcome partly because I walk in the footsteps of a previous British reporter, the UK *Guardian*'s W. J. 'Bill' Wetherby, who spread a lot of good will around.

For the next month I sleep on the floor of the Student Non-violent Co-ordinating Committee (SNCC) headquarters, a ramshackle house on a dusty side street where, night and day, helping with leaflets, driving and (God help them) cooking, I travel with some of the young firebrands, including my handholder Charles Sherrod, and the angry, jubilant Freedom Singers, plus a shifting crew of kids so young they look as if they're still in grade school, which many are. That is, when they're not out in the fields picking cotton to make their daily hundred-pound bale as set by The Man.

Some evenings are spent with the most targeted 'Nigra' in south-west Georgia, the lawyer and Navy veteran C. B. King and his stunning teacher wife Carol. C. B., who grew up in Albany and was educated in its segregated schools, returned to his home town after law school to challenge the system, at daily risk to his life. He's a magnet for impossible cases, paid or usually not – a murder charge, eviction notices,

Movement beatings or defending Freedom Riders – and is heartily detested by judges and prosecutors. Magistrates go ballistic at the very sight of King entering the courtroom in a stylish silk suit and carrying a slim legal folder, trailed by jew-commie-fum-up-nawth Dennis Roberts, weighed down by a ton of law books. Sidebar: the election billboard promoting the candidacy of a local judge reads: 'Re-elect Judge W. I. ("I DON'T WANT THE NIGGER VOTE") Geer'.

C. B., a master of the lost art of exploratory cross-examination, knows exactly what image he projects as the silver-tongued 'uppity nigra', which he cleverly plays to with guile, humor and legal finesse. One of his favorite tactics is exploiting Southern patriotism, inventing both non-existent legal statutes as well as non-existent Confederate heroes: 'As Magnus Tarleton Lee Jefferson, a famous general who liberated Nowheresville, Alabama, once said: "Regardless of how we feel about Nigras, our sacred Constitution, fought for by the leading citizens below the Mason-Dixon, requires that all be treated equally and this, most unfortunately, includes Nigras ..."' Without blushing, he'll refer to the white residents of the Deep South as 'The denizens of that Republic so dear to the hearts of every true Southern patriot ...' Such effrontery, so beguiling.

For C. B. it's quite personal. Years ago when his older brother Clennon tried to enroll at ultra-segregated Ole Miss, the University of Mississippi, he was beaten, arrested and tossed in a mental asylum. The authorities' logic was, a black man trying to get an education at Ole Miss had to be crazy by definition. C. B. got him out.

C. B.'s photographic memory is legendary and flexible. In the tiniest detail he'll cite a law, using words only he understands, and if it doesn't exist he makes it up on the spot in convincingly fancy language. He's smarter than the judges but also poorer. Racing around the state pro bono, it's hard for him to make a decent living because when a black plaintiff has a potentially juicy personal injury case, he'll hire a white lawyer on the (correct) assumption the authorities hate C. B. so much they'll automatically vote to punish his client.

It doesn't take a genius to see that Albany is a pressure cooker near to blowing its lid. One night while I'm at dinner with the Kings there's a screech of car tyres outside the house and, as if struck by the same lightning bolt, everyone but me drops to the floor. 'Get down here, young man, don't you know anything?' snaps Carol King. Afterwards C. B. explains, 'I want to live to raise my five children. We've been torched, firebombed and grenaded, shot at and punched out. We're responsible people. Appreciate you stimulating your extremity post haste next time.' Carol translates: 'Move your ass, Mr Sigal.'

In courtrooms I visit, white faces literally turn purple at the sight of him; when the police chief him calls him 'C. B.', C. B. turns this around to call him 'Laurie', which almost gives the chief a heart attack. No black man is ever called 'Mr' in Georgia so when judges call C. B. by his first name, Chevene, which understandably they mispronounce, C. B. calls them by *their* first names – until recently a hanging offense.

But these really are bad times. Reverend Martin Luther King (or 'De Lawd' as the SNCC kids dismissively call him) has come and gone without result. Chief Pritchett's clever strategy of clubbing demonstrators out of sight of TV cameras and conducting mass jailings, while farming out his prisoners to distant counties to make Movement lawyers sweat, seems to be paying off. SNCC kids are thrown into jail cells with known Kluxers who beat them; the kids are denied food and water or a decent toilet. A sheriff killing a black man is standard stuff.

(Albany is also the home town of track and field star Alice Coachman, the first black woman to win an Olympic gold medal, in the 1948 Games. The city gave her a parade but the mayor refused to shake her hand.)

You don't need to murder to intimidate. It's also done in all the small things, like the way insurance companies 'forget' your claim number or your land is stolen from you by tearing out a page of property records. Some counties around Albany, like Baker with 70 per cent black citizens, have no registered black voters at all. Still, Awlbaynee is no longer a submissive, sho nuff town – if it ever was; in the shebeens and pool halls and among street gangs I hang with – London's Bute Gardens and Islington with black faces – the young men talk openly about grabbing shotguns and making petrol bombs. 'Cracker blood is gonna run down the streets of Albany,' they tell me.

Reverend King's civil rights crusade is committed to non-violent love. But there's a lesser-known Southern tradition of blacks arming themselves in self-defense, and that includes the 'sainted Martin' whose Atlanta home holds a discreet arsenal of guns; MLK permits his bodyguards to protect him with a 'non-violent .38 police special'. Almost every rural household I see has guns. 'Uncle Shep', a black bail bondsman I talk to who deals with white authority, carries a .45, a .38 Smith & Wesson, straight razor and brass knuckles. Perhaps that's why the Albany police chief is slow to turn hoses on protesters: they are likely to return fire with something more lethal than water.

Movement heroine Fannie Lou Hamer's approach sums it up: 'Baby, you just got to love [racists]. Hating just makes you sick and weak.' But when it comes to threats from midnight terrorists: 'I keep a shotgun in every corner of my bedroom and the first cracker even look like he wants to throw some dynamite on my porch won't write his mama again.'

*

Over a hot steamy Georgia summer the audacity of SNCC veterans, some as young as nine or ten, is infectious. They shine with a sober exultation, exactly what I've been searching for in London, a surrender of self accomplished not with macrobiotic food and athletic Yogi feats but on an unvarying diet of red beans and fried catfish. Charlie Sherrod, the theology student whose character lights up the Young Albany movement, isn't kidding when he demands of one session:

> I want you to come to my funeral. You be
> prepared to die tonight when we get into those
> cars and ask people to register. You are the walk-
> ing dead. Don't you fool yourselves. You will
> not come back. Somebody will shoot you, run
> you off the road into the Flint river, beat your
> brains out with a baseball bat. Don't you fanta-
> size you're coming back a hero 'cause you ain't!

*

However, Albany has a sex dilemma. Miscegenation is deemed a capital offense by mob rule and state law. Yet

Albany's black and white SNCC youngsters who work and take risks together are of a hormonally charged age. It's a dangerous sitation while Georgia still has a 'fornication' statute on its books which means that an unmarried couple who have sex can be – and have been – prosecuted. A white girl having sex with a black guy is his potential death sentence, while a respectable white lawyer like C. B.'s intern Dennis Roberts, who brings his white girlfriend down from New York, is liable for arrest under the statute. It's obvious that some of the SNCC black guys and white girls and vice versa are making out. That is until Reverend-to-be Sherrod bans further interracial sex, not because he's a racist but because he's sensitive to the sexual dynamics of a lynching state. (From the 1880s to the 1950s in the South over 4,000 black men, women and children were lynched – often burned alive and the men castrated.)

Kids being kids, Sherrod's decree is soon ignored when the SNCC activists get together in the back seats of cars. I have a huge crush on the bravest of the brave, beautiful Diane Nash, a Freedom Rider, co-founder of SNCC and brilliant tactician, who has been beaten and jailed countless times. Still, she's a woman who tends to notice a guy hanging around holding an invisible bouquet of roses in his hand. One night before setting out in a voter-convoy to the nearby town of Eufalia, Diane takes me aside with a cautionary word: 'You looking at me like that won't get you killed. Me looking back at you will get *me* killed.' She smiles. 'Just so you know, I'm married, have a child and before that I seriously considered being a nun.' End of my love life in Awl-bay-nee.

But not of the many friendships I made there.

My only face-to-face with an Albany policeman is nothing like the later movie *In the Heat of the Night* with Rod Steiger as the fat, snarly sheriff. My cop is tall, handsome, white and slim.

He spots me strolling down the dusty street arm-in-arm with a young black woman – blasphemy in Georgia. I try and scoot her off in another direction as the cop car pulls up. He speaks to me over the rolled-down window.

'Sir?'

I keep walking.

'Sir ... sir?'

I slow down.

'How can I help you, officer?'

The car keeps pace with us.

'No, it's th'other way round. Chief asks how he can hep you.'

'Help me do what?'

'Like hep you pack. Chief says he'll even pay your train fare back to Chicago or New Yawk. Or wherever.'

'I take buses.'

'Chief says he can send someone over right now if you need hep.'

'I'm not ready to leave yet.'

'You a reporter?'

'That's right.'

'Like that other fella. Chief sent someone to hep *him* pack.'

'Is your chief looking for a diplomatic incident?'

'Pardon?'

'I'm legally resident in the United Kingdom where I work for a well-respected newspaper. My boss there is connected like you wouldn't believe – we're talking *ne plus ultra*. Anything happens to me here, the British Embassy will be in touch direct with your Chief.'

A thoughtful pause greets this before he tells me: 'Chief don't speak Eye-talian. Come on, fella. You don't belong around here. It's called "loitering with intent". Georgia Code 2010. That's a trial offense.'

I lean in to chat with the friendly officer.

'It's only a misdemeanor.' (I had this from the horse's mouth. Lawyers like Dennis have been coaching me on Suthin' law.)

'How you know that … sir?'

I smile. And wink at him. '*Ex ore equorum,* officer. *Ex ore equorum.*'

For the first time he glares at me, then shifts his police car into gear and drives off.

*

Some simple survival rules my friends teach me:

- never tell anyone where we are going or where we have been;
- disconnect the interior lights so we can't be seen when entering and exiting a car (that was how Medgar Evers got killed);
- never let a car pass you on the highway, no matter how fast you have to drive (Jimmie Travis was shot from an overtaking car).

*

Night after night, I attend church in rural Terrible Terrell, Damn Daugherty and Bad Baker counties, sitting alongside old black ladies and their husbands who are nervous of challenging the Man but here nonetheless, me singing along and holding work-roughened hands and riding out into the woods with the SNCC commandos to 'reddish' [register] voters. Voter registration sounds innocuous enough but the mere act of appearing at the county courthouse can get you badly beaten, even killed.

Yet like Lourdes, Albany heals the sick. Take one incident I witness: Diane Nash is teaching young black kids how to speak and debate in public. A boy raises his hand. 'I-I-I h-have t-t-trouble t-t-talking,' he stutters. Ms Nash looks him in the eye. 'If you believe you can, you'll talk.' Classroom 'Amens'. The boy's sister speaks up for her little brother, saying he's had this speech defect since birth. 'It don't matter,' repeats Nash. 'If he believes he can, he'll talk.' Jesus comes down to Albany then, because the next day I see the speechless boy in the front rank of a march on the courthouse, chattering non-stop with other marchers and singing freedom songs at the top of his lungs.

Neither the police nor the SNCC set any age limit on running a risk. When the Albany cops arrest two groups of young girls, aged twelve to fifteen, for lining up at the theatre's white entrance, they throw them into the distant Leesburg stockade, with no food and one open toilet. Then the deputy removes the single light bulb, leaving the singing protesters in the dark. One of the girls smiles at me through the bars. 'Thas all right, mister. Jesus is my light.'

How can you not be moved? The youngsters' complete conviction that they are doing the right thing – despite daily confrontations with violence – humbles me. Unaccountably, in the fraternal warmth of SNCC's 'beloved community', without any drama, my hitherto constant companions, Bruce-the-Typist and Brother William, start to waver round the edges and dwindle and finally shrink to oblivion in the red dust of Lee, Dougherty and Terrell counties. Gone. So long, fellas, I'll miss you. Same old story of a white man seeking his own redemption from black sacrifice? Better avoid that by making something of the story and of myself.

I still hear voices in my head, but now they're *a cappella* with the shouting gospels:

> *I'm gonna sit at the welcome table,*
> *I'm gonna sit at the welcome table one of these*
>   *days,*
> *Hallelujah!*
> *I'm gonna sit at the welcome table,*
> *I'm gonna sit at the welcome table one of these*
>   *days.*

I'm ready, Jesus.

My very last stop is to say goodbye to Albany's moral centre, Charlie Sherrod, at his interracial ministry at Koinonia Farm outside Americus. (Local whites keep burning down their roadside pecan stand.) He puts it to me I should stay to help their fight. 'You're sick, I can see that. Most white folks are. And so are my people. I'm not sure of this "black and white unite to fight" stuff. But maybe it's worth a try. Put yourself down here and see what works.' He gives me a second glance exactly as Dorothy Day did in

New York's Bowery, then smiles sadly. 'But sick as you are, I can see your mission lies elsewhere.'

How does he know?

*

PS Today, a park in Albany is named after Charles Sherrod. His wife Shirley, whose father was murdered by a white farmer, is former Georgia state director of rural development for the US Agriculture Department. Currently, Albany has a black police chief and a black woman mayor and the courthouse where Sheriff Campbell struck C. B. King over the head with a stick, almost braining him for the crime of being an African American in a suit and tie, is named the C. B. King US Courthouse.

NO, I DON'T KNOW WHERE JIMMY HOFFA IS BURIED

My 'birth calendar' demands that I stay in America a full gestational nine months, and I'm running out of money and time. Needing cash and digs, who better to lean on than my former union president when I still drove a taxi, James Riddle Hoffa?

'I don't talk to nobody nobody sent,' is how Hoffa greets me. Luckily, I've been sent. Hoffa checks my ID: 'Anything for a brother Teamster.' I hang out in his swish Louisiana Avenue office, and he lends me $500, and lets me sleep in a luxury Teamster-owned apartment because I've been 'sent' – spoken for – by our mutual friend Farrell Dobbs, the Trotskyist firebrand who was Hoffa's youthful mentor: 'who taught me everything I know and some things I was smart enough to forget,' in Hoffa's words.

'Farrell was a visionary Marxist, Jimmy. What would he think of where you are today?' I ask, gesturing at the soft lighting and marble floors. Hoffa laughs surveying his immense opulent office. 'He'd love it! Then he'd organize a faction against me, and I'd have to expel him from the union we built.'

Hoffa is fond of me because I remind him of his own early idealism; he enjoys having me around to watch him at mass meetings or working the phones. 'Take a good listen, kid. And then you, as an impartial witness, can go up to Capitol Hill and tell that cocksucker Bobby Kennedy I'm no crook!'

We speak the same language of violence and corruption, one in which certain things are accepted. It's how I was raised. You pay off one set of mobsters to beat up another who are importing scabs to break your strike; you don't ask questions about expense accounts; Good Government rules have no place in my dad's and Hoffa's and Farrell Dobbs's world.

Jimmy likes making fun of what he calls my 'naivety': 'Come be one of my assistants and you'll learn something for once in your life.' Our wrangling is probably an echo of arguments Hoffa once had sitting at the feet of the old Trotskyist Dobbs. 'That was Farrell's main problem, otherwise [he was] a genius. His ideals got in the way of serving the workers. Unions are businesses just like the guys across the table. It's all about the deal.'

On my last day in Washington, I walk in the ranks of the Albany SNCC kids' part of Reverend King's 250,000-strong 'March on Washington'. It's like Britain's CND marches on steroids – a best-of-America mix of civil rights and community workers, trade unionists, whole regiments of black and white students, Hollywood stars, and the otherwise unaffiliated who just picked themselves up and squeezed onto packed trains streaming into DC to attend this immense rally. Charlie Sherrod may no longer believe in 'black and white unite to fight' but he's here, walking hand in hand with me.

When we pass Teamster headquarters Hoffa's lieutenants in their expensive suits and pinky rings, enraged by the crowd belting out freedom songs, scream from the union's steps: 'Nigger lover!' The Teamster goons are as angry and nervous as the rest of the capital, which seems to have gone on siege alert; all along our route businesses have boarded up windows, police leave is cancelled in anticipation of a violent revolution, hospitals stock up on blood supplies, and President Kennedy is mustering thousands of soldiers and National Guard to stand by in the suburbs.

In the crowd I bump into the actor Sterling Hayden, a war hero and Joan Crawford's lover in *Johnny Guitar*, soon to be seen as the crazed brigadier general in *Doctor Strangelove*. In my previous existence in Hollywood I tried but failed to steal him as a client. If possible he is actually handsomer in the flesh than on-screen: Viking-tall, wide-shouldered and grey-bearded, he laughs when he recognizes me. 'Ah, yes, the kid agent. Thank your lucky stars you never got me. I'm the worm in the apple.' He grabs my elbow. 'Anyway what are we doing down here with the peasants? Come up and get drunk with the stool pigeon.'

Instead of packing into the crowd around the Lincoln Memorial, we spend the afternoon up in Hayden's hotel room while on TV Reverend King makes his stirring 'I Have a Dream' speech.

Sharing a bottle of bourbon with me loosens the actor's tongue. Sterling and I have the Blacklist in common, I confide. 'Did you rat?' he demands, his eyes intent on me. 'No,' I say, 'but it was a close-run thing.' He leans in closer. 'Who nailed you – your best friend, someone like me?' 'No, it was my own union president.' Sterling lets out a huge hee-haw. 'So much for working-class brotherhood!'

He can't seem to let it go, though. 'But you didn't rat like me, did you?' Self-hatred for betraying friends to the House Un-American Activities Committee over a decade ago is burning him up. 'I personally stabbed them in the back and ruined careers – all except mine. That's what I get for listening to my lawyer and shrink!' He's in town now not for the big march but on a stopover while he continues what he calls his nationwide 'repentance tour', speaking to civil liberties groups and along the way apologizing face-to-face to individuals he's harmed. Tonight he's not drunk, just self-lacerating. 'Will I ever get over despising myself? Simple answer. No. Never.'

Jimmy Hoffa doesn't hold my participation in the march against me – well, not for long – and lends me enough money to get to New York where he's arranged for a union-controlled job in a plastics factory. I work a punch press alongside Puerto Ricans who refuse to speak to me, the only Anglo, even on lunch breaks. It's killing my back but that's to be expected in the last days of manual labor.

Then I meet my dad for the first time in twenty-three years.

'Percy, you're not wearing shoe lifts, are you?' He opens the door to his small apartment and peers up at me. Who is Percy? I wonder.

This is my last stop in the US: Nelson Avenue, the Bronx.

*

Children like imagining their parents as they were before they got bogged down with kids and houses and the daily grind. I am conceived in a Pullman berth as the train rolls across corn-fields past Sinclair gas stations in the fastness of an American night. Dad and Jennie are running away from shame and dishonour, especially her large loving immigrant family who are bitter about the youngest daughter's choice of a big-talking man who abandons his legal wife and two small children to be with her. My poor mother! My dad is a hard man, a fear-less fighter for justice who is brought to his knees by his own volatile temper. He is painfully subject to raging frustration, teeth-grinding, piles, hemorrhoids, constipation, and trapped by a doomed lustful love. Jennie and he can't keep their hands off each other. With nothing but chutzpah and a rusty Colt .25 he fought Chicago's Capones and Detroit's Purple Gang to a draw, but normal family life is torture to him. He's absent from our lives, can't stand family ties, and I adore him with all my child's heart. His life-lessons guided me even when I didn't know it: this is how to be a man. On the few occasions he bent low to rub his permanent five o'clock shadow play-fully against my cheek, I almost fainted with joy.

In Detroit one of my black students, Rick, once took me home with him. At midday we found his unshaven slobbering father in a drunken sleep on the couch, vomit staining his overalls, snoring like a Bowery bum. Dennis saw me looking at his dad. 'I don't care what you think,' he said, 'he's the MAN!'

*

Negotiating long-distance, by phone and letters, it took two whole years for Dad and me, like Kennedy and Khrushchev in the Cuban Missile Crisis, to negotiate a Mafia-style meet. He was so unhinged by our impending reunion that he had to call an extraordinary session of his Bronx Social Democratic Federation to ask for the comrades' input.

He blocks me in the doorway, this little old guy with thick, beautifully combed jet-black hair, hardly any grey in it. My most vivid memory of him is as a cocky, cigar-chewing, bowler-hatted tough in spats who carried his rusty vest pocket .25 wrapped in a dirty handkerchief – Jimmy Hoffa would nod approvingly at that – and as a general organizer was known in his meat-packing workers' union as the 'little Jew'. The one time he let me come to court with him, where he was up on some slug-a-scab offense, he made a strange little gesture with his hand to the judge, who released him immediately because Dad had faked the Master Mason grip without ever being a Mason. No wonder Ma fell for him.

On his doorstep I move to embrace him, son to father, feel his lovely bristly stubble again, and he steps away. He's signalling he's not going to take any shit even from a long-lost son. His wife Sarah, in the background, urges quietly, 'Invite him in, Leo.' She's a darling, and after serving us tea and home-made coffee cake vanishes diplomatically behind a room partition.

Sitting knee to knee, sizing each other up for the opening round, awkwardly chatting, he insists on calling me 'Percy', which turns out to be his pet name for his 'real' son, my half-brother Phil – I have a brother! And a sister! Beatrice. Leo, when he ran off with my mother in a *folie à deux*, scandalized New York's sexually conservative, politically radical movement. There's so much I want to say to Leo, so much he doesn't want to hear.

Can I meet my brother and sister? 'Not in your lifetime,' he growls.

Who is he protecting, aside from himself? I'm dying to meet Phil and Bea. Like, who do we resemble? As I get older, I think: I look more like you, Leo Sigal. Same nose, same set jaw. This time he examines me from head to toe like I'm about to steal money from his back pocket. All he says is, 'I don't see it in a million years.'

How can he stay so angry after all this time?

It isn't my fault that he got the hots for a red-headed young factory worker (Jennie) who advertised herself as a wild Bohemian Girl then betrayed their joint dreams by turning into a Jewish mama like the wife he'd left behind. Oh, the irony! I can't help feeling sorry for a man constantly waylaid by life, remembering how he used to stumble in off the road, exhausted and broke after riding box cars, tramping all over looking for a job, needing his flame-haired mistress to pump life back into him. He'd take the son, though never called him by name, only 'the boy', if that was part of the bargain, for a few days at a time.

OK, years ago, he'd mailed a letter disowning me because, in a burst of adolescent longing, I'd written to him, from halfway across the country, to say that my life's ambition was to be a Labour guy. To fill his spats-covered shoes. What made him write me off?

Does he even know I'm a writer? He's cagey about the family history but surprisingly up to date on the English literary scene. 'How come you let that lady writer put the hook into you, Percy?' His small black eyes glitter with malice. Well, it's one way of staying in touch, I guess.

After a couple of hours of meandering conversation he abruptly signals it's time for me to go. He refuses to talk about the past or supply any of the missing pieces in our family history. Did he serve time in Leavenworth as I've heard? Why did Al Capone's brother Ralph run him out of Chicago? And his battle with the Purple Gang ...? He clams up as if I'm a detective. Except for saying, by way of apology: 'Hey, look, Percy. Understand. Physically I'm like Superman. Emotionally I'm a coward.'

'Walk him to the subway, Leo,' says Sarah as she emerges from behind the beaded curtain.

On the street we pass gang members hanging around a bodega who give us the hard stare. Dad, aged seventy-three, maneuvers things so that he walks dangerously close to them, to return the challenge. 'PRs,' he confides at the IRT subway stop. 'Tough guys. Or so they think.'

At the top of the steps I move in again to hug him. This time he doesn't pull back, just gives me the same cold-eyed look he threw at the Puerto Rican kids.

My old man is terrific. Sigals never give an inch.

I have always loved England, but never so much
as I do when returning from a trip over enemy
territory ...
 —Tail gunner R. C. Rivaz (killed in action)

Some of us need a little push, before we recognize we have the right to pick up a pen. In
my case it came from a book by the psychiatrists R. D. Laing and Aaron Esterson, *Sanity,
Madness and the Family* ... The people in it
seemed close enough to touch ... Each interview is a novel or play in miniature. So many
of these family conversations seemed familiar
to me: their swerves and evasions, their double-
ness ... For most of my life I had been told that
I didn't know how the world worked. That
afternoon I decided I did know, after all.
 Hilary Mantel, on how she first decided
 she was a writer, 'Author, Author: Every
 writer has a "How I Became a Writer"
 story', *Guardian*, 06 September 2008

'Please let me in!'

Mary Barnes, a forty-two-year-old former army nurse,
hammers loudly on the heavy wooden front door of
Kingsley Hall, a semi-derelict five-storey building on Powis
Road, London E1. She must be brave or desperate to want
to get in because the Hall we Philadelphians found looks
like one of Her Majesty's prisons, dank and ghostly.

Our first non-celebrity schizophrenic is this heavy-set
woman who is totally whacked out, given to flinging her
faeces all over herself and bystanders and me, after being

rejected as 'incurable' by a string of psychiatrists. As Kingsley Hall's lone caretaker (where is everyone?), I take Mary's hand and draw her in. She looks around in wonder at the grotty surroundings and breathes, 'Home. Home at last.' She twirls around like an overweight ballet dancer giving the place a 360-degree scan. And sighs, 'Safe. I'm safe.'

In the weeks and months to come Mary Barnes will become our star boarder, a beneficiary of 'regression therapy' she translates as being a baby again, a need catered to by her physician-advocate, Joseph Berke, a beefy compassionate New Yorker. Her 'journey' into infantilism resembles mine, though at least I have the decency when I crap myself to do it in my pants. Mary is my first major test of patience and humanity as a caretaker of the mad, which I blow. While she is having a whale of a time with Dr Berke, splashing noisily in the bath and painting walls with her turds, I stalk around the hall, now full of similarly loopy residents, like a prison guard. I carry a cricket bat concealed under my monk's robe. There's only so much shit, literally, I can take from Mary, who seems to want to daub it on my face. That's when I wallop her lightly; she seems not to mind, possibly because it's a respite from the overwhelming love bestowed on her by Berke and the other doctors who focus on her as our prize specimen.

My nine months away in the States travelling as a guest of Black America, most especially Albany, Georgia, restored my belief in the possibility of personal redemption through social change. 'Jesus is my light!' said the little black girl in the Leesburg stockade, and the little black boy lost his stammer because he believed, and the eighty-year-old black sharecroppers let their grandchildren lead them to 'reddish' to vote for the first time ever – what's that got to do with Kingsley Hall's 'therapeutic community'? How do Georgia's insanely brave souls connect with lonely, depressed Londoners? Would SNCC's beloved community believe that madness may not be breakdown but a break-through? Somehow I doubt it. What I don't doubt is that Charlie Sherrod, Diane Nash and the Albany teens dodging Chief Pritchett's clubs have taken me to a new place. Man, I tell you, even though we sweated blood for Kingsley Hall, it's definitely no longer my scene. But it's a happening scene.

Moths to the flame, Americans fly in: Tim Leary, Ken Kesey, Bill Burroughs, Allen Ginsberg & Co. Leary himself is tripping on 2000mg LSD while ordinary Kingsley Hall patients are dispensed DMT (Dimethyltryptamine), an Amazonian jungle herb ten times stronger than acid: after taking it just once I don't wake up for forty-eight hours. Astoundingly we don't kill anyone even though we've had our share of roof-jumpers. Nothing is made of these incidents, partly because the Hall is run according to the Inner-inner Circle's belief that life itself is but a bleak puri-fication ceremony on the way to extinction of Ego.

Albany, Georgia, this is not.

Laing is the light that illumines Kingsley House – or else fails to do so. When he is listening, warm, understanding and sympathetic, the light glows and he's a calm, wise shaman. Then, blink-blink, he's a drunken, foul-mouthed, brawling Scot. The light blinks, shuts off, glows again. He's spiteful, humane, empathetic, raging, psychotic and quantumly sane. Like a minor god he changes lives, destroys lives; he saves sanity, drives you mad.

It can get pretty chaotic in Kingsley Hall. In the hard-to-keep-track-of comings and goings a psychotic resident bludgeons Harry Pincus, an American volunteer 'student of deviance', forcing me to use my cricket bat to whack the berserker on the head, which is a clear violation of house rules, but a good deed that will soon be repaid a thousand times over. I'm pleased that the residents are wary of my weapon, but it sits poorly with the Philadelphia Circle. They think it's fine to slug one another in Mao-style 'speak bitterness' sessions but not to hit dangerous 'guests' or whatever we call them. Clearly I'm not a good fit for Kingsley Hall's 'intelligent schizophrenics'. So with utmost tact, Laing's close colleague, South African-born David Cooper, quietly urges me to cut my hours at the Hall in order to help, or observe, or be a patient, or *something* at his Villa 21, an experimental ward for young (under thirty) male acute schizophrenics at state-run Shenley Hospital in London's countrified suburbia.

HAPPINESS IS SPRAWLING IN FRONT OF A THREE-BAR ELECTRIC FIRE ON A COLD WINTRY DAY WITH A MUG OF HOT TYPHOO TEA AND SLICED WHITE BREAD SLATHERED IN LYLE'S GOLDEN SYRUP

David Cooper, a fan of Sartrean existential psychiatry, founded Villa 21 in the teeth of opposition from Shenley's hospital board. When it was built in the 1930s the hospital was seen as progressive in treating schizophrenics with up-to-date therapies like insulin shock, ECT and malaria fever. Today Shenley's doctors and nurses are proud of the institution's reputation for taking risks, but David Cooper and his Villa 21 have put them in a bind by pushing for change after change in the way schizophrenics are treated.

His V21 ward is deliberately dismantling institutional boundaries between staff and inmates, so as to give the latter more control over their own lives and treatment. Most radically, they are responsible for getting themselves up on time, making sure their ward is clean and looking after their personal hygiene, while those who choose not to take part in occupational therapy sessions are left to do exactly what they please. The result is liveable – with chaos and a grubby ward (though with none of that smelly Mary Barnes shit-flinging) full of the mad, half mad, nearly mad and perfectly all right young men who have somehow wandered into a diagnostic minefield.

Most of Shenley's more orthodox doctors and nurses are scared to death of the Villa's boisterous squalor, and take awkward detours on their way to the canteen in order to avoid possible contagion. In this they're like the nervous families of nearby Radlett, Frogmore and Potters Bar who for years have warned their children to be good or the men in white coats will take them away to Shenley. Granted, there is something a little spooky about the surrounding landscape, maybe once a country estate with darkly looming pines and laurels and lots of undergrowth to get lost in, plus a few decayed obelisks and the odd mysterious crumbling column or pagoda. No wonder absconding boys, already highly strung and edgy, decamp anywhere but to the nearby woods.

Once I settle in and have a good look around the reason for the management's paranoia is obvious because Villa 21 is hard-core musical theatre, not just one Lost Note but a Whole Fucking Chorus. 'Acting out' should be taken literally because, as I see it, young seriously ill schizophrenics are 'actors' in a comic drama of mental sickness where their theatricalizing, which can take the form of impersonating a crazy person, doesn't mean they're faking it but that they're committed to a profound spectacle, the climactic last act which they're desperately trying to write themselves out of. There's definite dramatizing of the self going on here. The mad will pretend to be mad to cover their real madness; or pretend to be sane, which of course is the most insane thing; or else a combination of the two.

Supercharged by my American rebirth, eager to take on tigers, for the next two years I commute like a suburban stockbroker between Villa 21's mad boys and Kingsley Hall's elite crazies, punctuated by spells spent observing the Philadelphia Association's internal faction-fighting and also continuing to hustle to meet bread-and-butter deadlines, the most pleasurable of these being for *Vogue* magazine, so as to pay my rent.

*

Vogue pays generously. At the Hanover Square office of the fashion magazine I'm a familiar figure in the cowled black monk's robe Doris sewed to protect me from what she calls the 'dark powers'. Since the publication is a fashion arbiter, barely anyone looks askance at my get-up, assuming I'm showcasing a new men's style. The teenage model Twiggy, dressing and undressing in the next plywood cubicle, is mildly curious. 'A bit warm in that, in't you?' My editor

Beatrix Miller closely examines me but all she says is, 'I'm not taking you with me to the Paris shows in that.'

From Hanover Square it's just a quick stroll to Soho's Wardour Street where I'm also the film critic of the Tory-conservative *Spectator,* which means I sit slouched in dark viewing rooms muttering gibberish at the screen, causing the other reviewers to sit as far away from me as possible. Most embarrassingly of all, those blasting six guns and dead bodies piling up on screen sometimes make me shit my pants, which wafts an unpleasant scent, causing me to play-act looking around for the farting miscreant. Only Mary Vonn, the *Catholic Herald*'s film critic, bless her nun's heart, has the charity to come sit next to me.

ENTER, LAUGHING

Cohabiting with real, halfway and faking-it mad actors at Kingsley Hall and Villa 21 gives me a fresh new slant on one of my many other freelance occupations, working as a drama critic.

It seems absurd for a theatrical know-nothing like me to pass judgment on a culture so rich in stage tradition. Editors pay me to sharpen my wits against those of theatrical professionals who quite likely carry Marlowe and Ben Jonson in their genetic code, whereas I flunked my college art history class to escape to the beach. My Hollywood brain is wired to a thirty-foot-wide white vinyl movie screen. It struggles to think of clever things to say about ordinary-sized humans treading bare boards while reciting 300-year-old poetry, much of which I'm deaf to at first. But deadlines are my true religion. When a job comes up that demands 2,000 words about, for example, the Royal Shakespeare Company's season of history plays at Stratford, I throw myself on the mercy of Kensington reference library and swot up on all the plays, from *Two Gentlemen of Verona* to *The Tempest*, the lot, plus the Sonnets. Will's beautiful metaphors are tough to handle until I take the plays home and speak them aloud, at the top of my voice, when it dawns on me that though none of the pieces are set in London, almost all of them feel like 'London plays', full of the town's noise, squalor and contradictions. I can picture as bit players the Bute Gardens boys and Islington thugs, Doris and me and the girls' hockey captain. Of course! Prospero's island is Shoreditch, the Forest of Arden is Regent's Park!

In desperation, and because I wasn't brought up with any knowledge of the classic theatre, I shamelessly eavesdrop on other critics during intermissions. Ken Tynan catches me spying. In the men's room he bangs into the stall where I'm sitting, frantically jotting down notes. 'Ah-ha! Plagiarist!' But he's laughing. 'David Astor told me to look after you. So stop sneaking around … if you don't know, ask me. But, please, do go and see my tailor.' In his classic dandy's frilled shirt, gold cufflinks, velvet trousers, he fingers my Marks & Spencer nylon wash and dry shirt and wrinkles his nose before sneering, amiably, '*Schmatte.*'

THE SAFE PLACE

Unlike Laing, according to whose moods Kingsley Hall runs or fails to run, Villa 21's David Cooper has the 'presence of an absence', his favorite Sartrean trope; he seems able to fade almost invisibly into the woodwork. He has this curiously passive talent for calming excitable patients by doing nothing whatsoever. The boys 'play' to his slight, neutral smile. When Cooper isn't around, the grunt work is handled by his genius – no other word for it – of a charge nurse, Frank Atkin, a former Liverpool lorry driver with a Scouser's instinct for calibrating the exquisite difference between real and stage violence.

The Villa offers its thirty or so young male patients safety at a price, which is ear-shattering noise, unmade beds, kitchen mayhem and a degree of personal freedom that drives some patients deeper into anxiety. Behave weirdly in a normal ward and retaliation by fist or needle is swift and assured; in David Cooper's wing you are excused everything, however bizarre. Inside the Villa time passes without anything apparently 'happening'. My take on it is that we're telepathically tuning into each other's unvoiced fabulations, unconsciously communicating through unconscious minds.

The atmosphere in the day room is like a Quaker meeting; you get up to speak your mind only when the spirit moves you. Tall spindly Jack Greaves (self-renamed after his Chelsea football idol Jimmy Greaves), as if infiltrating my dream-thought, will turn to me and say, 'Yeah, I think so too.' Or Brian #1 will switch on the invisible radio in his head, twisting his ear to get better reception, and announce the latest weather report: 'Cape Wrath to Duncansby Head, heavy squalls forecast including Orkney. Visibility poor, over and out.' And Brian #2 will call out, 'Nobody cares, do they? That I killed my parents!' Who arrive punctually every Visitors' Sunday.

Even after two solid years of mixing with the boys I have no idea if they are, as the anti-psychiatrists assert, a Corps of Discovery advancing the farther limits of human consciousness or just plain and simple sad cases, like David Cooper, Frank Atkin and me. All I'm sure of is that after searching so long for the 'real' England, in here I've found something close to it. And that, for reasons beyond me, being with them gives me the courage to cherish and keep safe vital parts of myself.

A SAFER PLACE

The boys like escaping from the hospital; all they have to do is walk away. So I redesign my monk's flat at Princes Square into a hostel for Shenley's fed-up, frightened or ecstatic schizophrenics. And later, as word spreads, I harbor runaways from other mental hospitals in southern England like Netherne, the Richmond Fellowship, and even the posh artists' and writers' refuge, The Priory. The absconders casually drop in and stay until they get bored or are overcome with 'freedom anxiety'.

As housekeeper I've cross-taped the windows against the inevitable thrown crockery and ordered in tons more Lyle's Golden Syrup and whole shelves full of sliced white bread and Typhoo tea – their comfort food. Especially on the weekends Hotel Sigal is crammed with guests, lazing on futons or curled up on the floor. Just like Villa 21, nothing much happens here except hanging about aimlessly, a bit of chat, some TV (I've plugged it back in) for *Match of the Day* and their favorite *Danger*

Man. We've only one female guest, 'Rory', a truant from a women's ward; but the boys never come on to her because, as an honorary male, she'll punch their lights out. The big problem isn't sex but boredom. 'There's nuthin' to do here,' they wail.

Solution: soccer drill in nearby Hyde Park, a bit unfair on the others since twenty-one-year-old Jack Greaves is a footballing prodigy once slated for a try-out with Chelsea's Junior Side, except: 'I forgot to wake up that day. Too bad, it's past, right?' On the grassy pitch amazingly nimble Jack is reincarnated as his goal-scoring hero Jimmy Greaves, whirling, dribbling, shooting ... vam! We lazily sit on our haunches to admire such football artistry, which embarrasses him. 'Just forgot to wake up that morning,' is all he says shyly before walking off.

It's easy to think of myself as Senior Warden or Head Matron in a shambolic hotel except the boys are taking care of me as much as I am of them.

Just once I experiment by taking some of the Shenley escapers to Kingsley Hall, to see if they fit in. It's a disaster because the working-class 'inartistic' boys are freaked by the no-holds-barred, Mary Barnes-shit-on-her-hair, psychedelic-poster carnival atmosphere of licensed regression, shouting and unpoliced wandering. They beg me to take them back to my flat's more normal brand of crazy.

Yes, there's a noise problem at Princes Square, but happily the building's other tenants are devout parishioners of the Established English Church of MYOB – mind your own business. The psychiatrist-musician on the floor above is so busy banging his girlfriends he's deaf to any action downstairs, and my basement neighbor, a classical music reviewer, has earphones on day and night. When annoyed tenants to either side of the building hammer on the walls, I make a neighborly call to explain we're an amateur theatricals group in rehearsal, which is not far from the truth. It also works when the local police, acting on a tip-off, drop in. 'Officer, see for yourself, we're all drama students.'

Family visits are the most upsetting occurrences for the boys and me. Kingsley Hall's premise is that families are always to blame, but somehow that doesn't seem to fit these ordinary mums and dads, numb with shock as after a traffic accident. True, some parents *are* killers. 'Franz', a tall blond Shenley boy, sports shoulder-length shaggy hair and smokes a lot of weed; his mother reports him to the police and in a remand centre officers scissor off the mop he was so proud of. He hangs himself in his cell. When I report his death, the other boys are so stricken they turn up my telly even louder. Go for it, John Drake, hit 'em harder Patrick McGoohan! Some boys are really angry with the departed Franz. After all, the whole point of being diagnosed and cared for is that you become less likely to kill yourself.

Youth suicide is in the sixties air, even though it's getting increasingly hard to check out of life since the domestic gas supply has been detoxified; head in the oven was once a favorite method. But kids will always find a way, won't they?

KARIN

She isn't Jewish but likes to pretend. She ridicules therapists as *eingebildet und hochmütig*, conceited and arrogant,

186

but can't seem to stay away from them, as patient or scold. 'Karin,' I say, 'if you dislike them so, why muck about? Go find other friends.' I keep warning her that the toxic mix of Kingsley Hall's disregard for boundaries and the core Philadelphians' androgynously bleak mind-set could be dangerous for her. 'Wasn't Hitler enough for you?' I add. Karin laughs, 'I was too young for Adolf, and my village was never bombed by you Yanks. The next village over but not us. Can't you see? I'm *glücklich* ... *lucky.*'

Lucky and suicidal. A girl not so much of the streets as of the yachts, where gentlemen friends pay for her company. 'Why not?' she demands. 'You think I'm a *Strichmädchen*? You're so old-fashioned. At least I don't dress like one of your hippies.' Indeed not. She prefers suede trousers, leather jacket, boyish cap: Jean Seberg chic.

'Karin Kappel' is a German-born party girl who calls me her 'GI buddy' because my unit once passed her village outside Darmstadt, tossing out Hershey bars and Wrigley's gum. She reminds me a little too much of the young girls German mothers used to bring to the wire fence of our compound, trying to bargain their daughters' bodies for a bar of soap or pack of Chesterfield cigarettes. My new London friend is part of the Hall's ever-circulating traffic of live-ins, friends of live-ins, friends of friends, visiting shrinks and curious observers. A free spirit, Karin drives a red open-top Austin-Healey Sprite Mark II and mooches around my flat and with the Philadelphians because 'I dig shrinks, they're so *verrückt* themselves.'

In her private life, away from her sugar daddies, Karin is the cherished pet of a North London network of extended Germanic families, not all Jewish, that fled to England

187

before the war. The pattern is, the husband arrives first and sends for his core family including his wife who sends for her sister, and then the sister's niece who sends for *her* sister, until a Hampstead menage is established where Karin finds loving safety with these unorthodox *gemütlich* clans ruled by a patriarch who holds it all together with the help of his 'wives'. My pal the Austrian-born poet Erich Fried, who fled to London after the Gestapo murdered his father, is one such patriarch, responsible for a series of wives, girlfriends and their relatives as well as his own six children. Erich and I talk all the time about how to manage our messy logistics.

During sex Karin's elfin face gets fixed in an expression halfway between a scowl and a smirk, disfiguring her Aryan *Schönheit*. Somehow this post-Nazi urchin got impregnated with a fantastic amount of the Third Reich's violence, of which she was innocent. She climbs on top and barks a mocking laugh: 'American GI … *Vorsicht!*' (Watch out!) And if I struggle she'll punch me hard. '*Sei still*,' (be still) she'll command, then sit back to laugh like a Valkyrie. She sees no reason why she cannot treat me as she does her financial benefactor, the one who keeps a yacht at Cowes.

It's the night before the Jewish New Year Rosh Hashanah when Karin tumbles into one of her serial depressions where her habit is to crash the Austin-Healey or swallow sleeping pills. In the recent past, alerted by her frantic phone calls, half a dozen times I've dragged her to Hampstead's Royal Free hospital where the nurses and attending physicians hate her; they resent attempted suicides who distract them from 'real' emergencies. The last couple of times I had almost to fight the doctors to get her seen and her stomach pumped.

Trouble is, if it happens often enough, over time you take such personal dramas as the norm. Tonight a very drunken, slurry-voiced Karin rings to wish me *Shana Tovah* (she speaks Yiddish better than I do) and goodbye. 'OK, OK, good night.' 'No, goodbye.' After hanging up, I think, goodbye? But it's pouring with rain outside and I'm sleepy and not up for calling a cab yet again.

The next call I get is from a Royal Free doctor who has treated Karin before. 'This time she did it,' is all he says before hanging up angrily. I was so used to her laughter, her jokes, her '*Mir geht's gut*' whenever I asked how she was; she made me feel I was intruding by checking up on her. *Geht's gut* ... what a lie.

*

Franz ... now Karin. Both young, and both dead because they chose to be. Do I share that death wish?

It's Rosh Hashanah eve. *Yes, now.*

GOING FOR GOLD

What better place to do it than dank, dark, creepy, life-enhancing Kingsley Hall?

Laing's Christ-like habit of presiding over candle-lit communal suppers is partly why I've stayed away from the Hall lately. Tonight, at the head of the table, he glances at each of his companions in turn: 'But I ask ye, "Who among us is our Judas?"' Ah, the Last Supper. Do the math. Twelve already sitting at table. Uh-oh, guess who's the thirteenth?

Even looking back, it's an enigma to me why I take a flying Fosbury Flop atop the Last Supper table. Or wrap an imaginary fringed shawl, a *tallit*, around me, to hop and jump like Tevye in *Fiddler on the Roof* and chant a joyful fake-Hebraic song/prayer? Or *tzadik*-like, cup my ear to listen to advice from God in the guise of a celestial railroad brakeman in overalls wearing a union button. As Laing says: this is it. A vision. Finally. Clean of drugs, ready for just this moment. The Revelation we were all anticipating ... who would go first? ... except I seem to be going over the top without any troops following me. Where are they? We'd made a solemn vow whoever 'went' first would pilot the other Philadelphians. A few seconds, a minute, half an hour – time stops. I'm alone up here, time speeds up, doesn't matter, until, exhausted, having shot my bolt, fed up that nobody's doing likewise, I climb down from the table and nonchalantly stroll out of Kingsley Hall to the fresh air of Powis Road.

Here is the message from who- or whatever the Railroad Brakeman is: GET YOUR ASS OUT OF THIS PLACE. LIVE A NORMAL LIFE. GO BACK TO YOUR WORK.

Outside on the top deck of a number 25 bus certain things seem clear to me:

1. I've had a 'manifestation'.
2. I'm nuts.
3. Pay attention.
4. I need a bath.

That's when I get jumped on my doorstep by six or seven of the Philadelphians, including Laing and one of his American heavies, who massively tackle me. They stick hypo needles full of the anti-psychotic Largactil into me, despite my futile screams of protest. ('But you promised! You promised!') The curse of being a movie buff is that screen images pop into your head at the most unsuitable times. As their drug siphons into my bloodstream, I scream: 'BUT I'M NOT GEORGE KAPLAN!' Which is Cary Grant's line in *North by Northwest* when the bad guys abduct him by mistake. One look at the severe, anxious expressions of the Philadelphian crew and I can see they're not movie fans but interpret my protest as another symptom. They drag me back to Kingsley Hall where they deposit my stupefied body alone in Mahatma Gandhi's old cubicle, to await my 'worshippers', a pilgrimage of psychotics, seekers, drifters, dopers and doctors. (Dr Esterson kneels to kiss my toe.) Freakos.

When they finally retire for the night, leaving me unguarded and shattered, I crawl up to the roof and – who knows for how long? – think about smashing myself on the waste ground below. Just it let go, fella. Like Karin, like Franz. So tempting. Without my summoning him my long-absent dad, the guy who can't remember my name, appears. There he is, inside my head, large as life, curling his lip at me: 'Punk! Loser!' Slowly, ever so slowly, suicide's seductive grip loosens, and I tumble backward off the ledge onto the balcony, saving my own life.

> ... many rape victims experience [PTSD] after
> their assault [which can include] irritability,
> an exaggerated startle response, outbursts
> of aggression, fixation on the trauma ... and
> disturbed dreams. [One study's authors note]
> a two-phase reaction, an acute phase ... lasting

from several hours to several weeks and including shock and disbelief and a long-term process
[of] chronic disturbances ...

Journal of Traumatic Stress, vol. 5, no. 3

CRAWLING BACK SLOWLY LIKE A TURTLE

As [Rip Van Winkle] neared the town, he
began to suspect that something was wrong.
The buildings were bigger, and there were a lot
more of them than there were yesterday. As he
made his way into the town square, he realized
that he didn't recognize anything ...

Washington Irving, *The Legend of Sleepy Hollow*

Home, alone.

Bruised and headachey from the Largactil, Rip Van
Sigal wakes up the next morning in his own broken-into
apartment and opens his eyes, really opens them, as if the
cataracts that had glued them shut had dissolved. Except for
sore ribs and an ugly shiner I feel something extraordinarily
unfamiliar: ordinary. Where has all the anxiety gone?

Don't worry, pal. It's still there.

What was it that voice said? Mustn't forget. Already it's
slipping away.

GO BACK TO YOUR WORK. LIVE A NORMAL
LIFE.

Easy for a guy in the sky to say. What *is* normal after all
this time? All I can think of is *revenge*. Stomping heads, stab-
bing hearts, the guys who jumped and tried to kill me must
not escape my wrath! But after all this fasting I'm weak as
a kitten and need to pump up in order to slug the bastards.

For expert advice, on wobbly legs I toddle along to Soho's Greek Street where the retired British heavyweight boxing champion, 'Our 'Enry', who fought Muhammad Ali twice and knocked him down once, and his twin brother George, hang out in front of a Gaggia coffee machine. Henry, a co-founder of the Anti-Nazi League, says to me, 'You look flabby as 'ell. Want to beat up someone? Not in a million years, looking like that.' On his say-so off I go to the Regent Street Polytechnic to join a boxing club, except that kids half my age jab me insensible without even trying; and pub fights, my usual gym of last resort, aren't the fun they used to be because the rozzers now carry a shoulder mic and shout into it: 'Officer needs assistance!' which brings in a riot squad of rugby-toned cops. Confess it, Sigal. The violence that once charmed you has lost its appeal.

END OF THE MAD, MAD AFFAIR ... WELL, NOT QUITE

I may want to say bye-bye to foolishness, but it has a few parting gifts to bestow, such as Voices in the Head, Demons on the Ceiling, and OCD in all its glorious permutations. A notebook purchased from W. H. Smith records: MUST HAVE ONLY THIS, NOT TOO LITTLE AND NOT TOO MUCH SPACE between ruled lines; the rye bread MUST be German-baked Mestemacher not Dimpflmeier; step on a pavement crack and the world will explode ... and so on. Hallucinating and ventriloquizing the dead, I assume, will pass away (pun intended). 'Becky', a drop-in visitor, cries, 'Oh my god, you're speaking in the voice of my brother Stanley. I buried him last year.' (Faints.)

It's just leftover garbage.

In its own good time it would dribble away if not for these frequent drop-ins, usually Americans with communicable hysteria who come calling because of a trans-Atlantic rumour that I vibrate a holy energy like Maharishi Mahesh Yogi only am (slightly) better-looking. Like my long-time friend 'Ken', a super-cerebral MIT physicist, who descends for the privilege, as he calls it, of gazing soulfully at me. 'I see it now,' he breathes. 'The light! The light! You ARE Jesus!' Is the whole world on acid? Even a sober *Life* magazine journalist, Shana Alexander, pops in to absorb my 'aura' and writes about it in a full-page column. What aura? Half-crazies are driving me, well, crazy.

Finally, the Levines of Manhattan arrive on my London doorstep. 'Oh, Art,' the wife Dorothy sighs, 'isn't he wonderful?' The husband sobs. What can you do with people like that?

LAND OF COCKAIGNE, UPSIDE DOWN

I've come awake to a new and foreign London. All this time I was so into the Other World, I'd been deaf to the clamour of a real-estate war all around me, McAlpine and Balfour Beatty's jackhammers and bulldozers razing and tearing apart my town.

Eyes clearer, legs a bit shaky, brain still fogged, testing, testing, one two three four. Whoops, don't fall over! I take a lead-footed dizzy stroll along Hereford Road and Pembroke Villas, ground not yet solid beneath me after several years of (it seems) slipping and sloshing over imaginary ice. As usual passersby brush past, ignoring the man talking to himself.

Next big adventure, climb aboard number 15 bus, past St Paul's and all the way out to Limehouse. Riding familiar bus routes through the Portland cement jungle – O, where are you, Clippie Jean? – numbers 7, 8, 15, 24, C2, 59 and 73, is like fitting myself back into a comfortable easy chair. This new London – new to me – is way out of scale, the magnitude of the devastation impressive, like a Second Blitz, with huge black holes in the ground waiting for 'redevelopment' that resemble the craters left by the Luftwaffe. Whole streets of devastation, you can see through to the river now. When I fell asleep central London was mostly low-rise. New tower blocks are forty-two storeys high. Are they mad?

Walk, keep walking. Clear your head. With Ordnance Survey in hand, I cross the river and head for Crystal Palace. Numb legs, never mind. Walk it off! Bridges – Albert, Westminster, Waterloo – give me back London as it was.

Past Stepney where East End 'slum clearance' has bulldozed old familiar neighborhoods in favor of 'streets in the sky': vertical tenements designed for whom by whom? Who decides what's a slum? Even in my own grandly shabby Notting Hill the Georgian-era houses are being 'done up' – for whom? What happened to cheap, grubby, cheerful, spivvy London?

And why at the last cinema show I went to didn't people stand up for the National Anthem? What's happening here?

Wake up, Rip!

*

... testing, testing, one step at a time, at first red buses then Green Line into the back country of High Wycombe and Crawley ... Up North exploring this strange new landscape by (more expensive) BR, I'm unnerved to see how few working coalfields remain. One day, it seemed, I was drinking in working men's clubs in some of the liveliest towns in Britain; the next, they were in ghost towns. In Manchester, Liverpool, Bradford, Leeds, Sheffield and Birmingham, whole neighborhoods have simply gone. Medieval cattle markets are bulldozed in favor of 'pedestrianized' shopping precincts, which give carbuncles a bad name.

Where – in heaven's name! – do these new clothes styles, this new music, new skylines, for God's sake, new *everything*, come from? Chelsea boots, PVC mini-skirts, five-inch-wide ties. When I checked out it was the Platters singing 'Harbor Lights'. Now ... The Who? Are they kidding?

AT THE OLD GRIND

If you 'have' schizophrenia or its afterbirth, a condition millions of people share, how do you re-enter the labor pool and function 'as if' normal?

Yes, I still hear voices and vocalize grunts and growls at inopportune moments, disguising them as an asthma attack. And, yes, sometimes I bang on my Corona typewriter in frustrated rage, thinking it's a musical instrument so where's the tune? And one night, half-naked, I crawl out on my balcony to drop down on the pavement on all fours, claw the air like Spring-heeled Jack and snarl at a passing woman who, thank God for blasé London, calmly steps around me with a cool: 'Fuck off!'

Calculating my limits, what's safe, what's not, scared of overstepping an erratic line, I insist on competing for freelance assignments by haunting El Vino's, Fleet Street's gossip shop-cum-job fair where any form of strangeness is dismissed as merely having one too many. In the smoky crowded bar I'm careful to present myself as one of the boozy herd, and if another customer behaves bizarrely I hear myself chortling with the others, 'Oh, weird.'

The practical (i.e. financial) problem I face is how, aged forty, I can adjust to a whole new world out there of 'alternative youth journalism'. One magazine is actually called *Fuck You*. (Does it pay?) The 'production process' itself is geekily robotic. Only yesterday my ancient Corona #3 typewriter fed 8x10-inch pages to an underpaid, middle-aged editor wearing an eye-shade who fed them into a massive, union-manned, German-made hot-metal press; now all you need is an IBM Selectric typewriter and offset litho to create an 'underground' paper full of Eastern devotional ads and Herman Hesse quotes.

Someone up there must love me because I'm re-hired as a drama critic, which alas requires adjusting from the old-style 'well-made' Rattigan or Robert Bolt play, easy to follow and no shock to the nerves, to the current fashion for Brechtian 'breaking down the fourth wall'. With the agent Clive Goodwin, I'm in the front row of the Aldwych theatre reviewing *US*, a Peter Brook protest play starring Glenda Jackson, when actors dressed as American soldiers in camouflage storm the aisles, cursing the audience and calling us: 'Imperialist baby killers!' Why is this? Clive yells, 'You poncey bastard, get that fucking rubber bayonet out of my face!' and we both punch our way out and run, laughing, from the theatre.

Where is Vietnam anyway?

Sanity's fixed goalposts in the sixties are shifting faster than the bent mind can catch up with …

Incident #1: one night in a White City BBC2 studio, while I'm debating with Marxist scholars Ralph Miliband and Isaac Deutscher, the camera's terrifying Great Satan red eye picks me up and hurls my body onto the floor at the feet of a live audience, who stare goggle-eyed. After the show the producer congratulates me for providing 'great television', and invites me back.

Incident #2: on Thames (commercial) TV the other guest is a best-selling nature writer who pokes me a little too hard in the ribs to make a point. I hit him and am caught on camera. Post-show, the producer is over the moon. 'Now that,' she cries, 'is what I call television!'

How to navigate such a scene?

You never know who's watching. Sir Laurence Olivier calls to ask if I'll help write a play for him. Who, me? So 'young-blood left-wingers', Ken Tynan and Roger Smith, and I dream up an extravaganza on the Cuban Missile Crisis to be staged at the Old Vic. Contrary to the actor's reputation as cold and distant, we find him a dream to work with: easy, vulnerable, charming, with that truly royal knack of making you feel as if you're doing him a favor by condescending to work with him. Olivier adores (his word) our play, and visualizes the Cuban nuclear Armageddon as a musical comedy with Fidel Castro, Nikita Khrushchev and John Kennedy as three debonair men about town in white tie and tails, like Jack Buchanan in a 1930s revue, curtain up on them tap dancing down a Busby Berkeley-style glittering staircase.

Alas, inside the theatre, Olivier gets down on his hands and knees with a tape measure and regretfully informs us that it can't be done without the first four rows of the stalls being removed to make space for our extravaganza. 'And, dear boys,' he laments, 'I'm just a hired hand around here, and my guv'nors the trustees would never go for a plan that reduces the number of tickets sold. Sorry.'

There goes my career as one half of the next Rogers & Hammerstein.

THOSE JEWS!

In 1290 England's Jews were expelled by royal edict and not readmitted for several centuries. Ever since, a sort of lazy anti-Semitism has lingered among all classes. Even a social-ist like William Morris lambasted Prime Minister Disraeli as the 'Jew wretch'. And let's not even speak about Karl Marx's 'On the Jewish Question': 'What is the worldly reli-gion of the Jew? Huckstering. What is his worldly God? Money.'

*

Tonight, there is a reunion of some former New Reasoners at Mervyn Jones's house off Blackheath Common where we all sit around watching the World Cup Final on TV. I'm ecstatic when England's Geoff Hurst heads in his hat-trick goal, beating the Hitlers ... I mean Germans ... and winning our first World Cup in twenty-six years. I scream, yell, pound my chest. Edward Thompson, Mervyn, Ralph Miliband and John Saville tut-tut at my lack of 'comradely internationalism'. The evening gets 'tired and emotional', i.e. drunk. Edward reclines on a couch like Manet's Olympia, and stares fixedly at me across the room until he bursts out, 'Pretty little Brooklyn Jew!'

What? 'Hey, Edward,' I laugh, not taking it seriously. I'm from Chicago after all. He won't be joked out of it, rolls off the couch and lunges toward me. His wife Dorothy and Mervyn intervene. We take it into the back garden, where after a lame swing or two at each other, it fizzles out. Where is this coming from? Simmering, simmering. Others in the room have heard the exchange but only Mervyn comes over to me. 'Poor Edward spends too much time in museums. Or else England doesn't win a World Cup every day. Put it down to that. Let it go.' Still, God bless Geoff Hurst and Bobby Moore!

BUT THE MOST ENDURING WOUND IS ...

... a lost sexual identity. Call it gender confusion because I've lived and worked in an atmosphere of misogyny, misanthropy and androgyny to the point where I no longer know what kind of man I am, which is probably clean off the Kinsey Scale. Where do you go to find your lost manhood? Obviously, to the North, where men really are men.

Editors have a genius for knowing what's on my mind even before I know it myself.

Bingo! A magazine editor dispatches me to investigate one of England's few successful enterprises, Northern working men's clubs, and I'm off touring my favorite region.

PS My assigned photographer is Princess Margaret's ex-husband, Lord Snowdon, whom I urge to travel with only the barest minimum of equipment and leave behind his usual coterie of assistants so as not to draw attention to his royal self. Instead, he zooms off with two pretty female aides, a white parabolic umbrella and a massive load of complicated cameras. On his first night in the steel town of Sheffield, a club member cheerfully slaps him on the back: 'Hey, Tony, what'll you have?' Startled, Snowdon flees back to London and handwrites me an apologetic note. The gist is that he experiences a friendly back slap as physical assault. In the end I ask Mike Cohen the Jewish street-fighter to take the photos.

GOD BLESS YOU, REVEREND BASTARD

I've rediscovered something in the Northern clubs, something I've forgotten while living in London – the quiet defiance of people determined to make their own lives and their own styles.

There are sixty or seventy clubs dotted around just one city, Sheffield: in the centre that's been developed out of existence, in the respectable suburbs, and in the working-class estates and surrounding hillside villages. They have names like Sheffield Loco, The Limes, Crookes, St Philip's Social and Brinsworth Ex-Servicemen's. And beyond the South Riding hills there are many more like them – with a total membership of five million.

In effect, the working men's clubs are a self-regulating, financially sound, parallel government to Whitehall, with their own rigid code of ethics and rules of behavior. As times get harder and traditional neighborhoods disintegrate, as jobs in steel or coal or shipbuilding are lost, the clubs play an ever more important part in the lives of their members, help to anchor them.

Club history stretches back into the mists of the early Industrial Revolution. As more people moved to the towns, as new industries changed the character even of the smallest villages, the clubs seem to have become part of the proliferation of new workers' organizations – rudimentary trade unions, mutual improvement societies, mechanics' institutes and libraries. This was part of the move towards self-help as well as, perhaps, a by-product of the evangelical sects that swept the country in the late eighteenth century. The paternalistic aristocracy and new mill owners encouraged the club movement in order to keep workers away from the twin evils of gin and revolution. Even though Temperance was the watchword, almost immediately the clubs sold alcohol, a practice introduced by a Dorsetshire clergyman blessedly named Horlock Bastard ...

Many of the present clubs retain names that suggest a now-forgotten political intransigence: Attercliffe Radical, Grimsby Social & Reform, Dewsbury Socialist, Burnley Irish Democratic League Social. In South Wales everyone calls the Blaenclydach Marxian 'the Max'; in a glass case it still proudly displays a first edition of Karl Marx's *Das Kapital*. But a Rhondda miner sighs ruefully to me, 'What a pity no one can get to that book anymore. Our club secretary, foolish man, went and lost the key. He says it was a mishap, and I say it was a prophecy.'

*

On the working men's club circuit I'm a groupie of one comic in particular, a huge star up North, prince of the realm, although he's barely known in the 'other country' of London and the South-east. He shares a club stage with the former stripper and lady wrestler Battling Mollie Malone.

Gradually, tonight in Oldham, the act builds to his patter, a mixture of ethnic slurs and what he calls 'mucky', a seemingly inexhaustible cast of transvestite butlers, phallic Black Panthers, ineptly circumcising rabbis, farting policemen, effeminate cabinet ministers (by name) and slow-witted Irish animal buggerers.

All around me women are laughing as hard as men, teenagers joining in as eagerly as their dads. Working men's clubs may be the only places in Britain that bridge the generation gap.

This comedian's dad was a Yorkshire miner who disliked his son being on the stage. 'To him you were rubbish if you didn't work with your hands. Maybe that's why the audience is always ready to turn on you. They don't make in a week what I make in a night. They want their money's worth, in blood.' Tonight after ultimately losing his audience, he smiles at me tiredly. 'Eeh, bah goom,' he puts on a thick Lancashire accent, 'but it beats workin' anyroad.'

The distinctive quality of all Northern comics is their intimacy with the audience. They are, quite literally, constantly in touch, by jumping off the stage and moving among the tables. The audience expects to be hauled from their chairs and used as props in the act. A middle-aged comic/magician in Wolverhampton tells me: 'I haven't done original material in twenty years. Concert secs [secretaries] would chuck me out if I did … I need the smell, the touch, the feel of those bastards out there – I need to get in among them

– see if they crack – bend them to me. If necessary shout at them: SHUT YER BLOODY GREAT GOBS! Break their bloody will before they break mine. They respect that. We're hard people up here. Inside hard.'

AN ECOLOGY OF THE FIST

Liverpool is only a short distance from Oldham but in culture and skin color a different cat. 'Polyglot Liverpool', the home port of the Mersey Beat and the Beatles, was built on the slave trade. The city is known for its 'half-castes' or 'Liverpool colored' who live, more or less segregated, in the postal district of Liverpool 8 by the docks. For as long as anyone can remember blacks, often West African seamen, have intermarried in Liverpool and produced generations of startlingly handsome mixed-race children. Half-castes, who can trace their descent to the Albert Dock slave block, are siege-minded, and bristle with hostility towards police who freely repay the compliment with baton and boot.

I spend tons of time in Liverpool 8, sleeping on the floor or in the spare room of families for whom today 'half-caste' is no longer an acceptable term since black American GIs from a nearby USAF base have begun educating the kids about Black Power. In Wakefield prison I visit my best mixed-race buddy, 'Henry'. He is banged up for tossing dynamite into a Top Rank dance hall that allegedly discriminates against blacks. Neither he, his family nor his friends see this as a crime.

Finally, Liverpool is the only major British city where the working men's club scene is violent, rife with murder, arson, kidnappings and corruption. Bouncers, the hard men on the door, are the real club rulers. 'You don't want to get the wrong idea about us,' a gorilla-in-a-tuxedo says. 'We're just like your average docker or bus driver except we train for this job. Like what American footballers do. Traditional, like … We're almost an arm of the law. Yobbos and trouble-makers come and we smash their faces if they take liberties. It's a vocation, like.'

A few kilometres from Liverpool along the M62 is …

MAN… MAN… MANCHESTER…

… with its solid Victorian values, that's where I'm sure to rediscover my misplaced sexuality, right?

Scene: a pub in Cheetham Hill, Manchester, drinks with old friends, club comics, strippers, jobbing musicians. Raucous laughter, singing along. We're boozed up and happy.

A stunning woman in an over-the-top evening gown decorated with sequins and beads snuggles in next to me. She and I flirt, and I silently pray: Thank you, God, for giving me back my long-lost hard on. She's a bit on the hefty side but just what the doctor ordered, with the loveli-est throaty seductive voice, a bit of Eartha Kitt crossed with Ava Gardner. Under the beer-laden table I gently place my hand on her thigh, causing her to smile at me encouragingly. My hand as if on cruise control moves over her thigh. I am who I was! She turns to gaze into my eyes and growls in a deep bass voice, 'Mate, one inch more and you're in for the surprise of your life.'

Everybody at the table falls about shrieking with laughter at my expense. I've been making love to a man. Bunny Lewis, the most famous drag queen in the North of England. Oh, no.

Bunny places a muscular arm around my shoulders. 'Easy does it, lad. It's happened to better men than you.'

Over time Bunny, who prefers 'impressionist' to 'female impersonator', and I develop not exactly a romantic relationship, let's call it 'erotically charged' – but is it lesbian or homosexual or neither? Bunny works days as a dock laborer at the Manchester Ship Canal, nights as a club performer. His Marlene Dietrich vamp and Marilyn Monroe lisping 'Let's Make Love' are right on. And – here it gets complicated – so is his take-off of Britain's best-known female impersonator Danny La Rue, who – just to get things more muddled – takes off women who parody him. I'm not the only confused fan because sometimes yobbos in the audience boo and catcall, but if a heckler dares jump on stage, I've seen Bunny deck him with a straight punch to the jaw.

As part of his loyal entourage I keep returning to the Northern club circuit just to take in Bunny's act and slip backstage to help him choose and dress up – as I did for Doris – from his pricey collection of gowns, dresses and jewellery. Like most romances this too must end. Bunny's dresser, also a dockworker and part-time club bouncer who outweighs me by a ton, is jealous. Bunny kisses me goodbye, saying, 'Don't make any more trouble for me than I can get into myself, darling.' I joke that I've been planning a big future for us, and he waves me off with: 'In your dreams, lad.'

When rambling North you lug along a suitcase crammed with regional clichés. The 'flat cap and whippet' cliché; the 'where there's muck there's brass'; 'Eh oop, 'ow's tha doin'?' Yorkshire pud and *Room At The Top* ... all of that. When I was first in Lancashire, mill women still wore wooden clogs they'd rather die than be seen in today. The North is a Methodist church plus drinks and footie. You can't go past the Watford Gap without falling victim to, or being converted by, the religion of Football Association soccer. Every industrial town I enter has its local passion, and the best way to orient yourself is to stand in the icy rain in the grandstands of Crown Ground, St James's Park or Hillsborough. I'm a Manchester City fanatic, keen on the team's champion 'diver' (injury faker) Francis Lee, and – the only foreign player in all of Division One – their amazing goalkeeper who broke his neck but did not end his career. Bert Trautmann, a former Hitler Youth and German paratrooper was awarded the Iron Cross in WW2 before becoming a POW in Lancashire. The English fan, otherwise unashamedly racist, will forgive anyone who can save a penalty kick.

For me the North is always a safe harbor, a glass of Mackeson's and a good warm feeling. Until ...

HEATHCLIFF AND CATHY AND THE MARQUIS DE SADE ON SADDLEWORTH MOOR

Encounter magazine's Mel Lasky often knows where my head is at and assigns me to cover 'a story just made for you', the tabloid-sensational 'Moors murder trial' at Chester Assizes where Ian Brady, twenty-eight, and Myra Hindley, twenty-two, are charged with killing and raping five children between the ages of ten and seventeen in and around a place I know well, Saddleworth Moor in the Peak District, not a million miles away from Thurcroft. The turf is doubly familiar to me because I have friends in squalid Gorton, the Manchester suburb where Brady and Hindley first met. In Chester the attorney general, Sir Elwyn Jones, rises to read IN A VERY LOUD VOICE from Ian Brady's diary:

> People are like maggots. Small, blind worthless
> fish bait.
> Rape is not a crime, it's a state of mind, murder
> is a hobby and a supreme pleasure.
> You are your own master. You live for one
> thing, supreme pleasure in everything you do.
> Sadism is the supreme pleasure!!!

How did I miss it? Murder, paedophilia and child torture palpitating just under the skin of Northern cheeriness, all that 'luv' and 'pet' and matiness? Up to now the moors were my second home, somewhere I felt safe to wander at will.

When I study them in the dock, Brady and Hindley couldn't be more ordinary, which is why hearing those extracts from his diary propels me, unprofessionally, in a blind panic back to London on the first train. What's the problem, since without flinching I sat through days of gruesome testimony at the Nuremberg War Crimes Trial, where Hermann Göring stared me down, and I didn't run away? But this, at Chester, there's something so terrifyingly familiar about Brady's there-are-no-limits philosophy. I'd come so close to it myself.

Back in Bayswater the flat feels terribly lifeless without the Shenley young men on a mental high taking their ease on my floor. This tomb I built for myself is destroying me, but I dare not, cannot, move because of what's out there in the real world, a world of Ian Bradys.

Please, get me out of here. Somebody, help.

James Garner does.

I'd climb out of my coffin to pick up an editor's phone call. At just the right moment a magazine pays me to hang with the film director John Frankenheimer on his *Grand Prix* movie locations at Formula One race tracks all over Europe. *Grand Prix* zooms from England's Brands Hatch to Monaco to Autodromo Nazionale Monza outside Milan, Italy, with its killer banked curves that play their part in the film's plot. (Look closely, I'm visible in crowd scenes.) And the girls! The race tracks' supercharged glamour draws beautiful mini-skirted Young Things with a yen for F1 drivers. 'Are you a driver?' a clone asks me. I smile, she smiles back. 'Oh, you liar.'

A camera set-up at Monza has co-star Yves Montand at the wheel of a Ferrari supposedly racing against Garner's car. But the real Montand suffers an acute anxiety attack, causing his vehicle to be ignominiously towed by a camera car rather than force the Frenchman to do his own driving. Even at a crawl Montand in the Ferrari's cockpit is pale and sweating, and his pit crew pretend not to notice the dark stain on the crotch of his fire-retardant suit. The next set-up calls for competing driver James Garner's car to go screaming down the track and, as planned, burst into flames. Garner insists on doing his own fast driving, which goes horribly wrong when there's a safety malfunction, and the actor is almost incinerated. When Garner crawls from the burning car he's pissed himself too, but despite his fears, a true professional, finishes the shot. What a guy. Tape recorder over my shoulder, I sidle up to Garner who is still covered in flame retardant.

'Jim,' I say, 'what made you stay in the car when it was on fire? Why didn't you bail?'

He gives me his trademark *Maverick* grin. 'And spoil the shot? Listen, I got a bullet in the ass in Korea. Purple Heart brings me in an extra ten bucks a month. I may not get a medal for this job but it sure pays better. Anyway, the camera didn't catch it but I was crapping my pants at the end.'

Bret Maverick is a crapper too! Inspired by his example, I hurry back to London, grab my duffel and typewriter and catch a plane to New York. After all, why stay in England for serial killers when I can go where they mass-produce the stuff?

PART THREE

The Stationmaster

Simon & Garfunkel's 'Sound of Silence' at #1. US draft-card burners first arrests. In London, Ronnie Kray is convicted of shooting a rival gangster in the Blind Beggar pub. First B-52 bombing of North Vietnam.

NEW YORK, NEW YORK, IT'S A WONDERFUL TOWN!

It's said that astronauts behave oddly back on earth after they've been to outer space. Who is weirder, the space voyagers or the earthlings they left behind?

Scene: Upper West Side, Manhattan. Summer of Love, a day after I've flown in. A sparkling dinner party hosted by a celebrated editor-and-author married couple with stellar guests from law, academia and publishing. Without warning a guest, the Judge, a heavyset man with a beard and a steel hook for a hand, lurches across the dinner table and grabs my throat with his hook, screaming: 'Stalinist!' Say what? I rear back, dragging his 250 pounds across the table and smashing plates – I'm in better shape than I thought – as we both crash to the floor in an absurd wrestling match.

Note: not one person moves to stop the assault. They all watch impassively like zombies in *Invasion of the Body Snatchers*. 'Get this fucker off me!' I scream. Eventually, the Judge tires of clawing at me and conversation resumes around the table. That is, goes on without any reference to the brawl that scattered china and cutlery all over the dining room.

And I'm the crazy one?

It's three years since I was last here. I'm too restless to settle. Antsy as a Calaveras County frog, I jump all over the city from borrowed apartment to nothing to Lower East Side to Park Avenue to 97th and Broadway to 271 Central Park West to miserable little hotels where I drape my wet undies on the steam radiator, sleep wherever I can including Central Park benches and Tompkins Park, and when it rains all day curl up in the balcony of the New Yorker movie house on 84th and Broadway. Its owner Dan Talbot likes my work and lets me in for free.

I'm homeless because my first sanctuary caved on me.

The Levines are the Manhattan couple who visited me in London to soak up my holiness. Having money – Art owns gas stations – they invite me to mentally dry out with them at their Upper East Side apartment. Slim and dark, Dorothy is an aspiring literary wife who graciously surrenders her office and typewriter to the Visiting Great Writer and seems to be content to linger in the doorway, gazing and sighing her admiration. Grateful for a refuge, I pound her typewriter just to hear the noise. What she can't see, because I cover it up, is that I'm not writing but on long rolls of

Associated Press copy paper copy the names of every writer I can think of so that it looks like

Proust

Fielding

Hergesheimer

Colette

Hamsun

O'Hara (and so on, over and over again)

Dorothy Levine hangs about the open door to her office staring hard at the genius at work, seeing this manic activity as something it is not, serious literary productivity, which drives her crazy. Finally, one day, after Art has gone to his office, she invites me into the living room where she poses dramatically by the fireplace, one hand on her hip, the other wrapped around a vase like a threatening projectile. 'If you don't fuck me,' she announces, 'I will scream rape.' She chases me round the coffee table, sneering at me. 'You hypocrite! You two-timer! I see you going out every night to fuck anything that moves!'

'I'll scream!' she warns again. I scuttle out. Returning to the Levine apartment that evening, please God they're asleep, I walk into a coven, a clutch, a circle of a dozen or so men and women waiting in the front room. Wile E. Coyote backpedals. 'No, come in,' smiles Art. 'This is all for you.' The Levines have cordially invited in a 'crisis intervention team' of friends who are psychiatrists, social workers, a lawyer, teacher, etc. – a cross-section of Manhattan's caring class. 'We know you're in deep, deep trouble,' portly Art says, 'and everyone in this room wants to help you with your problem.' What problem? The Levines exchange glances. Dorothy chimes in, 'You're a very troubled man, Clancy.' Shades of Kingsley Hall! In five seconds flat I duck into my room, pack my duffel, grab a huge roll of AP wire-service paper and dash out into the night, escaping with my life once again.

And that's when it all changes for good.

BEN SUC

Trailing streams of AP paper, by animal instinct I some-how find myself in Greenwich Village, on the corner of MacDougal and Bleecker, almost crashing into Country Joe and the Fish, who are strumming away to a street-corner crowd of shaggy-haired, bell-bottomed youths with wispy Fu Manchu goatees, their female companions clones of Janis Joplin. Country Joe shouts, 'Victory to the NLF!' A bunch of stripped-to-the-waist young guys around me, all sideburns and glassy smiles, torch their draft cards with a cigarette lighter. Who are these hippie scum? I search their flushed, exalted, scratchy-bearded faces, callow, intense, oozing sexual energy, Ivy League stamped all over them, elite twits on a binge. A rush of class envy, of primitive sexual jealousy, floods me. Suddenly I'm for anything they're against.

Someone in the crowd warbles …

> … *O say can you see*
> *By the dawn's early light …*

Insanely, our National Anthem spills from my mouth, parting the crowd as if I'm a skunk in heat. Country Joe stares down at me. 'You're damn right, brother. Heil, Lyndon!' And he shoots his arm out in a Nazi salute. The crowd laughs. The draft-card burners set up a chant, 'Hell no, we won't go!'

Go where?

A goatee-ed boy steps out of the crowd and punches me in the stomach – oof! – not with his fist but a paperback book. 'Wake up, stupid!' Arrogant little twerp, I should smash his face. On a Washington Square bench, I settle in the sun with his frayed Penguin copy of *The Village of Ben Suc* by Jonathan Schell. One book can't change your life, can it? I flip through the pages in disbelief. Fucking Dr David Cooper is married to a Vietnamese and never said one word. But I don't blame him, it's those keep-out-the-world, triple-thick orange velvet drapes at Princes Square that shut everything else out.

Who knew? So *that's* what the London play *US* was about. Next stop the 42nd Street library reading room, trawling through old newspapers where I learn that my old unit, 8th Regiment 4th Infantry Division, is deployed in a 'free-fire zone' around Đắk Tô, Pleiku and An Khê, wherever they are. Must look at a map, still not even sure where Vietnam is. Apparently 'free-fire' means shooting anyone without first checking if they're hostile. My guys. For years I've kept in my wallet as a good-luck charm a cloth replica of the 4th's four-leaf clover ivy patch, part of my identity.

Warm blood seeps back into my deep-frozen brain.

And just because I once wore the same patch, do I have a responsibility to act now?

GI BLUES

Fort Drum outside Watertown in upstate New York is a nine-hour Trailways ride from Manhattan. At a soldiers' bar on Arsenal Street, looking in vain for 4th Division troopers, I hang around men just returned from Vietnam or who are 'on levy' for their first tour. They suspect I'm CIC, army counter-intelligence, but don't give a shit, which is my first clue.

In one night, just by listening while I down beers, I acquire a whole new vocabulary: dink, slope, REMF, treeline fire front, Zippo raid, hooch, asses in the grass. Uncensored, the troopers speak freely of search and destroy missions, ambushes, Claymores and, once the drink takes hold, lost and shredded buddies. They take it as read that low-level GIs like them are sacrificed by higher command, live bait to draw fire from a cleverly camouflaged Viet Cong enemy, so that US air power and artillery can add up the 'body count' that promotes majors into colonels and colonels into generals.

It doesn't take me more than an hour or two of beer-time to grasp that this war is being fought by the eighteen- and nineteen-year-old children of factory workers, secretaries, waitresses, truck drivers and coal miners from small towns I never heard of. Of the dozen or so I talk to none has been to college, and several never finished high school.

*

> Oh, didn't I mention I got shot twice? Up in
> the Highlands near Cambodia. I was always the
> point man, the lowliest schmuck in the whole
> platoon. Desert? Go AWOL? Are you crazy? In
> 'Nam I was too depressed to go to the toilet let
> alone run away.
>
> – 'Robert', 25th Division infantryman

*

Voraciously curious and comfortable to be back in a military environment, almost unchallenged I wander around a few bases and their adjoining GI coffee houses at Forts Benning, Meade, Jackson and my old Fort Hood camp, talking to point-of-the-spear infantry riflemen: the boonie rats. These guys may be the same age as the hippie anti-patriots I ran into in Greenwich Village but they're a world apart. They go when called.

I had *loved* the US Army, chickenshit and all, but my bronchial lungs and 'nervous condition' would have meant I wouldn't last a week on these Vietnam jungle-combat patrols: incessant rain, cutting trails with a machete and praying your Medevac isn't late.

It's dead easy to eavesdrop on kids in uniform who brag about cash bonuses, up to $10,000, to anyone who 'frags' (throws a grenade at) an over-enthusiastic officer demanding a body count at the men's expense on high-casualty patrols into bad-guy territory. Apparently corruption is the soldier's fact of life: heroin-smuggling, brazen blackmarketing of US weapons sold to Cong sympathizers who turn the guns on their American salesmen, the deeply resented disparity in tours of combat duty (six months for officers, one year for enlisted men). It takes no military genius to see that the war against the Vietnamese Communists is turning into a civil war *inside* the American Army with enlisted men versus 'lifers' (career officers and NCOs), and lieutenants and captains increasingly colluding with their men to avoid death traps. With desertion almost impossible, private cease-fires are negotiated outside the wire. As one Fort Benning Green Beret tells me, 'Everyone in 'Nam including my fucking sergeant carries a weapon. What, desert, you crazy? They'd shoot my nuts off before I got out the gate.'

*

The Vietnam War will last almost twenty years with 58,000 GI deaths and more than three million Vietnamese dead. Of the 27 million American men who come of draft age during this time, only 2.5 million are sent to Vietnam. Unlike WW2 when everybody, rich and poor, served, there are ways to escape military duty in the Vietnam conflict. Among those who claim exemption from combat are George W. Bush, his adviser Dick Cheney (five deferments to finish college) and Donald J. Trump (four deferments to finish college, plus a medical deferment for heel bone spurs).

It takes no military genius, based on what I hear, to figure out that the American 'big battle' strategy against hit-and-run peasant guerrillas is a catastrophe.

*

Bitter-sweet to think this killer war is making a place for me in America again. GI underground newsletters like *Fed Up*, *Protest & Survive*, *Harass The Brass*, *Fort Polk Puke*, etc. – a hundred of them and still counting – certainly could use my editorial assistance. What syntax, what grammar! But, as I quickly discover, the guys don't take any fault-finding from someone not their own age. When I say I was an MOS 745 rifleman in the 'Good War', they look at me as if I'm a Martian.

So I fly back to the Smoke.

THE LOST BOYS OF QUEEN
ANNE STREET

> Civilians who 'entice' or 'procure' or in any
> substantial way assist US military deserters are
> liable to severe punishment, including prison
> terms and fines.
> > Title 18, Section 1381, Uniform
> > Code of Military Justice

London is a perfect hideout if you're running away from the US military or helping those who do. We may not have cheerful GI coffee houses but we do have something even better: the determined apathy of the average citizen. Nobody bats an eyelid if you walk nearly naked down High Holborn (really!) or, like me, stroll through Notting Hill in a monk's robe. Remember Goodge Street Tube station when the crowded lift failed to operate and we were so reluctant to appear panicked that nobody dared press the red alarm button?

Number 56 Queen Anne Street, just off Oxford Circus in the West End, is today a set of Grade II-listed, high-end offices. In the late 1960s, during the Vietnam War, this elegant Georgian building houses, among other tenants, the Royal Asiatic Society (established 1823), as well as my own London 'station' on the underground railway – the escape line for GI deserters.

Harry Pincus drags me here to save my life.

He and I first met at Kingsley Hall when I'd 'neutralized' (whacked with a cricket bat) the patient who ambushed him, and he returns the favor when, one foggy evening, he finds me regressed and wandering homeless and in despair in Swiss Cottage, and brings me home with him to Queen Anne Street where he has a spare room. Frantic for a rest from myself, I choose to believe Harry's fiction that the civilian-clad youngsters of military age and their girlfriends, lying around, making love or sleeping in the spacious front rooms, are hippies on a 'gap year'. What he's actually doing, in this luxury apartment, conned out of God knows who, is providing a haven for those with no place to go, a sanctuary for American war resisters, 'self-retired' military and draft dodgers.

Campus-jock handsome, Harry is such a gifted spin artist I shut myself in the flat's airy back room and ignore the goings-on elsewhere. That is, until one afternoon, on the corner of Queen Anne and Welbeck Streets, a grubby, unshaven little man – yes, in a dirty mac – with an Oswald Mosley mustache, approaches me and, in a stage-Yorkshire accent, introduces himself as 'Sergeant Brent' of Special Branch. Politely, he shows me his warrant card, and suggests that I'm up to my neck in a deportable offense. 'So, squire, it's up to you.' Pause. 'Desertion, eh? Nasty business that. You'd be talking to Mr Hitler now if our boys had behaved the same way in the war.'

I run back to the house, sweating with anxiety that I might lose my precious room. Harry, what have you got me into? Fifteen years younger than I am and half a head taller, with the pop-eyed good looks of the actor Jeff Goldblum, he wraps a reassuring arm around my shoulders. 'Relax,' he soothes me, 'we're the best thing that's ever happened to you.' And this turns out to be true.

HARRY PINCUS COLLAPSES, MAKING WAY FOR 'THE CRAZY OLD MAN IN THE BACK ROOM' TO TAKE OVER WHATEVER IT IS

Since he's been rumbled anyway, Harry comes clean by taking me on a tour of the flat's labyrinth of high-ceilinged, almost ballroom-sized rooms. Bodies, asleep or stoned, lie sprawled on couches or on the living-room carpet while a multi-colored bubble Wurlitzer jukebox in the corner wails the Lovin' Spoonful's 'Did You Ever Have to Make Up Your Mind?' There's a strong scent of weed mixed with odours from the Cordon Bleu cooking school on Marylebone Lane below. The TV is on all the time, showing gruesome images of the war our charges have either escaped from or never wish to witness.

Harry calls Queen Anne Streeet a 'foco', or vanguard commune of a revolution, which is the case mainly in his head since deserters have more practical things to worry about, like evading serious jail time.

He is by now pretty much out of it, his big eyes spooked by acid, exaltation, anger, joy, sadness and despair, alternating with spasms of common sense. He's on a journey

– indeed the same one I was on – and will not deny himself what he believes I have seen: the Third Eye of God. Stubborn, gentle, raging, compassionate … Harry's trying, like all of us, to unknot his contradictions. At a recent Labour Party Conference in Brighton he'd grown so frustrated by the delegates' lack of sympathy for the deserters' cause that in a rage he'd busted up the ballroom furniture and was thrown out on his ear. Although I'm ten years his senior he's been like a real father to me, offering refuge, friendship and understanding, but when he flies off on a self-destructive binge, it's my turn to play Daddy – been there, done that.

Night after night, in his red-brocade-hung room, he and I have these long, exhausting arguments about his search for God's Third Eye. 'Don't do it, Harry!' I'll plead. 'I've been there and it's a killer!' He'll give me his charming, heedless smile. Nothing I say slows him down. Those knowing, glazed eyes … what I once looked like.

He sleepily murmurs, 'Roger and over to you, Clancy.' And is out cold, leaving me in charge as I believe has been his intention ever since he tracked me down in Swiss Cottage.

But what exactly does a 'stationmaster' do?

This one learns on the job. Fast.

In my hearing the inhabitants of Queen Anne Street and their girlfriends refer to me as 'the crazy old guy in the back room'. Yes, I must look slightly mad as I dash about the flat at all hours: hoovering, picking up rubbish, stacking mattresses, scrubbing dishes, paying or delaying a mountain of bills, ordering in basic comfort food, plunging toilets. Then there's taking morning roll call for who's dead or alive or vanished or zonked; collecting passports real or fake before they're lost or stolen; searching the flat for weapons and narcotics (don't ask); going down to Boots the Chemist for Tampax and sanitary pads for the girlfriends, and performing the many other Sisyphean tasks needed to keep teenage things – and my disordered mind – in order. They just laugh, call me a 'sanitation Nazi', look upon my efforts with some amusement as a waste of energy. Oh, yeah, let them do it then, the lazy fucks!

I learn to prioritize better and the housekeeping is delegated in favor of:

> smuggling American deserters in and out of the
>   United Kingdom, avoiding Dover for less
>   busy ports like Harwich and Newhaven;
> arranging false papers;
> finding safe houses in the UK;
> babysitting our less stable 'packages' (AWOLs
>   in transit) and personally accompanying those
>   too shaky to travel alone;
> and liaising with my opposite numbers in other
>   foreign cities that have a runaway GI problem.

Unlike Sweden and France, which offer safe haven, in London we're constantly alert for police snatches because of a Visiting Forces Act that encourages UK cops to 'detain and arrest' American AWOLs. Harold Wilson's Labour government, mindful of its pacifist wing, winks at the law, but the British police, who detest the prime minister, enjoy the easy sport of plucking a deserter – instantly recognizable by his buzzcut – off the street and turning him over to the US Military Police and a federal jug. Cat and mouse. With British connivance we've already lost many deserters, including American boys dug deep into the British fabric with jobs and native wives.

My wallet is stuffed with an emergency list of on-call helpers: Quakers, Unitarians, pacifists, pastors, street people, students, the vegetarians and sandal-wearers George Orwell sneered at, even retired military officers.

Recently, I've run across the tattered notebook I always carried with me for deserter emergencies, including a list of those who could be relied on to offer a meal, a sleepover and help with the onward journey to runaway Americans. I'm omitting the real names:

> Manchester, Peace Pledge Union (grumpy?)
> 'Springalong', Kettering, Northamps (Quaker)
> Lancs (mystic Vegans)
> Otter Ferry Tea Room, Tighnabruaich, Argyll
> Liverpool, street organizer
> Cheshire (War Resisters Intl)
> Oldham (on dole but can help)
> Mill Hill, London (Libertarian teacher)
> Birmingham Univ (leftish kid)
> Birmingham (Quaker)
> Old Vicarage, Grantham
> Labour Party, probation officer's son
> Local priest, Portsmouth
> Derbyshire ('keen Christians')
> Worcester (Quaker)
> Retired Regular Army officer, Penrith

The anti-war movement favors nice, clean-cut, middle-class draft dodgers over working-class anti-heroes. Few boys see their outcast experience, as I will come to do, as a rite of passage. Given their predicament, deserters soon learn to be skilled liars, perpetually pulling fluid identities out of their hat like stage magicians. You don't like this name? Try that or the other, take your pick, I'll be whoever works.

Kingsley Hall and Villa 21's mad are duck soup compared to these runaway GIs who truly believe anyone over thirty is the enemy. Nothing in my life to date has prepared me for these war-crazy youths. Some days, I'll trawl nearby Hyde Park for kids who look lost and have short haircuts. Even though the Street Offences (anti-homosexual) Act has just been revoked, you can still get arrested for enquiring of a young American boy: 'Need a bed?' It makes me sound like a Bayswater hooker.

Business is rarely slow because our address is circulated on a contraband SAFE CONDUCT pass scattered among the US Seventh Army in Europe and GIs in Vietnam.

*

> I got wounded three times. AK 47 in the chest, a Bouncing Betty … I had practically to shoot my way out during Tet. After the hospital, my next duty was Germany. I go to collect my pay, and a buddy says, 'John, you're on levy.' That's army talk for 'Nam. I figured my luck was gone. They was shipping a dead man. Borrowed a hundred bucks and took off for Paris. These American students turned me over to CIMADE, the French Protestants, who sent me to a Quaker farm to sort myself out. I couldn't have split in 'Nam. Everybody has got a gun, including the guy who gives you the orders.
>
> – John Herndon, infantryman

*

Combat vets like John Herndon are too stressed to stay at Queen Anne Street more than a few days. Often nearly mute, with the infantryman's thousand-yard stare, they soon move on to God knows where. Since it's almost impossible to desert from Vietnam, except wounded from a hospital ward in Japan or Hawaii, the few who manage it come through like restless zombies and vanish fast.

We exist in a curious timeless dimension where outside events – Israel's Six-Day War, the long hot violent summer 'war at home' when blacks rise up in more than a hundred cities, NASA's space probes – barely impact on minds focused on sheer survival.

In my stationmaster guise I evolve a classically English accommodation with the secret services on our case: MI5, MI6, Special Branch, CIA, FBI, US Navy and Army Counterintelligence as well as US Seventh Army Counterintelligence, not to mention the local Marylebone police who come pounding up the stairs in response to neighbors' complaints about the blasting Wurlitzer, or when the marijuana clouds wafting out of the front windows become too noxious.

Deserters like to suspect one another of being CIA. Our intake is a paranoid's dream, riddled with fantasists, liars, charlatans and the rare government spy easily spotted by his 'tell', a rant designed to entrap us into conspiratorial violence. And, yes, occasionally the 'Met', or its Special Branch, will infiltrate us with an undercover cop pretending to be a Kansas-born deserter in an absurd Dagenham accent. Now and then a teenage fantasist slips through, insisting – it's always the same grisly tale – he was a helicopter side-gunner spraying bullets on all those poor Vietnamese peasants. Mostly these kids turn out to be truants from Middle America, flipping on too many Sergeant Rock and Fantastic Four comic books. My all-time favorite is a sixteen-year-old from Tennessee who calls himself Kid Blue. Last I hear from him, he phones (he says) from the US Embassy in Grosvenor Square where CIA agents are torturing him. 'Help! They're murdering me! Help me . . . help – arrrggghh!' I never hear from Kid Blue again.

Rage against the Vietnam War drives a whole generation outside the law. But even among the outcasts there's a social pyramid. At the very top are the civilian draft dodgers and resisters I've least in common with: student-deferred, high-flying, affluent, suburban-bred, high-SAT scorers with loads of college-admission-'PQ's' (personal qualities) – like the Ivy League card burners I met at Country Joe's sing-along in the Village. Way down below, military deserters usually have no money, little or no education and outlaw ways of looking at life. When AWOLs disintegrate it's drunk in a Stockholm snowdrift or London gutter; the Student Smarties (as I think of them) have nervous breakdowns.

Inexplicably, the Smarties seem to crack up more than the deserters, who are natural-born losers. Most AWOLs don't expect much from life or from themselves so what they get is no surprise; but Frank Aller (Oxford, Rhodes Scholar), and Harry Pincus (Amherst, London School of Economics) and their friends tend to buckle under the stress of their parents' aspirations and their own Vietnam melancholia.

Long after our commune breaks up a number of these high achievers suffer breakdowns, and worse. Somewhere, high in the psychic sky, where such things are determined, the trajectory of a fine prospective career meets the war's lightning bolts of brute force, and Icarus falls to earth.

PS To medical officers many draft dodgers, but almost no deserters, pretend to be, or are, gay. The only homosexual deserters I know remain deeply closeted rather than expose themselves to 'company punishment' at the fists of a livid sergeant.

THE ODD COUPLE

Half my age, Kevin O'Gara and his shadow sister 'Charlene Davis' are the guts of the American anti-war movement. They don't march in parades or get their picture in the paper but find their own ways of defying death in the paddy fields 8,000 miles away. Kevin, a three- or four-time loser (grand theft auto, felony DUI, twice a deserter), is bracingly unsentimental about his fellows. 'Let's face it, Old Timer. We deserters are no "band of brothers". We all have different agendas. How many of us have real political convictions versus facing criminal indictment for slugging a sergeant or stealing a car, like me?'

Tall, slim, sexy Charlene and massive ox-strong and alcoholic Kevin used to be an item when she found him half-frozen, drunk and buried in snow on a Stockholm street and brought him to Queen Anne Street. Chronically furious with me, she doesn't see why I won't sleep with her too. 'You're such a hypocrite, Clancy. I see it in your eyes. You give us these big moral lectures, but all the time you just want to fuck the babes here. I came all the way from

Sweden to fuck you and you tell me to get a room at the YWCA? You are such a rat!' Kevin advises me to ignore Charlene. 'She's peeved because you won't screw her. And,' he laughs, 'you probably look like her father.'

Kevin and Charlene dig each other. He may, or may not, have served in Vietnam ('I was pissing at the side of the road and I saw this gook, probably VC, on the other side of the road, pissing too, but when he didn't shoot me, I didn't shoot at him. That's the full extent of my combat experience'), but fled to Sweden, acquired the language and drove a school bus while earning a credential to nurse terminally ill children. Unscrupulous, misogynistic and seriously depressed, he is also brilliantly alive, shrewd and unpredictable. What does Kevin think of Charlene? 'She gets off on saving guys' lives. How queer is that?'

OH, NO, NOT ANOTHER WRITER'S BLOCK

Queen Anne Street is so time-consuming I haven't written a word since arriving. The trouble with not writing is that the less you do, the harder it is to start again. No sooner do I unzip the ancient Corona than the demons inside violently bang it shut. Which leaves me plenty of time to bitch at other people's efforts, all those leaflets full of EXCLAMATION MARKS!! And WE DEMAND, DEMAND! AMNESTY NOW! OUT OF VIETNAM NOW NOW NOW! Inevitably, a day comes when Harry, fogging over but still with enough verve to feel offended by my sermons, shouts, 'You're the fucking writer. So write!' He tosses a scribbled draft of his current leaflet at me and takes off for the pub.

I almost shit my pants again.

Nearly twelve hours later, ankle-deep in crumpled balls of paper, I'm still in my room doggedly sweating over no more than fifty or sixty words. Until, bleary-eyed, late the next morning, as if it's a mere nothing, a bagatelle, an afterthought, I toss my piece of paper at Harry who is breakfasting in the kitchen. He glances at my effort then gives me his most evil smile. Sonofabitch! He's done it again, this time suckering me back into being a writer.

I AM HARRY PALMER

Scarlett O'Hara's 'After all ... tomorrow is another day' was also Harry's motto. Relax, it's all good. But I'm a worry wart. It's hard not to fret when young AWOLs mock and insult you, their girlfriends parade semi-nude to drive you crazy, and you're surveilled up the kazoo by spooks in dirty macs. Jarring on the nerves.

A trick I learned long ago, originally from my mother for whom 'keeping up a front' under stress was important, is temporarily to 'be' somebody else, like a movie star maybe, John Wayne or Burt Lancaster, who would never stomp around screaming 'Flush the toilet! Wash the dishes! Don't throw condoms out the window!' Currently, to ease the transition of power from Harry Pincus to me, I'm trying to be Michael Caine in the spy film *The Ipcress File*. Sartre or somebody says, 'You are who you pretend to be.' Caine/Palmer is what I'm not: unflappable, expressionless, sexy and stylish. I trot round to 22 Wigmore Street to opticians

Curry & Paxton for a pair of horn-rims, to Aquascutum for Caine's three-quarter-length Prince of Wales plaid raincoat, and buy a new InstaBrewer coffee-maker exactly like the one Harry Palmer uses after he wakes up each morning with a new bird.

I am Harry Palmer, but without the bird.

*

> At Fort Jackson in South Carolina, I told my
> sergeant how I felt about Vietnam, and he put
> me on permanent KP, diving for pennies in a
> gasoline drum …
> Finally, in my army fatigues, I walked away
> from camp and followed the railway line
> north. There was a reward for [informing on]
> escaping GIs. But the only ones who spotted
> me were some old black guys working on the
> tracks. 'We
> know what you're doing,' one of them shouted,
> 'and it's a good thing.'
> – 'Tim', a disciple of the radical
> Jesuit, Fr Berrigan

*

Tim took one way out. Greg Farkas took another:

'I'm a white male, Hungarian American, from a blue-collar family.

'I enlisted in the army in 1965 for three years. I was a light weapons specialist.

'In country I went to the 173rd Airborne Brigade in the Central Highlands (think the movie *Platoon*). I was an E-4 and was promoted on the battlefield to Sergeant E-5 (buck sergeant) as a fire team leader of three or four soldiers.

'The Central Highlands were brutal. We would go out on thirty- to forty-five-day missions, with no change of clothes. They would rot off eventually and be torn apart by the elephant grass.

'The biggest battle I was in, a regiment of NVA ambushed one of our companies and wiped it out almost to the man. Of about sixty or seventy troops, only about eight were left alive. We were the first company in. The jungle floor was soaked in blood. A trooper came running out with two hand grenades in his hands and fell to his knees crying because he hadn't needed to use them, on himself. Many of the GI [dead] had been wounded [first]; the NVA finished them off with head shots. We got hit that night by heavy mortar fire. A position directly above ours got hit and the only thing left of one soldier was a smoking boot with his foot in it.

'Being a line doggy is hard, real hard. We never even heard about the underground papers and coffee houses, etc. We resisted incompetent leaders, be they non-commissioned officers (sergeants) or officers who would endanger us [needlessly], by fragging 'em. Fragging is lobbing a live grenade at someone.'

[He cites an argument among the GIs.] 'The debate was over whether to frag the Company Commander. To settle the thing, somebody put forward that maybe we could unite around giving him one more chance, just give him a warning, and everyone generally agreed. Somebody left a grenade on the CO's bunk with a note tied to it, "Quit fucking with us." About a week later, the CO opened the door to his hooch and a charge went off and blew him away. For a while after that, everybody was nice to us, everybody was friendly – it was like a fresh breeze blowing in the air. None of us ever figured out who fragged the CO.'

[He transfers to a Long Range Recon Patrol or LRRP, pronounced Lurp.] 'In Lurp we watched each other's back without trying to be fucking John Wayne glory hounds. We smoked killer weed and opium and would paint the black liquid opium on our weed cigs.

'Our base camp was outside Bien Hoa and we'd go into the bars on pass and drink in the same bars as hardcore VC, who were taking a time-out like us – beer – weed – massages – blowjobs – whore houses. We [VC and us] had our own version of the famous Christmas Truce in WW1.

'Armed to the teeth – bad attitudes; a mutual enemy – no, not the VC but the fucking establishment officers and sergeants!

'I had earned a Purple Heart by being shot across the nose. On my last mission, we got hit and were in a life-and-death shoot out. One VC bullet hit a buddy's white phosphorous [willy peter] grenade; it exploded – killing him and wounding me.

'In a Philly hospital I chugged a whole bottle of Robitussin cough syrup. One day, I'm resting in my hospital bed when the MPs snatched me up and threw me in the brig [jail] for a couple of days to see if I'd go cold turkey. I would have killed those fucks with my bare hands if I could have.

'This put me on the path to resisting.'

– Greg Farkas, from Queen Anne Street, wounded in
eye and knee

Before Harry collapsed I'd no idea how broad a front of lost souls we covered: most of Europe, in fact, as far east as the Bug River on the Ukrainian border with Poland, all of Scandinavia (up to Lapland!) and the parts of North Africa closest to Spain. Pretending to have Michael Caine's cool, I embark on a Euro-inspection tour to see if our guys are safely tucked in, in jail or else frozen to death in some Swedish snowbank.

First stop my equivalent stationmaster in Paris.

Barrel-chested and square-built like a longshoreman, 'Max Watts' – real name Tomi Schwaetzer – is a rock-solid, coldly analytical revolutionary in the Victor Serge mould, and my reality check as well as my teacher-on-the-job.

Max, in his other life an oil industry geophysicist, is over-qualified as a den father for runaways. His doctor father shot himself when Hitler marched into Austria; Max's mother and sister made their way with him to the United States where he was drafted into the Korean War, split to France and joined radical sects until finding his métier in anti-Vietnam War work. His thing isn't desertion but RITA, resistance *in* (not out of) the army, spreading subversion among serving soldiers; but he'll harbor any AWOL for any reason once they walk through the door of his 'office' at the Quaker Centre, 114 bis Rue de Vaugirard. Which is why the French Sûreté (its FBI) routinely deport him to Corsica during any political crises, and US counter-intelligence just as routinely tap his phone, with reason because he runs an efficient escape line for American GIs to whom he is fiercely devoted and about whom he is icily clear-headed.

'The working-class, often juvenile delinquent GI,' he lectures me, in a fist-pounding way that reminds me of my father, 'has had *beaucoup d'éxperience* of getting around authority figures, from social workers to sergeants. Watch your step, Sigal. If you force him, he'll phony up a political interest and then fuck you. You must let him figure it out for himself. Help the guy, but don't mess with his mind. Or you'll have a suicide on your hands. You have no idea of the mental cost of turning your back on everything familiar you've ever known.'

Oh, don't I really?

Max's partner in crime is a tall grey-bearded Englishman, Tony Clay, also at the Quaker Centre and commanding a deserter 'battlefront' like mine stretching from the English Channel to Siberia, from Norway to Tangiers, a system inspired by CIMADE, the Protestant relief organization that sheltered shot-down Royal Air Force and American pilots in WW2. It's easy for a GI from the US Seventh Army in Germany to stroll into France, but that is where his troubles begin because President de Gaulle likes spitting in the eye of President Nixon by receiving deserters but doesn't really want them running around loose. Without language or marketable skills, an AWOL is at the mercy of his nerves and well-off expatriate Americans who grow quickly disillusioned helping, and sometimes getting ripped off by, high-school dropouts 'with issues'.

Most deserters aren't draftees but have enlisted to escape the draft's guaranteed ticket to Vietnam, or maybe jail time for a petty crime like joyriding, or else simply to get out of the house. 'Understand where they come from,' Max instructs me. 'They believed the recruiting sergeant so they expected something better, but they get the same shit, and have at least one more year to get mad about it.'

He drills me in a whole new Movement vocabulary. RITAS are politically motivated Resisters-in-the-Army. 'One in ten, maybe … Make it one in a hundred.' Most are apolitical FUFAS, fed-up-with-the-fucking-army, too freaked to make it in 'the world'.

SETTLERS are the minority, capable of learning a language and holding down a job; AGENTS, spies or paid informers: 'Not to worry. The Americans don't want to close us down entirely because we drain off their least desirable assets. We're their junkyard.'

'That Max,' I confide in Tony Clay, 'is something else. I mean, he could be a control freak or a double agent or a paedophile in love with young boys.'

'Or all three.' Max, eavesdropping, steps in through the side door of the Quaker Centre. 'However, I'm glad to see you've started thinking like a cop.'

Before leaving Paris, I drop in on a couple of rich American friends to beg alms for the cause: James Jones, author of *From Here to Eternity*, and Irwin Shaw (*The Young Lions*), who I nail in Jim's apartment on the Île St Louis overlooking the Seine. Wrong move. Both Jones (Pacific) and Shaw (Europe) are WW2 combat veterans.

Jones's naturally pugnacious jaw hardens as I conclude my pitch, and he stalks out of the high-ceilinged living room. Shaw, ski-bronzed and football handsome, leans against the grand piano. 'You,' he says affably, 'must be out of your mind. Jim's Regular Army. He loved the service. It gave him everything. He's still carrying Jap shrapnel in him. This guy is one loyal American. He hates deserters.'

'And you?' I ask.

'Oh, I'm a liberal, not at all like Jim. But deserters? The miserable fucks deserve everything they get. But, as I say, I'm a liberal. I'm still talking to you. Jim probably wants to shoot you.'

A VISIT TO THE UNDEAD PAST

I wrap up in Paris by paying my respects to the woman I loved, the artist Riva Boren Lanzmann, who, as the unofficial daughter of Simone de Beauvoir and Jean-Paul Sartre, brought me into their *Les Temps Modernes* circle where I lost all my money at the poker table. The 'Sartres' were keen for us to have a love affair, not so keen when it escaped their control. Today Riva works in an atelier off Avenue de Choisy. But Vietnam, now my war, is one too many for her considering that both her parents had been *dénoncé* and murdered, and my sick pleasure in street rioting sticks in her bruised memory. Among other things, it's what broke us up. I loved Paris in the springtime but it didn't love me.

Does Harry Palmer hope in his heart of hearts she still feels something for him? Some hope.

Will she help me with the escaping American soldiers? 'You have a nerve,' she replies. 'You almost got me killed – by my jealous husband with his silly little gun and by that bomb the paras threw at us in Concorde. If you are involved, there is violence. You are a blood addict, like Dracula, like most Americans.' Delivered straight with no venom.

Her long brown hair has streaks of grey in it now. Still the most beautiful woman in France.

And what about our old Café de Flore crowd? She shrugs. 'As usual. Fatter, older and sleeping with their own wives for a change. Boring. They don't even go to the Flore anymore. Tourists like you chased them out. They hang out at the Coupole now. Want the address?' Oooh, nasty.

'So you're with the deserters?' She puts on her exaggerated John Wayne accent acquired from movies: 'Well, pilgrim, it figures.'

France's *années noires* never ended for her; she spent the Nazi Occupation hiding with other girls in attics, closets, on the streets. And then the cold, snowy day we trudged from one Paris *commissariat de police* to another whose petty bureaucrats sent her on a vain hunt for the elusive *document de l'Holocauste* that might prove Riva's parents had been deported and thus entitle her to a small stipend. Finally, back at the Fifth arrondissement *commissariat*, she had turned white with rage and told the desk sergeant: 'You were quick enough to take them away!' Then burst into tears, the only time I saw her cry.

We kissed – not on the lips, alas, but like polite acquaintances.

RED PATRIOTS

Surely I'll have better luck at the Renault factory in Billancourt where ten years ago this tiny crew of workers, calling themselves Socialisme ou Barbarie, opened their hearts to an American mangling their sacred language.

Compared to the lofty Sartre–de Beauvoir crowd they couldn't have cared less about my emotional and linguistic stumbles. Amazingly, Jean-Louis, Yvon, François, Georges and Daniel are still on the line assembling 4CVs; a little older and a little greyer but with their revolutionary zeal intact. In a small café near the plant they stun me by refusing to provide a safe house for one or two deserters lost on the Paris streets. Jean-Louis, who looks like Yves Montand and has the best command of English, has a whispered conference over the wine with his comrades.

'Hey, look,' Jean-Louis sums up, 'we 'ave *confiance* in you. But we are in the *guerre, vouz savez,* war ... before. *Resister ou s'évader ou travail d'esclave pour les Boches.* (Resist or escape or slave labor for the Germans.) *Vos déserteurs sont lâches.* You know, *frousssard?*' He flaps his arms wildly like a bird. The others laugh. *'Poulet.'* Ah, chicken. The American runaways are cowards and turncoats apparently.

'Come on, guys, what about Vietnam? Y'know, *la guerre injuste,*' I plead. After another whispered conference Jean-Louis (reluctantly) agrees to accept one American and, if it works out, who knows? Clearly these French reds are also patriots.

*

Yeah, I guess I'm a sex slave. I stumbled across
this soldier's dream, a Frenchwoman to care
and cook for me. But I don't have papers or a
job. She keeps me in this closet until she comes
home from work and expects me to function
like a movie star. She has these photographs
of Montgomery Clift all over her bedroom.
Like he's President Kennedy or the Pope. Man,
I'm too wore out even to report weekly to

the po-lice. Right now, I don't know which is worse, 'cause I'm in the stockade whichever way I go.

– 'Bobby', eighteen, AWOL in Paris

THE GENERAL INSPECTS HIS TROOPS

GOEIEDAG, SOLDAT! GUTEN TAG, JOE! HEJ, GI! HALLA DAI, YOU GI!

All over Europe, especially in formerly Nazi-occupied countries, young people of a GI's own age are the foot soldiers of resistance. In Holland, for example, American 'self-retired' soldiers know where to go because Dutch youngsters, overwhelmingly pro-American and anti-war, hang around the Centraal train station holding out leaflets with the coded message INADAMMYUGO2PROVOS.

'In Amsterdam you go to the Provos.'

An anarchist youth group offers them food, a bed and papers forged on a printing press operated by ex-resisters of the German Occupation. Maybe there's a guilt thing going on here because, contrary to the Dutch national myth, proportionately the Netherlands may have sent more Jews to a Nazi death than any other European country.

My checklist so far reads: Belgium unsafe, Holland terrific, Ireland OK if you can fake an Irish grandmother, Denmark fine because young people nearly toppled the government when it tried to arrest two American runaway GIs. Russia first embraced but then expelled the four AWOL sailors from the USS *Intrepid* aircraft carrier who sparked the original GI movement. Your ordinary American teen-age dope-smoking rock 'n' roller was a KGB nightmare.

241

The only thing I regret about the end of the Vietnam War is that I then lost touch with Pieter, Dirk, Hans-Goran, Dieter, Bo, Finn, Ulrike, Willi, Kenji and Ichiro, Françoise, Bengt, Jon, and all the other underground railroad conductors who are the true descendants of the religiously inspired Nazi-era martyrs Hans and Sophie Scholl. My own deserters are more like the 'Edelweiss Pirates', the tough, lawless young corner gangs who were the *real* anti-Hitler Resistance.

A short ferry ride from Copenhagen across the Baltic lies Malmö at the southern tip of Sweden. It resembles Duluth on a bad day: a dirty, snowbound, industrial city where African American deserters, many of whom enlisted as a 'career opportunity', hole up in a colony all their own. Why in Malmö of all places? I wonder.

My local contact, a self-retired US Seventh Army military policeman, who is also the Black Panther rep and married to a Dane, says, 'Man, you want to know why we live in a shithole like this instead of a big city like Stockholm? A lot of us are country boys. We like the South ... any South. It tests us, this place. These Malmö folks they are *Swedish* Swedes, not like those big-city dudes up North. In Malmö, they don't like foreigners. Or Americans. Or deserters. And they especially don't like foreign American deserters who happen to be black. Have a good day now, you hear?'

*

Our army that now remains in Vietnam is in a state approaching collapse ... avoiding or having refused combat, murdering their

officers ... drug-ridden and dispirited where
not near-mutinous. Conditions exist ... that
have only been exceeded in this century by the
collapse of the Tsarist armies in 1916 and 1917.
Col. Robert D. Heinl, Jr., 'The Collapse
of the Armed Forces', *Armed Forces
Journal*, 7 June, 1971

SNOW THERAPY

Stockholm's long, bracing winter launches me back on
to my feet, literally. Every morning, to talk to deserters
and their social workers, I jog miles in the snow – on
snowshoes! – in the sub-zero climate, and flourish.
There's no cure for a lifelong anxiety 'disorder', but in
the cold clear Swedish air the eternal terror of imminent
doom shrink-freezes down to manageable proportions.
Something like it happened before in the humid heat of
Albany, Georgia when Brother William and Bruce-the-
Typist miraculously vanished in the red dust. Always
trust mutations.

My street-tutor Kevin O'Gara, who has endured several
Swedish winters, had sent me off with a cheerful, 'Since
you're a crazy cocksucker, you'll just love the Swedes.'

I do.

*

First of all, the age of consent is fifteen in
Sweden. There's no double standard. Girls
fuck the way boys do. Everybody knows sex

is more fun dirty. So the fun is gone out of it
here ... [In Sweden] there's no guilt, except
about religion. You can't do anything for the
Swedes because they have everything they
need. That just closes off possibilities for an
American ... Sweden is exactly like American
suburbs without the sexual hang-ups. Vikings?
Vikings? You mean those people on the
subway?

 – 'Victor', deserter, son of deaf factory-worker
parents in upstate New York

*

'We Swedes mean well,' Bengt, my student handler, sighs. 'We
really want to help. But they [the American kids] don't always
make it easy. For example, the bank robbery last week ...'

What bank robbery?

Bengt laughs. 'This deserter goes into one of our suburban
banks and pulls a fake gun. He's tackled and captured – by a
fourteen-year-old girl. Get the picture?'

*

Movement protocol demands I kiss the ring of the local
stationmaster – 'Mike' – (perhaps his real name), who is
neither GI nor deserter but an ideologue all-out to 'politi-
cize' lost young men under his influence. A small, intense
American in his angry forties, he insists on meeting in a
gloomy Kingsgarten café whose only other customers at
nearby tables appear to be his Praetorian Guard of young
Americans, wearing parkas and sulky expressions. Unlike
Max in Paris, Mike inhabits a world of festering paranoia
and factional intrigue. Exile politics, always overheated,

boils over in Sweden where there is so little else to do in the long winter months. Toward the end of my visit Mike and some of his boys entice me to a basement apartment in the Gröndal district and hold me prisoner until I agree to 'repent' my bourgeois crimes, and admit that, yes, I am a CIA spy. Rather than get beaten up I beg forgiveness for my sins then run like hell. (Mike and his crew gave the same treatment to *New Yorker* reporter Dan Lang.)

*

I wore a peace symbol all the time I was in
Vietnam.
Even when I got wounded. I saw the war
through a [tank] turret slit. Boom ... and a puff
of smoke. I never knowingly killed an enemy,
though I guess I did. For a lot of us, it all goes
back to the Summer of '67 – remember, Summer
of Love? I was still a civilian. Cut my hair long,
read *Animal Farm* and Tolkien. Before that, I
was Pony League and junior varsity football in
high school. When my father died, I stopped
going to church. I felt I was losing contact. All
my friends were getting drafted; I enlisted. Man,
my home town wasn't San Francisco, where you
went to jail [instead of being drafted]. In my
town you got your notice and went. In 'Nam
I drove convoy, like cavalry guarding wagon
trains ... We got ambushed at Thunder One base
a mile from Lai Khê. Big-time NVA attack. Did
I kill anyone? Never saw them. Maybe didn't
want to. You have to realize, we were nothing
but a bunch of hippies in the tall grass.
– 'John', on a student grant at
Uppsala University

This is the fourth winter for Sweden's 400 or so American deserters who are starting to understand they are settling down as just one more immigrant group, like the Finns, with its own class system and quarrels. It's so easy for them to fly into Stockholm's Arlanda airport and request humanitarian sanctuary, but so hard to survive the ongoing physical and emotional cold, the inescapable 'Nordic depression', far away from *Johnny Carson* and their home towns.

There's nothing I can do for the Sweden-based deserters that the government isn't doing better. As far as I can see, the biggest problem is the 'soul clash' between the Swedish character and the American one, and only God Himself can resolve that.

On my very last night in Stockholm, after inspecting the troops in Gothenberg and Uppsala, yet another crew, this time of African American AWOLs including black American civilians, invite me to a party in Kungsholmen in the city centre. They, too, corner me in an incense-scented, candle-lit room, bent on whipping my ass for being – what else? – CIA. When one of them pulls a small shiny object from his leather jacket, I surprise everybody, including myself, by again channelling Michael Caine's Harry Palmer and jumping out of a second-floor window into – thank you, Jesus! – a thick drift of soft snow. Fleeing down a cold dark alley at midnight, with a pack of ideologically juiced- up brothers on my heels, makes me think that perhaps it's time to gracefully depart this bleak and lovely land.

The thought of that 'small shiny object' haunts me all the way to Ireland.

ERIN GO BRAGH!

After doing business with the humane and efficient Swedes, the Irish can be exasperating. Eire until recently was a shelter for American deserters, especially those who can thinly claim a great-great Irish ancestor. But some boys are panicking because heavies from the militant Irish Republican Army are now threatening to 'kneecap' them on suspicion of being informers or dope dealers. Alarmed to hear about this, after returning from Sweden, I take a ferry across the Irish Sea to negotiate a deal in a supposedly safe house somewhere on Dublin's outskirts. In a bare room, lit by a naked light bulb, a representative from the Official (Marxist, political) IRA, who looks like the elder brother of Victor McLaglen's 'Gypo Nolan' in John Ford's *The Informer*, sits down around a table with my guide, a Trinity College professor of archaeology, and me. Mr Official IRA places a pistol on the table to let me know he means business (or has seen the same movies I have).

He warns that any agreement reached with his group may not be honoured by rival Republican factions like the Provos (more violent, less political) and even crazier active service units, like the Irish National Liberation Army who later will bomb Margaret Thatcher's hotel, missing her but killing several others.

The good news is I'm dealing with the slightly less crazy IRA who do not, unlike the Provos, outsource political murder to paid hit men skilled at 'OBE' (one behind the ear). The

Trinity professor has told me the only reason the IRA agreed to a sit-down is that a reputation as an arms smuggler precedes me. Back story: when novelist and New Reasoner colleague Mervyn Jones and I traveled together on an archaeological dig on ancient ring forts in the Republic's Co. Longford, we were driven to the site by Proinsias Mac Aonghusa, a Dublin-based writer and broadcaster, who detoured north across the border into Ulster, to 'pick up some shopping for the missus'. On a lonely country road he opened his car boot to reveal Armalite rifles destined for whichever IRA faction Mervyn and I didn't want to know. But word had duly leaked to the gunmen that I was a trusted soul.

In the semi-dark Dublin house I implore Mr Official IRA to go easy on deserters who are very young, emotionally unstable and new to a free life. OK, he agrees, but in exchange for not shooting Americans he demands that we take into Queen Anne Street some British Army deserters from the Northern Ireland 'Troubles'. No? Well, how about smuggling more weapons to the IRA, preferably M16s? I say I can't do that either. He loses patience and declares the IRA will continue to enforce its own forms of discipline on American AWOLs. Meeting over.

Before he departs the Official IRA man says: 'Your name is Clancy. You Irish?'

No, Jewish.

'That's all right then. Bob Briscoe, a Hebrew he called his self, was a good IRA man and Lord Mayor of Dublin in his time. He trained your Israeli people in guerrilla tactics against the focken' Ainglish.'

So, if I'm Jewish I'm almost Irish then, and you'll help my boys?

'Fock 'em. You won't help us, we won't help you.'

Afterwards the Trinity College archaeologist takes me aside. 'You're well out of it. The IRA are a bunch of crazy fuckers. They shoot anybody. Probably the IRA shooters themselves are undercover agents for the British Army.'

There's nobody more paranoid than an idealistic Irishman. *Éirinn go Brách.* Ireland forever.

IT'S MAY '68 AND ALL BETS ARE OFF

It's May '68 and Europe is exploding. Paris is afire: petrol bombs and barricades on boul'Mich. In Prague kids hurl Molotov cocktails at invading Soviet tanks. Resistance spreads to Berlin and Mexico City where government snipers in the plaza at Tlatelolco mow down hundreds of rebellious students during the Summer Olympics. In Vietnam a US major says, 'It became necessary to destroy the town to save it,' and TV anchor Walter Cronkite broadcasts his opinion that the Vietnam War should be abandoned 'with honour'. President Johnson reputedly says, 'If I've lost Cronkite, I've lost Middle America.'

Four thousand miles away Chicago cops (God bless you, Officers Henderson and Blanton!) are running amok, smashing anyone at the Democratic National convention who isn't wearing a blue uniform. Promptly, almost within hours of the blood-letting, we at Queen Anne Street receive a whole new intake of long-haired alleged Weathermen, strutting around showing off their scars, still eager to fight anyone, any time, anywhere. Revolution is in the air, but housekeeping goes on forever.

Stay cool, Harry Palmer.

MONEY FOR THE GUY, PLEASE, YOU FOOL

As our pad rapidly fills up with Chicago convention survivors I run around London fund-raising to keep us fed. Up in Hampstead, the small Group 68, well-off, well-intentioned Americans, want to 'do something' about the war. I'm forever going down on bended knee to fellow expatriates like this, who smile fondly on well-bred draft dodgers but are wary of 'the whole deserter thing'. Sometimes for good reason.

Like at their latest meeting, when I put out my wheedling hand for a deserter named 'Chip' and his apparently pregnant wife who must flee to sanctuary in Sweden. The allegedly desperate couple milk us for $750, and the next we hear is a picture postcard of the beach at St Tropez with written on the back: 'There's a sucker born every minute.'

NO LUCK HERE EITHER

Pockets empty, I'm forced to tap personal friends, including Doris. Our roads have parted but, on occasion, our bodies still converge. As usual we sit opposite each other at her kitchen table, negotiating who we are these days. Peter pops in, and as in the past I want to say hello with a play-wrestle but his stern expression announces he's too grown up for such horseplay. (Indeed, he's as tall as me.) Instead, he recites a Sufi joke he's picked up from his mum. A what? 'Ma says they're even funnier than Jewish jokes. Here, I'll tell you one.' Which he does, though it leaves me unmoved. 'Ma says you don't have to understand it. That's the point,' he explains. Uh-huh. Sufi mysticism? Doris says briskly, 'There's no formula for humor. Remember when we were comrades? Spelling everything out got us stuck in such awful literalness. That's what it's about, darling.'

All I see is pound notes flying out the window on the wings of Sufi angels.

REVOLUTIONARY CRIME AND THE KRAY TWINS

Les evenéments français of May '68 infect us all with the fever of insurgency. 'Propaganda of the deed', revolutionary excitement without revolution, also infects London's previously non-violent activists who now see any form of restraint as a middle-class sell-out. Bomb-throwing London anarchists take over posh squats; rebels with Oxford degrees drive past the US Embassy and shoot out its windows. Radical sects spring up like mushrooms. LAWLESS ANARCHY! scream the British tabloid headlines. At Queen Anne Street things go unnaturally quiet when, within weeks of each other, Martin Luther King and Bobby Kennedy are assassinated. Suddenly, in London, anything goes if it is politically motivated.

Crossing the blurred line between crime and commitment is surprisingly easy.

'Nigel', a young professional burglar and talented locksmith from Hackney, lives on the proceeds of what he now calls his 'political act' of breaking and entering in country houses and London mansions. Lately he insists on dividing cash from the spoils between himself and 'the Movement' at Queen Anne Street. Even though he's on the run for shooting a policeman during a robbery, I don't seem to feel any compunction about accepting 'for safekeeping' some of his loot, stuffed in a brown paper bag. I almost suffer a heart attack when I look inside it later on. There must be hundreds in there. Gosh, that money comes in handy.

*

Traditionally, London crime is concentrated in the East End or south of the river, but in the late sixties anarchy, murder, arson and extortion travel 'up West', where killers hobnob with Cabinet ministers and film stars. So it seems only reasonable to try and coax donations from hardmen like the Kray twins who, luckily for me, once were military deserters themselves and have indicated a mild sympathy for our situation. These criminal psychopaths are presently clapped up for multiple murders, Ronnie in Broadmoor-for-the-criminally-insane and Reggie in a regular prison, but by falsely claiming to the floor manager of the Krays' Knightsbridge club, Esmeralda's Barn, that their hated rivals, the Richardson gang, have pledged and the twins don't want to look cheap, I'm able to extract a little of the green stuff to add to Nigel's munificent stash.

So far my own 'crimes' have been trivial, like arranging forged passports (see *The Day of the Jackal* for technical details) and digging up Hyde Park to bury deserters' hash stashes.

Police tip-off: if you take a shovel and go to the Tyburn Brook by Hyde Park's Serpentine you'll find a tuft of grass sticking up. Underneath are carefully sealed baggies I buried by the light of the moon.

Visiting a severely bruised Nigel, on remand in Wormwood Scrubs after being recognized by the police and cornered in a Tube tunnel, I'm stunned when he reaches across the table to pat my hand and says, 'I'm fine, don't worry. Duffed up a bit but I've already paid a warder to bring us a bottle of wine. It's you I'm worried about. How can you keep living this way? Get a wife to take care of you.'

Even strangers notice?

The very next day Kevin O'Gara's friend Charlene is as usual mad at me. 'I thought you were a serious guy. Look at the mess you've made of your life. Like a bum. What a shithead! *Why the fuck don't you help the guys by getting married at least!*'

First Nigel, now Charlene?

Marriage to 'help the guys' isn't my idea of romance. But age (early forties) and 'social inappropriateness' are catching up with me. This struck home on my last trip to Paris when Amy, a deserter's twenty-year-old girlfriend, came along as my platonic travel companion, and Jim Jones and Irwin Shaw both gave me leering winks that could be translated as: 'Oh, you randy old goat!' Why should they donate money to a paedophile?

A matrimonial brainchild slowly buds. What about Doris? She already knows my faults and always wanted to get married. No, probably not. What's a Sufi marriage like anyway? Does the man get more than one wife? Can't see Doris standing for *that*. Then how about Charlene? When I hint around about it, both she and Kevin practically fall down laughing.

The search begins.

Except … I wake up one morning with 'Glory', a student nurse. 'Honey, how old are you?' I ask. 'Eighteen,' she murmurs sleepily. I do the math. She's into Jethro Tull and … what? Vanilla Fudge! A klaxon alarm goes off in my head.

HOW TO ORGANIZE A WIFE FOR YOURSELF

Action stations! I throw myself on the mercy of Catherine Hall, Stuart's scholar wife, who suggests I stop fooling around and focus on someone 'suitable to your political history'. And this someone is where? At next weekend's first National Women's Liberation Conference at Ruskin College, Oxford, Catherine suggests.

On a cold and drizzly late-February day, off I go hunting the Snark of happiness or self-annihilation, I'm not sure which.

> Women in labour keep capitalism in power.
> Down with penile servitude!
>   – graffiti on Ruskin College walls

I've never been so adrenalized (and horny) as during this thunderous, exuberant, foot-stamping weekend at Ruskin. Among the 500 or so attendees there are only five or six brave male souls. Like me, they hunch over and try and make themselves invisible. 'I'm on assignment … I'm on assignment,' I plead with women who are giving me dirty looks.

'You're a spy!' objects a woolly-hatted female wearing carpenter's overalls. I have visions of Dickens's vengeful Madame Defarge knitting at the foot of the guillotine.

Many of the women at the conference, drawn from wimmin's history workshops and local discussion groups, have that certain look: middle-class, straight, academically intense, long hair, ankle-length velvet coats over crocheted mini-skirts, faces flushed with exultation and obstinate self-assurance. I listen to their demands – for equal pay, abortion on demand, community-controlled nurseries – with only half an ear, because I must constantly crane my neck in search of my wife-to-be.

My mother, a union organiser and single parent, habituated me to smart, militant women with a mouth on them, as had snarly, defiant movie stars like Joan Crawford and Barbara Stanwyck. But the buzz at Ruskin – and then at the Oxford Union where the conference is moved to accommodate a larger than expected crowd – almost knocks me down. It's like being at the Finland Station in 1917 when Lenin's train chugged in to start the October Revolution.

Some women at the conference pick up on this spy nonsense and loudly demand the expulsion of men from the hall, but Mary Holland, an *Observer* colleague, bless her half-Irish heart, stands up to the shouters for us Few.

Happily, in the face of the platform's scornful denunciations of the 'male patriarchy', and despite the palpable rage that runs like an electric current through the conference, down on the floor I encounter almost no personal hostility. Some women even take pity on me: 'You poor lad.' Apparently they know what it's like to be mocked and shoved aside at meetings.

Two things happen as a result of the conference: many women who have always considered themselves mad come away feeling sane, perhaps for the first time in their lives; and I find a wife.

I'm slouched in my chair, behind enemy lines, guiltily examining my bloke's psyche, so at odds with the hall's atmosphere, when this stunning brunette smiles – actually smiles! at me. 'Don't take it personally,' she says in a rich, friendly voice. 'I wish we were as tough as we talk.' My heart swells. A voice can be even more compelling than a face.

Entering a serious relationship with a smart, fully committed feminist who has a sense of humor is an adventure in accommodation and self-censorship. Your eyes must *not* stray, your mouth must *not* betray. But would I, could I, make myself over into a 'liberated man'? Some of the 'new men' I run into, the lovers and husbands trying their best, strike me as enfeebled by guilt. And at the one meeting of a men's support group I attend in Camden Town Hall, the atmosphere is so grimly depressed it reminds me of a back ward in an asylum I worked in.

Coupling with a militant, ironic feminist is exciting. New emotions, new politics, fresh pain. It recharges me with energy to accomplish my own work.

NO MORE 'SHOULDS'!

When money gives out I hatch a truly brilliant scheme. At a free Rolling Stones concert in Hyde Park, we'll beg from the anticipated mob of hippies, street freaks and war-averse American students on vacation. With all those kindred spirits gathered on the grass (in both senses), we're on to a surefire way to pluck a fortune in donations. To help us rattle the cans a contingent of young American 'Rhodies' – Rhodes and Fulbright scholars – arrive to trawl through the crowd and mooch. One of them is Frank Aller, a straight arrow whose Oxford room mate and best friend is Bill Clinton: scraggle-bearded, fattish and vaguely on our side. Frank, in his neatly pressed Brooks Brothers suit, looks (and is) so incorruptibly ethical that on demos we often put him instead of volatile Harry in front of the TV cameras. Frank drags Bill Clinton along to Hyde Park where Bill flirts with the girls – this is not hindsight – and is always somewhere else when it comes to hawking leaflets on street corners.

On that lovely sunny Saturday, about twenty of us gather to sweep through the 250,000 fans in the park. Every hippie, freak and doper in the United Kingdom, Europe and the Americas seems to be there. We collect endless saintly smiles, hugs and peace signs, while up on the jerry-built stage Mick and Keith set loose as many white butterflies as have survived the long wait in confinement. By dusk, in total, we collect a grand total of six petition signatures, $30 in US currency, £12 sterling and some coins. What a shower! Peace, brothers and sisters.

*

The Hyde Park fiasco breaks Harry's spirit; it doesn't do much for mine, either. A miasma of Movement fatigue descends on us, intensified by infantryman-journalist Ron Ridenhour's exposure of the My Lai Massacre and Nixon's not-so-secret bombing of Cambodia. A commune has a natural life, and ours is coming to an end. But we have one last hurrah when President Nixon comes to town.

Disguised in suits and ties to look like Young Republicans Abroad, we gather on the north side of Brook Street opposite ultra-svelte Claridge's Hotel where Nixon is staying. Our plot is to lure him onto the hotel balcony in front of the TV cameras then suddenly expose our anti-war placards. And there he is! Upstairs, hemmed in by aides and secret servicemen, on the balcony, waving to nobody in particular with his death-rictus smile, all teeth and hatred. The police hold us back and we politely obey according to plan. Just then Harry, former Amherst varsity player, ducks past the police cordon and makes straight for the Art Deco doors leading to the marble lobby, bellowing: 'NIXON MURDERER! NIXON BABY KILLER!' He's like a blind Samson, bobbies and Special Branch and secret servicemen all over him, fists flying. Blood streams down his face; his protruding eyes glow with the joy of battle. The cops push us back while they concentrate their fury on him with kicks and punches. I've never seen Harry look so light of heart.

In the midst of it all I glance up and am transfixed by the detached stares of Nixon and his henchmen. Instantly, I recognize two Nixon aides as my UCLA drinking-buddy classmates: ramrod-stiff, crew-cut Bob Haldeman and jowly John Ehrlichman, gatekeeper and dirty-tricks adviser respectively. Bob is wintry-eyed and controlled. But it's the look in Ehrlichman's eyes that strikes me: hot, angry, outraged. Viewed from below, his jutting, pugnacious jaw looks like Mussolini's. 'Hi, John! Hi, Bob!' I yell at them, and then scream out UCLA's fight song:

By the old Pacific's rolling water

We straggle back to the house to watch ourselves on the *Six o'Clock News*. There we are, posters and all. The world has noticed. And then it's over.

*

A few days later I find a dead body in the porcelain claw-foot tub in the main bathroom off Harry's red-draped bedroom-cum-seraglio. The gold-plated taps are full on and the tub is overflowing. 'Omigod, Harry's done it!' I cry. Charlene dashes in, slushing over hundred-year-old William Morris tiles ankle-deep in bathwater, and tugs at the taps to grab the corpse's hand, checking for vitals, then slaps its face. 'The bastard's OD'd,' she says.

Ever so slowly, with a lazy, Neptune-like stirring, Harry rises up in the bath to stretch his athletic body, drenching us. Peering down with a hazy, crazy smile, he sloshes his way out of the tub to give me his best regal hug. 'That's always been your problem, Clancy,' he says. 'You let the little things get to you.'

Charlene returns from downstairs to report that Harry flooded a whole wall of priceless books and tapestries in the Royal Asiatic Society's library. A few minutes later, fully clothed and seemingly composed, he leads our remorseful little delegation down a flight of stairs, past portraits of long-dead maharajahs, for a penitential chat with the RAS librarian, 'Miss Evans'. Even now, as moisture from upstairs darkens the flock wallpaper of her beloved library, Miss Evans, once she sees our stricken faces, manages a heroic degree of forgiveness. Should – she gets the words out with some difficulty – we agree to pause the midnight parties, and remove the jukebox, and contribute 'however modestly' to the cost of repairs, a 'rapprochement' (her word) should be possible. My heart swells with relief and gratitude. But something about Miss Evans's manner – her sheer niceness? – rattles Harry.

'NO MORE "SHOULDS"!' he roars, banging his fist on the inlaid teak conference table and towering over her. '"Shoulds" are breaking the heart of the world!' He can't stop himself from indicting at the top of his voice British imperialism in Cyprus, Kenya, India, and anywhere else that comes to mind. For good measure, as he stomps out of the library, he flings over his shoulder a promise that under no circumstances will we, her upstairs tenants, support British collusion in the Vietnam War by silencing the jukebox. At the door, he turns back to face Miss Evans, who is trembling with shock and anger, and bestows on her his saintliest grin. Our eviction notice arrives the next day.

Whenever I have Big Thoughts about our little operation at 56 Queen Anne Street, a final image snaps me back to reality. The last time Harry and I see each other, in Marylebone Lane, just after our foco breaks up, I'm outraged to see that he 'borrowed' my best pair of cavalry twill trousers. So we stand on the narrow pavement, shouting at each other like fishwives, arguing the merits of bourgeois property rights versus … oh, I forget what. I demand my pants back and, without hesitation, Harry slips them off in the middle of the passing lunchtime throng and hands them over. Then, mustering his dignity, he strolls away in his jockey shorts.

Because I don't have XX chromosomes, by definition I can't be an equal partner in the Women's Movement. On the other hand, since I cannot *not* participate, the next best thing is to eavesdrop. When Margaret has male-excluded, consciousness-raising meetings at her place (into which I've moved from Queen Anne Street), I place an empty water tumbler to my ear and press it against the wall to pick up gossip through the plaster. Threaded through their high-minded discussions, including a plot to disrupt the Miss World contest, is exuberant chat about orgasms and penises and why do men think doing such-and-so in bed is so erotic when in fact it's a turnoff? My ears burn when, amid whoops of laughter, in excruciating anatomical detail, they exchange Chaucerian tales of their men's sexual shortcomings. How I envy the women's free and easy sisterhood.

I'm blessed because Margaret turns out to have an ironic view of the Women's Movement while also remaining committed to it. Even so, I tread carefully. Some of her friends are furious with her, feel she's betraying them by living with a man; a newly converted lesbian actually slaps her face at our house-warming party. Self-defense karate classes test my nerve to the max. One night at a North London gym, another guy and I watch from the sidelines as 'our' women violently throw each other around, practising kung fu-style kicks and parries, part of their assertiveness training. Margaret, kicking high and punching the air, glows with exertion and exhilaration. My man friend and I glance nervously at each other. Session over, the women stream into the locker room to change, and my new friend and I turn for the exit. But his girlfriend, stripping naked, just laughs: 'Don't be such fogeys, you two. Stay!' Naked women's bodies glowing with healthy exertion shouldn't be a problem. So why are this guy and I blushing madly?

Margaret gives me entrée to a new world of women basking in their new power. A lot of them are tough, difficult and, like my mum, sassy. But such is the moth's love for the flame that I'm enchanted – in the original sense – by their vivacity and sheer joie de vivre. It's fun being around them, absorbing their positive vibes. Best of all, Margaret and her sisters demand nothing from me, I'm like Ralph Ellison's Invisible Man, and at this early stage of the 'second wave' there isn't much of a party line. It takes a bit of getting used to, this being ignored and looked through as if I'm not there, even when I march with them for women's equality through the streets of London. Oh, you hypocrite, from cad to Liberated Man in one mighty bound.

There are mis-steps aplenty, of course. Margaret hates it when I compliment her adorableness. 'You still don't get it, Clancy. Being called "beautiful" is just another put-down.' The flour bombs and rotten fruit hurled at the stage during the Miss World contest at the Royal Albert Hall in London are only weeks away.

PS We marry at a register office round the corner from Sherlock Holmes's mythical 221B Baker Street. It would take all of the famous detective's powers to deduce why we pledged our troth when most other couples we know are simply setting up house together. I pushed for marriage over Margaret's resistance. She defies the ceremony by showing up in a funereal black dress; the ring-and-license that legitimize our union have deathly connotations for her. A bunch of deserters, including Kevin, come to our wedding party. So Margaret knows what she's getting into, and so do I.

ROSA LUXEMBURG MEETS GERMAINE GREER

Time: a year later. Scene: a table at the Garden Café near Queen Mary's Gardens, Inner Circle, Regent's Park.

Two women and a man sip weak tea. The older woman carries a cane for her wonky knee.

Despite my protests Margaret wants to meet Doris who is equally curious about Margaret. I dread the outcome when a strong feminist confronts a mother of feminism who is famous for denying her ideological children. (Doris has taken to rubbishing 'lazy and insidious feminists' who 'demean and insult men, the silent victims in the sex war'.)

Thank God Doris dressed for the occasion in a rather fetching Chanel-style navy-and-gold crocheted sleeveless shift – who's choosing her clothes these days? Modern, assured, confident. Margaret, who'd look spectacular in a wooden barrel, is in knee-length Italian boots, a shortish Scottish plaid skirt and a Biba psychedelic blouse – a suitable contrast in styles and world-views.

Immediately, as if I'm not present, they chatter away like old friends, laughing over shared jokes, so far none at my expense.

'Hey, I'm here too,' I mutter.

'Oh, you,' says Doris.

'Oh, you,' says Margaret.

The energy they exchange is a force field from which I'm excluded. Bored, I get up to stroll around the park, leaving them to gossip. They barely notice.

Half an hour later I return, and they're actually holding hands. And we wonder why men are the way they are?

IT'S THE SMALL THINGS THAT TRIP YOU UP

We're together until an afternoon tea party with one of Margaret's women friends in the kitchen of our house. The *Observer* comped me two scarce tickets to a Glyndebourne performance of Gershwin's *Porgy and Bess,* which, being busy, I return unused to the editor. Foolishly, I mention it. 'What?' Margaret demands. 'What?' her friend echoes. Margaret accuses me, 'It never occurred to you that Maggie and I might want to go? *You never even offered.*' The end is signalled in her blue-green eyes – the glance she exchanges with Maggie. Oh, God, despite my best efforts, I'm still The Man Who Thinks Only of Himself.

I should have seen it coming.

*

Sometimes, I think Margaret and I broke up because our fate was so closely tied to the National Union of Mineworkers. We fed, sheltered and picketed with their members. We made friends among the colliers at the pit closest to us in Betteshanger, Kent. In odd moments I wonder if the miners' defeat had something to do with our own. But there I go again, falsely blaming the intensely personal on The World Out There.

The world is a lonely liberating place after divorce. It's like finding yourself on the Hollywood blacklist: suddenly you're on your own, way off in some other alien universe without structure or signposts. What you do have is a jet pack of sex pheromones wafting out to attract other marital castaways.

This big blonde with a Souf Lunnon accent picks me up at the National Gallery where we're both gazing at Seurat's *Bathers At Asnières.* A little problem: she likes being slapped around, whacked and bruised. A bridge too far for me. And – deal-breaker – she insists on doing it on the sitting-room couch only on Tuesdays and Fridays for the re-runs of *Emergency Ward 10*, so she can watch over my shoulder during.

Where, oh, where, are Jean from the number 88 bus, Philippa the glider pilot and Amanda Sunshine the potter, now that I need them?

I pray they're still out there, if under different names and faces.

Some weeks later I realise I have underestimated the draw of a single man newly exposed to the female element in the London literary scene. Prestigious book-world ladies of a certain age come around to audition me, no other word for it, it's like a job interview to see if I'm fit enough for them to stake a claim on my Swedish-snowshoe-toned body. Without shame or embarrassment they look me up and down like a prize bullock. Not all of them have the same funny bone as lovely Edna O'Brien: 'My last lover seduced me by pretending he was impotent. Clever bastard. What's your dodge?'

Have you ever fallen for three women except they are the same person? 'Freda Balcon', novelist and journalist, looks like a great Aztec queen, dark and imperious. I'm smitten with all three Fredas because she's also 'Anne Charteris', the heroine of her divorce novel *The Hungry Vessel*, as well as the actress Julie Christie who plays Anne Charteris in the movie, and of course Freda herself – whoever that is – at any given moment.

Our romance is engineered by my best 'ginger' (ginger as in ginger beer, 'queer') friend, the writer Colin MacInnes (*Absolute Beginners, City of Spades*), with his malicious sense of humor. Colin and I cover the same London turf and constantly bump into each other to compare notes. He introduces Freda Balcon to me in a pub where she sits with bowed head as if awaiting the executioner's axe. Freda says and does nothing, but lets her magnetic good looks do all the work. The fragility of 'Anne Charteris' combined with Julie Christie's brittle charm are irresistible.

'Let's go to the house,' she says to me, abruptly dismissing Colin. She is enigmatically silent on the drive to her home in Primrose Hill. Is she as choked with desire as I am? I haven't had a woman in eons.

After Freda's Mini stops in front of the tall terrace house at the top of a hill, she lets me kiss her then takes me firmly by the hand and leads me under a canopy of heavily branched trees and up the stone steps. It's cold out. We run into husband William outside the front door together with a lissom, leather-jacketed Young London Thing. (Actually, William and I know each other from joint TV appearances.

I like his habit of calling me Clancy on camera as if we're old friends.) Bless his urbane heart, William is unperturbed by our apparently accidental meeting but Freda goes all googly-eyed and sprightly.

Gripping my elbow hard, she practically steers me toward her husband. 'Isn't it beastly out? We must see to the Mini, it's coughing like an old asthmatic. I've got your things in the back. Is Sammy staying in tonight or is she with the Redgraves? Nanny *still* hasn't got Auberon's formula right. Oh, yes, hello, darling.'

William, balding and portly as a Dickens character, greets me warmly, even affectionately. 'Nice to see you again, Clancy. If you're not doing anything for Christmas Day, get Freda to have you over.' Courteously excusing himself, he opens the massive front door, painted a chic Sanderson mauve, and ushers the *Vogue* model clone inside. He then shuts the door in our faces. Freda stares at it.

From that moment on I never get another clear look at her face. Totally silent, she turns away from the dim transom light and leads me round the side to a glass-sided extension that is her writing studio. Is she angry? Grieving? Lustful? The large split-level studio has a railed balcony to which Freda guides me by the glow from the main house's side windows. There's a bed, or rather a camp cot, in one corner. She lies on it and, wordlessly, pulls me down on top of her. I keep trying to see her face. The act, once I remove her tweeds, is dry, remorseless, mute.

Well, I think, that's only a first go, she's used to fat William. Later, still in the dark, she makes us mugs of Darjeeling on a small Belling stove. I sit on her cot, feeling the rough blanket under my naked behind, and shiver. From beneath the blanket she solemnly clinks mugs of tea with me.

'What's she like then?' Freda breaks the brooding silence.

'What's William like?' I fend her off.

'Oh, William,' she mutters bitterly. 'He's as unvarying as the seasons. Sensitive, virile, anonymous. He's possessed me since the first day of our marriage – would you believe I was a virgin? I *love* being owned. But once he'd established his rights he lost interest – except in the children. Can't fault him there. What's Doris like, in a situation like this?'

Like what? I think on my feet.

'Oh, you know, modern and heartless. Unforgiving.'

She talks on and *on*, about William and herself, the exciting hopelessness of them together. She cries, drily, refusing sympathy. 'If you want to help me,' she repeats fiercely in the semi-darkness, 'tell me about *her*.'

When I do, she abruptly changes the subject. 'It's the children, you see.' She weeps discreetly. 'I'm supposed to love them. No, worse, *like* them. It's my duty. I'm a good maternal soldier. I do *try*. William refuses to see what's going on. They all adore him. And why not? The children disgust me. They do. I fall apart every Christmas. It's their greed, do you understand? Their greed.'

Freda says she's signed herself into a private mental hospital after the last three Christmases. Twice William allowed doctors to administer ECT, to shock her out of her depression. 'I wanted it,' she tells me. Then, in the third person: 'Freda needed to be punished. Because if they hadn't put her away, she would surely have slaughtered the lot of them. Their faces when they receive the presents! That's what the doctors' electricity is supposed to expunge. How can anyone in their right mind be happy with a family at Christmas?'

There, there, I say.

'When I was a small child it was all so much better, don't you see? Father took us all to Christmas Eve service, we each had to put a farthing in the silver collection plate. There was the choir. Sometimes, not often, snow. Christmas was part of our piety. I was a very devout little thing. Presents were small and lovely but not'—She stops abruptly. 'But you're a Jew,' she protests.

That's OK, I tell her, I've seen it in movies.

In the dark and cold I try to focus on which one of her is coming apart. Sounds more like Anne Charteris than Julie Christie or Freda Balcon. I put my hand on her.

'Oh, yes. Right there …'

Afterwards, she says softly, almost wonderingly, 'But you're greedy too, aren't you?'

My Aztec queen has gone. 'Do you want me to call William?' I ask.

'It's not urgent,' she says briskly, slipping from the cot and wrapping herself in the scratchy blanket. I dress. In the dim light from the big house I can see her perched on a high wooden stool in front of a long table. I know without looking there will be marked galleys on it.

'Are you, uh, going to the hospital this Christmas too?'

'This year I was really efficient. I had myself topped up before.'

William's a bastard for signing you into ECT, I say.

'It's that – or cccchh!' She makes a throat-cutting gesture. Yawns.

'Can I kiss you?' I ask.

'No,' she says.

I want to take a last look. I stumble over the Anglepoise, feel for it and switch it on. The glaring yellow light stabs her face, inches away. She blinks but otherwise doesn't flinch. Slowly, I lift my hand until it forms a plinth to her marvelous face with its Mexican eyes. A stone sculpture. A carving. Freda takes advantage of the flood of light to examine me too. I smile, gallantly. But she's too preoccupied to return it.

'Goodbye,' she says. 'Please don't mind. Not your fault.'

As I feel my way down the stripped pine steps to the door, she says, with real feeling, 'I hope St Nicholas brings you everything wonderful, Young Prince.'

Outside, the Prince makes his way down the path. I stand sentry on the pavement gazing up at the large house, blazing with light, its nice big family cosy inside.

As I walk to Gospel Oak to look for a taxi or an early-morning train, I think: I belong here as much as they do. Yes, I do. I *do*.

DOING WHAT COMES NATURALLY

Back on the dating scene, I phone Doris. She comes over with her hair worn in a tight grandmotherly bun! We snuggle up close on the couch having drinks. I put my hand on her knee, checking her out for a total makeover: that hair for a start, burn the flour-sack dress, how about Christie Brinkley-style transparent shoes? Well, maybe not stiletto heels, and absolutely no Laura Ashley, a little eye shadow … There's a momentary pause. She gazes deep into my eyes. 'Oh, sex,' she sighs. 'I'm through with all that, Clancy. It's just too damn much trouble. Don't you find?'

No, I don't find. 'Oh, well.' She exhales an even heavier breath with her signature shrug.

'Are you sure?' I say.

She half-shuts her eyes, the way she used to, indicating that as usual I'm being an idiot.

EPILOGUE

Editors hold my future in their hands. The phone rings, I leap from my coffin. The *Observer* is devoting its entire magazine to the '84 Summer Olympics in Los Angeles. True to its frugality, the paper dispatches only one reporter, me, against Rupert Murdoch's *Sunday Times* flying over a dozen reporters and photographers.

Twelve against one? Love those odds.

EPILOGUE'S EPILOGUE

I'm back to being my real age as I write this, not reliving my prolonged English youth when together with millions of other people I took part in the great social democratic experiment of our time.

In *Lost Horizon*, a novel by James Hilton that was made into a Frank Capra movie, the hero crosses over the snowy Himalayas into an idyllic valley called Shangri-La, sheltered from the bitter climate and where the normal aging process is on hold. He is astonished at this alternative to the selfish civilization he left behind, and wants to stay forever. But, reluctantly, he recrosses the mountains and returns to his home country where he remembers selectively only what he wishes to recall of that enchanted time …

Where are we all?

Jean the bus conductor marries her route supervisor in church and doesn't invite me. Amanda Sunshine's pottery becomes fashionable. Oswald Mosley's neo-Nazis split into whites-only National Front grouplets. David Astor sells the *Observer* to an American oil company but continues his charitable work. Don McCullin, the slum kid who took me into his Islington mob, becomes an award-winning war photographer in Vietnam. Shirley Williams is one of the 'Gang of Four' that abandons the Labour Party to form a 'middle way'. After leaving prison for sabotaging the National Front presses, Mike Cohen becomes a photographer for the Communist daily *Morning Star*. Melville marries again and has more children. David Cooper's Villa 21, probably anti-psychiatry's most enduring contribution, lasts only four more years before the hospital shuts it down. His charge nurse, Frank Atkin, the Villa's linchpin, I've lost touch with. R. D. Laing exits Kingsley Hall with a new wife and turns to mysticism. Drag queen Bunny Lewis goes on tour as far afield as Malta. In America, both Dorothy Day and Grace Lee are on their way, respectively, to Catholic and secular sainthood. With the Vietnam War over, Kevin O'Gara clears his police record and discovers his true vocation as a licensed nurse for terminally ill children. He marries in Canada. 'David', who swaggered around Queen Anne

Street in Buffalo Bill fringed buckskin and liked to incite pub brawls, becomes – of all things – a US federal prosecutor before returning to England and becoming a rural councillor. Oklahoma farm boy and MIT graduate Fritz Efaw, head of our paper organization UAEB – the Union of American Exiles in Britain – is nominated for US vice president at the '76 Democratic convention after being arrested for draft evasion; in front of TV cameras the paraplegic Vietnam vet Ron Kovic (played by Tom Cruise in *Born on the Fourth of July*) embraces him: 'Welcome home, Fritz! 'Max Watts', my opposite number in Paris, emigrates to Australia after the Vietnam War ends and, a (very) skilled helmsman, in protest against American hegemony, steers his boat into the path of a US nuclear-powered guided missile cruiser in Sydney Harbor. Our friendly London spook, Sergeant 'Brent', goes back to his real love, the Art Fraud Squad. My two best police 'sources', a Caledonian Road foot bobby and a City of London chief inspector, who kept us informed of impending raids on Queen Anne Street, both retire honourably. After being beaten by prison warders for escaping again, Nigel hangs himself.

Of our 'cricket team', Occy is a successful actor-playwright, and Ernest a disciple of Danilo Dolci the 'Sicilian Gandhi', as well as a bespoke furniture-maker and environmental activist. My plan to kidnap Peter Lessing and take him back with me to America fails to pan out. His mum wins a Nobel Prize. Harry Pincus, my rescuer and the founder of our Queen Anne Street foco, returns to New York to work as a drugs counsellor where he commits suicide. Frank Aller, Bill Clinton's room mate at Oxford and apparently the least likely of us all to self-destruct, on returning home to Oregon shoots himself.

For them the war never ended.

'My' North of England, its moors, mines and mills, is now a shadow of its old Spartan self. Half the long-established working men's clubs up and down the country have gone, replaced, if at all, by rock music venues. My visits to mining villages ended with the closure of Kellingley, Yorkshire, the last of the nation's deep pits. The process was referred to as 'deindustrialization'; I call it something else. Sheffield, Hull, Rotherham, Barnsley, Wolverhampton, have been hollowed out if demographically added to. Manchester City football club is now owned by an Arab sheikh, their rival United by an American tycoon. Teams I once followed like City, Stoke and Crewe Alexandra are now mired in paedophile scandal as if the Moors Murders and Yorkshire Ripper were a prediction, not an anomaly.

I remain umbilically attached to certain parts of London. It never lets you go. Only last week I developed a sympathetic toothache on learning that National Health bean-counters are closing down my old Kentish Town emergency dental clinic. How could they?

A Note on the Type

The text of this book is set in Linotype Stempel Garamond, a version of Garamond adapted and first used by the Stempel foundry in 1924. It is one of several versions of Garamond based on the designs of Claude Garamond. It is thought that Garamond based his font on Bembo, cut in 1495 by Francesco Griffo in collaboration with the Italian printer Aldus Manutius. Garamond types were first used in books printed in Paris around 1532. Many of the present-day versions of this type are based on the *Typi Academiae* of Jean Jannon cut in Sedan in 1615.

Claude Garamond was born in Paris in 1480. He learned how to cut type from his father and by the age of fifteen he was able to fashion steel punches the size of a pica with great precision. At the age of sixty he was commissioned by King Francis I to design a Greek alphabet, and for this he was given the honourable title of royal type founder. He died in 1561.